CW00351600

OFFICIAL
ENGLISH LEAGUES'
FOOTBALL
RECORDS
2011

First published by Carlton Books Limited 2010
Copyright © 2010 Carlton Books Limited

Carlton Books Limited
20 Mortimer Street
London W1T 3JW

A CIP catalogue record for this book is available from the British Library.
10 9 8 7 6 5 4 3 2 1

ISBN: 978-1-84732-614-0

Editors: Martin Corteel, Conor Kilgallon
Editorial Assistant: David Ballheimer
Designers: Darren Jordan, Stefan Morris
Picture Research: Paul Langan
Production: Rachel Burgess

Written by: Press Association Sport

**PRESS
ASSOCIATION
Sport**

Manufactured under licence by Carlton Books Limited
Printed in Dubai

Players, from left to right: Nathaniel Clyne, Crystal Palace;
Cesc Fabregas, Arsenal; Lee Hughes, Notts County;
Shaun Harrad, Burton Albion

OFFICIAL
ENGLISH LEAGUES'
FOOTBALL
RECORDS
2011

CARLTON
BOOKS

Contents

Overleaf: Manchester United take on local
rivals Manchester City at Old Trafford.

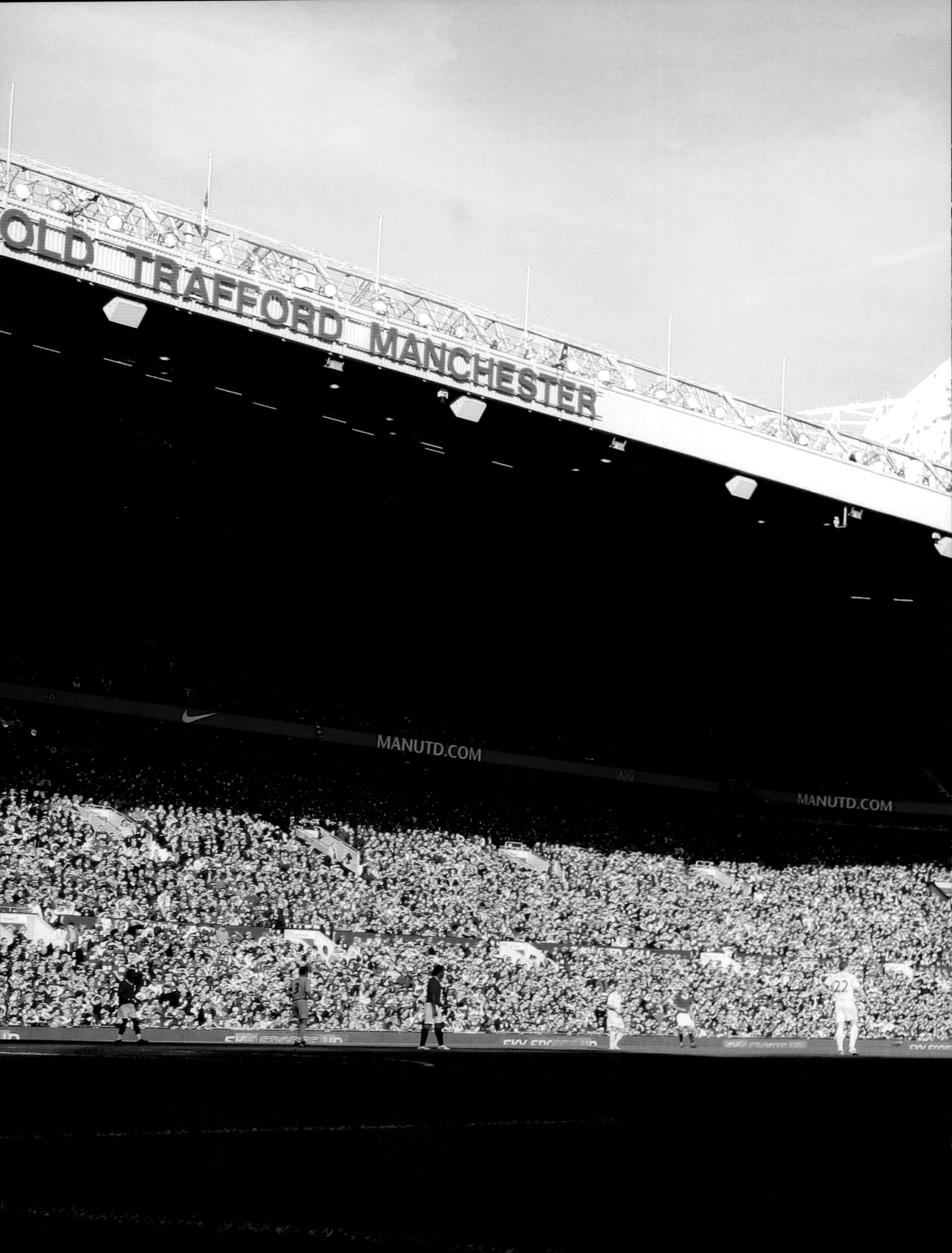
OLD TRAFFORD MANCHESTER
MANUTD.COM
MANUTD.COM

Introduction

Welcome to the debut edition of the *Official English Leagues' Football Records 2011* – a book crammed full of stats and facts covering every aspect of our beautiful game.

English football has witnessed many memorable moments, matches and players since the first Football League season took place in 1888 – and all of those are covered here. From the amazing 32-game winning record that led one side to the fourth-tier title back in 1976 to the Premier League game that broke new ground when it finished 7–4, no detail has been spared. In fact, each division and every one of the 92 clubs that make up the npower Football League and the Barclays Premier League have their own dedicated pages, containing every record and piece of trivia you could wish to know.

The top flight is covered in the most detail, with reviews of the 2009/10 campaign in all four divisions and the cup and European competitions followed by a comprehensive look at the all-time stats that have lit up the Premier League since its formation in 1992. Look out for interesting sections on things such as top goalscorers, leading appearance makers, transfers and attendances.

As well as all-time records for every division, each Premier League and Football League club's history has been explored in detail – from Arsenal to Yeovil – with some fascinating stats and key moments picked out.

You will also discover interesting and quirky facts about England's major cup competitions, from the oldest association football competition in the world, the FA Cup, to The Football League Trophy, currently called the Johnstone's Paint Trophy, which has been running since 1983.

A book like this also has to have a cut-off point. Football, by its very nature, is never standing still, and such is the fast pace of the modern game that when the season is in progress, records can be set or broken every week. That is why all the stats and information used here are correct up to and including the end of the 2009/10 campaign. This explains, for example, why Barclays Premier League new-boys Blackpool, along with Newcastle and West Brom, can be found in the Championship section, whereas relegated trio Hull, Burnley and Portsmouth are included as top-flight clubs.

Every effort has been made to ensure that all appearance data and goalscoring records are 100 per cent accurate, although anomalies in the records pre-dating the modern era, particularly those involving players from the late 1800s and early 1900s, are unavoidable and have to be taken into account.

Hopefully, you will have great fun reading this book.

Action from the Barclays Premier League clash between Liverpool and Aston Villa at Anfield on August 24 2009. Villa won the match 3–1.

Review of the Season 2009/10

The 2009/10 campaign was one to savour, not least for fallen giants and underdogs. Newcastle, who have twice been runners-up in the Barclays Premier League era and have finished in the top seven in eight of their 16 full seasons in the competition so far, made it back to the top flight in style. The Magpies ended the campaign 11 points ahead of Championship runners-up West Brom, who also made a timely return to the big time.

Elsewhere, Leeds finally made it out of the third tier at the third time of asking, going up automatically after two years of play-off hurt. They took second spot in League 1 behind champions Norwich.

Blackpool and Dagenham & Redbridge were the surprise packages of the campaign, sneaking into the play-offs in their respective divisions on the last day of the season and going on to secure promotion. The Seasiders knocked out Nottingham Forest in the Championship semi-final after a stunning performance in the second leg and then went on to beat Cardiff in the final at Wembley. Meanwhile, Dagenham hit Morecambe for six in the first leg of their League 2 semi-final at Victoria Road before getting the better of Rotherham to earn a place in the third tier for the first time in the club's history.

Most of the headlines, though, came in the Barclays Premier League, where Chelsea became the seventh team in English football history to win the double, pipping Manchester United by a single point to lift the league crown before going on to beat Portsmouth 1–0 in the FA Cup final. The top tier also waved goodbye to Portsmouth, Hull and Burnley, with the Clarets suffering relegation after just one season.

Further down the divisions, Millwall were third-tier play-off winners, while Rochdale ended a 36-year spell in the bottom tier by finishing as runners-up to The Football League's oldest club, Notts County. Sheffield Wednesday were relegated back to the third tier after six seasons in League 1 and were joined by Plymouth and Peterborough, with Posh managing only eight wins all campaign.

Stockport collected just 25 points as their off-the-field problems hindered their chances of staying in League 1. Southend, Wycombe and Gillingham were also relegated, with the Gills losing out on the final day of the season on goal difference.

The Football League bid a fond farewell to Grimsby and Darlington, although the Mariners battled until the last day of the season before their fate was sealed.

The cup competitions were equally thrilling. Chelsea's FA Cup triumph brought the curtain down on the campaign domestically, but before that, Manchester United celebrated Carling Cup glory with victory against Aston Villa at Wembley, while Southampton claimed success in the Johnstone's Paint Trophy.

It was a disappointing year for English clubs in Europe, with the top flight's big guns making an early exit from the Champions League. Only Fulham managed to sustain a challenge in the inaugural Europa League, but having made it all the way to the final against Atletico Madrid, the Cottagers could not overcome the final hurdle.

↓ All smiles for the Chelsea players in May 2010 as they celebrate winning the Barclays Premier League for the first time since 2005/06.

↑ It was double the fun for Chelsea when they beat Portsmouth 1–0 at Wembley on May 15 2010 to win the FA Cup and claim the first double in the club's history.

↓ Jermaine Beckford (left) scored the only goal of the game as League 1 outfit Leeds stunned Manchester United 1–0 in the third round of the 2009/10 FA Cup at Old Trafford, before later earning promotion to the Championship.

↑ Newcastle were the class act of the Championship, romping to the title with 102 points – 11 clear of second-place West Brom.

Barclays Premier League Review

Chelsea enjoyed the most successful campaign in their history, securing a first double and becoming only the third team in the Premier League era to achieve the feat.

Carlo Ancelotti's first season in English football also saw the Blues break the record for the most goals scored in a single season in the competition. They netted seven or more on four separate occasions, with Didier Drogba winning the Golden Boot and Frank Lampard recording the most assists. The England midfielder, who scored 10 penalties, also moved up to third in Chelsea's list of all-time goalscorers.

The Londoners, who won the title by a point from Manchester United, had a 100 per cent record against the rest of the so-called 'Big Four', with highlights including a 3–0 win at Arsenal in November and 2–1 success at Old Trafford five months later.

Wayne Rooney became the first Englishman since Kevin Phillips to score 25 goals or more in a top-flight campaign, netting 26 times in the Barclays Premier League in total, but United were forced to settle for second place.

Arsenal got their campaign off to a flying start with a 6–1 win at Everton, and they topped the table at the turn of the year. Ultimately, though, they fell away, finishing 10 points behind United and 11 adrift of champions Chelsea.

Tottenham were one of the success stories of the season, holding off the challenge of Manchester City to land fourth spot and Champions League qualification under Barclays Manager of the Season Harry Redknapp. They also recorded one of the biggest wins in Premier League history, as Jermain Defoe scored five times in a 9–1 victory against Wigan.

Big-spending City, meanwhile, parted company with manager Mark Hughes in December and brought in Italian Roberto Mancini, who led them to fifth place.

Liverpool endured their worst season since 1998/99 and could only manage seventh under Rafael Benitez, who left the club at the end of the campaign and subsequently took charge at European champions Inter Milan.

Across Stanley Park, things looked bleak for Everton when they sat two points above the relegation zone at Christmas, thanks in no small part to a mountain of injury problems. However, an impressive run of just two defeats in their last 24 Barclays Premier League games saw David Moyes' men finish eighth.

Elsewhere, Birmingham turned St Andrew's into a fortress, while Darren Bent was a one-man goal-machine for Sunderland – although a stray beach ball had to take some of the credit for deflecting home his strike against Liverpool in October!

Hull parted company with manager Phil Brown and brought in Iain Dowie until the end of the campaign, but he couldn't prevent the Tigers from going down. Others to lose their top-flight status were Burnley – the 43rd side to play in the division – who struggled on their travels, and Portsmouth, who endured off-the-field problems that saw them deducted nine points on the way to finishing bottom of the table.

TOP SCORERS

Didier Drogba	Chelsea	29
Wayne Rooney	Manchester United	26
Darren Bent	Sunderland	24
Carlos Tevez	Manchester City	23
Frank Lampard	Chelsea	22
Jermain Defoe	Tottenham	18
Fernando Torres	Liverpool	18

⬇ Sunderland paid Tottenham an initial £10million to secure the services of Darren Bent for the 2009/10 season. The striker repaid them in style, scoring 24 of the Black Cats' 48 league goals.

WINNERS AND LOSERS

Champions: Chelsea
Runners-up: Manchester United
Champions League qualifiers: Chelsea, Manchester United, Arsenal, Tottenham
Europa League qualifiers: Manchester City, Aston Villa, Liverpool
Relegated: Burnley, Hull, Portsmouth

↑ It's that sinking feeling for Hull's Caleb Folan after a 1–0 home defeat to Sunderland on April 24 2010 confirms the Tigers' relegation from the top flight.

↑ Tottenham's Jermain Defoe netted a Premier League record-equalling five goals during his side's stunning 9–1 victory over Wigan on November 21 2009.

⬅ Roberto Mancini's arrival at Manchester City to replace Mark Hughes as the club's boss was one of five managerial changes in the Barclays Premier League in 2009/10.

Barclays Premier League Table and Awards

Team	P	Home					Away					Pts
		W	D	L	F	A	W	D	L	F	A	
Chelsea	38	17	1	1	68	14	10	4	5	35	18	86
Man Utd	38	16	1	2	52	12	11	3	5	34	16	85
Arsenal	38	15	2	2	48	15	8	4	7	35	26	75
Tottenham	38	14	2	3	40	12	7	5	7	27	29	70
Man City	38	12	4	3	41	20	6	9	4	32	25	67
Aston Villa	38	8	8	3	29	16	9	5	5	23	23	64
Liverpool	38	13	3	3	43	15	5	6	8	18	20	63
Everton	38	11	6	2	35	21	5	7	7	25	28	61
Birmingham	38	8	9	2	19	13	5	2	12	19	34	50
Blackburn	38	10	6	3	28	18	3	5	11	13	37	50
Stoke	38	7	6	6	24	21	4	8	7	10	27	47
Fulham	38	11	3	5	27	15	1	7	11	12	31	46
Sunderland	38	9	7	3	32	19	2	4	13	16	37	44
Bolton	38	6	6	7	26	31	4	3	12	16	36	39
Wolverhampton	38	5	6	8	13	22	4	5	10	19	34	38
Wigan	38	6	7	6	19	24	3	2	14	18	55	36
West Ham	38	7	5	7	30	29	1	6	12	17	37	35
Burnley	38	7	5	7	25	30	1	1	17	17	52	30
Hull	38	6	6	7	22	29	0	6	13	12	46	30
Portsmouth	38	5	3	11	24	32	2	4	13	10	34	19

ROO BEAUTY

Wayne Rooney dominated the individual top-flight awards in 2009/10, and was honoured for a fantastic season when he was named the Barclays Premier League Player of the Season. The Manchester United sensation was also named Player of the Year by both the PFA and the Football Writers' Association.

⟶ *Wayne Rooney enjoyed a prolific season for Manchester United in 2009/10, bagging an impressive 26 goals in 32 Barclays Premier League appearances.*

⤳ *A hat-trick on the last day of the season, during Chelsea's 8–0 win over Wigan, helped Didier Drogba to the Golden Boot in 2009/10 with 29 goals.*

CECH'S GOLDEN GLOVES

Chelsea shot-stopper Petr Cech took the Barclays Golden Glove prize for the top goalkeeper, although his Liverpool counterpart, Jose Reina, ran him close. The Spaniard also kept 17 clean sheets, but he made more appearances than the Chelsea man so came second overall.

TOP DROG

Didier Drogba won the Barclays Golden Boot for the second time in his Chelsea career in 2009/10 with 29 goals – he also triumphed in 2006/07 (with 20 goals). Team-mate Nicolas Anelka (19 goals) had won the prize the previous season, with Cristiano Ronaldo (31 goals) taking the accolade in 2007/08.

BLUES ON MERIT

Chelsea received a special Merit Award for becoming the first team to score over 100 goals in a Barclays Premier League season. The Blues' tally of 103 saw them become the first team to reach three figures in the top flight since Tottenham in 1962/63.

↑ *Seventeen clean sheets in 34 appearances for Chelsea in 2009/10 were enough to earn Petr Cech the Golden Glove prize for the second time in his career.*

⤳ *The Chelsea players mob Didier Drogba (right) after the Ivory Coast striker netted the Blues' third goal during their emphatic 3–0 away victory over Arsenal on November 29 2009.*

HARRY IS TOP MAN

Harry Redknapp won the Barclays Premier League Manager of the Season award after guiding Tottenham to a fourth-place finish and their first-ever qualification for the Champions League. Spurs were bottom of the table when Redknapp took over in October 2008, but he has turned things around at White Hart Lane in spectacular fashion. It was the first time since 2000/01 (Ipswich's George Burley) that the Manager of the Year had not claimed the Premier League title.

⟵ *In only his second season at the club, Harry Redknapp led Tottenham into the Barclays Premier League's top four and a place in the coveted Champions League.*

Championship Review

Newcastle's stay in the second tier proved to be brief, with Chris Hughton's side securing promotion back to the Barclays Premier League with six games to spare.

The Magpies adjusted to life in the Championship with ease, finishing the campaign with 102 points and winning the title by an 11-point margin. They claimed 30 victories, boasted an unbeaten home record and scored the most goals of any team in the division, with Kevin Nolan and Andy Carroll leading the way at the top of the club's scoring charts with 17 each. The north-east outfit's last home game of the season, against Ipswich, attracted a crowd of 52,181 – the highest attendance in the Championship overall.

West Brom, who had been relegated from the Barclays Premier League alongside Newcastle at the end of 2008/09, also earned an instant return to the top flight. The Baggies went unbeaten in their last 12 games to clinch the second automatic promotion place.

Blackpool proved to be the league's dark horses, enjoying a fairytale campaign to go up via the play-offs. Many pundits had tipped Ian Holloway's men for a season of struggle, but after securing the final play-off spot on the last day of the regular campaign, they went on to stun Nottingham Forest and then Cardiff to complete a remarkable feat.

The Seasiders recovered from an early setback to earn a 2–1 win in the first leg of their semi-final clash against the Reds at Bloomfield Road, and the second game at the City Ground was a classic. Forest were leading twice, but both times they were pegged back, and three goals in seven minutes – two from DJ Campbell to complete his hat-trick – put Blackpool firmly in command. Dele Adebola pulled a goal back at the death, but it was too little, too late for Forest – who had finished third and equalled a club record of 12 consecutive home wins during the regular season – as the tie ended 6–4 on aggregate.

Blackpool's first promotion to the top flight since 1970 was secured with a 3–2 win against Cardiff at Wembley, with all five goals coming in an exhilarating first half.

Middlesbrough, the third team looking to bounce back to the Barclays Premier League at the first attempt, parted company with Gareth Southgate in October, and they were unable to maintain a promotion challenge under his replacement, Gordon Strachan.

At the bottom, Sheffield Wednesday and Crystal Palace were involved in a dramatic final-day decider at Hillsborough, with the South Yorkshire club needing a win to avoid relegation at the expense of their opponents. Darren Purse gave the Owls hope when he equalised with three minutes remaining, but they couldn't find a winner, and a 2–2 draw sent Alan Irvine's side down to the third tier.

Plymouth, who appointed former club stalwart Paul Mariner as head coach in December to replace Paul Sturrock, finished 23rd, with Peterborough bottom of the pile.

↑ *Victory in the 2010 Championship Play-Off Final meant that Ian Holloway led Blackpool to the top flight of English football for the first time in 40 years.*

WINNERS AND LOSERS

Champions:	Newcastle
Runners-up:	West Brom
Play-off winners:	Blackpool
Play-off runners-up:	Cardiff
Relegated:	Sheffield Wednesday, Plymouth, Peterborough

↑ *Chris Hughton made a stunning start to his managerial career, leading Newcastle to the second-tier title to regain the Magpies' top-flight status.*

TOP SCORERS

Nicky Maynard	Bristol City	20
Peter Whittingham	Cardiff	20
Gary Hooper	Scunthorpe	19
Kevin Nolan	Newcastle	17
Andy Carroll	Newcastle	17
Charlie Adam	Blackpool	16
Michael Chopra	Cardiff	16
Gylfi Sigurdsson	Reading	16

← *Nicky Maynard enjoyed the best season of his career in 2009/10, netting 20 goals in 38 league appearances for Bristol City to end the campaign as the Championship's joint leading scorer.*

↑ *Crystal Palace's Darren Ambrose (left) and Sheffield Wednesday's Luke Varney battle for the ball during the crunch relegation clash at Hillsborough in May 2010.*

League 1 Review

Norwich recovered from an opening-day humbling at home to Colchester to win the League 1 title. Bryan Gunn was relieved of his managerial duties after that game and replaced by Paul Lambert, the man who had masterminded The Us' stunning 7–1 victory. The Canaries went on to claim the championship trophy by nine points, winning 29 games, scoring more goals than any other team (89) and keeping 19 clean sheets along the way.

Leeds, who had topped the table from August to February, suffered a dip in form following the turn of the year and finished as runners-up. The Yorkshire club made life difficult for themselves in what turned out to be a must-win clash on the last day of the season against Bristol Rovers. Max Gradel was sent off in the first half and Darryl Duffy fired the visitors in front, but Simon Grayson's side recovered to snatch a 2–1 victory, with Jermaine Beckford scoring the winner – his 25th league goal of the campaign – in his last game for the club. That match, which brought an end to Leeds' three-year stay in the division, was watched by 38,234 fans – the biggest League 1 crowd of the season.

Millwall, Charlton, Swindon and Huddersfield contested the play-offs, with the third-place Lions coming out on top. Kenny Jackett's men edged a tight semi-final against the Terriers, with Steve Morison and Paul Robinson scoring in the second leg to secure a 2–0 aggregate win and a place at Wembley. There they took on Swindon, who had earned their spot with a 5–4 penalty shootout win against Charlton.

Striker Charlie Austin proved to be an inspired signing by Swindon boss Danny Wilson, joining from Poole Town in the summer of 2009 and scoring 19 goals in his debut season in The Football League. Austin's total was 11 less than Rickie Lambert, who finished as the division's top scorer on the way to helping Southampton to a seventh-place finish, despite the club having started the season with a 10-point deduction. Saints certainly didn't struggle for goals, netting just four less than champions Norwich.

Stockport ended the term at the bottom of the table, 18 points behind Southend and two more adrift of Wycombe, with the Hatters' fate sealed well before the last week of the season. That left Exeter, Gillingham, Hartlepool and Tranmere to battle it out to avoid the drop in a final-day showdown on May 8. Wins for the Grecians and Rovers assured their safety, while Hartlepool, who only found themselves involved in the scrap after losing three points for fielding Gary Liddle against Brighton in April when he should have been suspended, managed a 0–0 draw at Brentford. That was enough to send the Gills down to the fourth tier on goal difference.

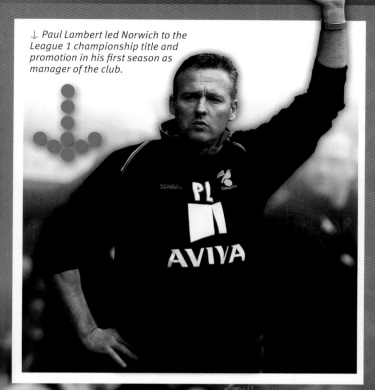

↓ *Paul Lambert led Norwich to the League 1 championship title and promotion in his first season as manager of the club.*

TOP SCORERS

Rickie Lambert	Southampton	30
Billy Paynter	Swindon	26
Jermaine Beckford	Leeds	25
Grant Holt	Norwich	24
Lee Barnard	Southampton	24
Steve Morison	Millwall	20

⇡ *Charlie Austin (left) with 19 goals and Billy Paynter (right) with 26 goals combined with great effect for Swindon in 2009/10 and helped take the Robins to the League 1 Play-Off Final.*

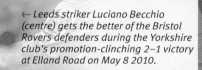

⇠ *Leeds striker Luciano Becchio (centre) gets the better of the Bristol Rovers defenders during the Yorkshire club's promotion-clinching 2–1 victory at Elland Road on May 8 2010.*

WINNERS AND LOSERS

Champions:	Norwich
Runners-up:	Leeds
Play-off winners:	Millwall
Play-off runners-up:	Swindon
Relegated:	Stockport, Southend, Wycombe, Gillingham

⋯⟶ *Gillingham goalkeeper Alan Julian contemplates life in League 2 after the Kent side lurched towards the bottom of the League 1 table and relegation.*

League 2 Review

Notts County finished the season without either Sven-Goran Eriksson or Sol Campbell, but with their hands on the League 2 trophy. A takeover at The Football League's oldest club had resulted in former England boss Eriksson arriving as director of football at the start of the campaign, and he was soon followed by Campbell, who dropped down from the Barclays Premier League to the bottom tier of The Football League in the most surprising transfer of the summer. It seemed that County would subsequently cruise to the title, but football is never that predictable. Campbell made just one appearance – a 2–1 defeat at Morecambe – before leaving the club and eventually making a return to the top tier with Arsenal.

Meanwhile, a shaky start resulted in manager Ian McParland leaving in October and Eriksson soon followed him out of the exit door. The season was to have a happy ending, though, as the appointment of Steve Cotterill and the goals of Lee Hughes turned County's fortunes around. They suffered just two league defeats in 2010 and clinched the title with a 5–0 victory at Darlington in April – one of five wins by that scoreline during a memorable campaign.

County's title victory saw them overhaul long-time leaders Rochdale, but winning their first promotion since 1969 was all that really mattered for the Lancashire club, who had been seven points clear at the top of the table after a run of six straight wins in November and December. Bournemouth clinched the second automatic promotion place, despite spending the season under a transfer embargo. It was a dramatic improvement for Eddie Howe's side after they had only just avoided relegation the previous season.

Dagenham & Redbridge completed an historic achievement, with promotion via the play-offs sending them up to the third tier of English football for the first time. They clinched the final play-off place before reaching Wembley in style. A 6–0 first-leg victory at Morecambe, inspired by Josh Scott's four-goal haul, meant that the second leg was a formality, although Morecambe took great pride in finishing fourth – their highest-ever league placing.

Rotherham also reached the play-offs, overcoming the blow of losing manager Mark Robins to South Yorkshire rivals Barnsley to book their place in the end-of-season shootout. They made it to Wembley when the impressive Adam Le Fondre's two goals were enough to edge out Aldershot. The Daggers twice took the lead in the final but were pegged back before Jon Nurse grabbed what proved to be the winning goal with 20 minutes remaining.

At the other end of the table, Darlington had to wait until October 17 for their first league win and went on to suffer relegation. And it was a similar campaign for Grimsby, who were given a glimmer of hope after a late-season surge but were ultimately sent down after losing to Burton on the final day of the campaign.

The tragic death of Macclesfield manager Keith Alexander in March, however, ensured that matters on the pitch were kept firmly in perspective.

WINNERS AND LOSERS

Champions:	Notts County
Runners-up:	Bournemouth
Promoted:	Rochdale
Play-off winners:	Dagenham & Redbridge
Play-off runners-up:	Rotherham
Relegated:	Darlington, Grimsby

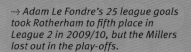

⟶ *Adam Le Fondre's 25 league goals took Rotherham to fifth place in League 2 in 2009/10, but the Millers lost out in the play-offs.*

⇡ *Thirty league goals from striker Lee Hughes propelled Notts County to the 2009/10 League 2 title – 10 points clear of second-place Bournemouth.*

TOP SCORERS

Lee Hughes	Notts County	30
Brett Pitman	Bournemouth	26
Adam Le Fondre	Rotherham	25
Chris O'Grady	Rochdale	22
Shaun Harrad	Burton Albion	21
Chris Dagnall	Rochdale	20

⇣ *It's tough to take for Darlington's Stephen Foster after a difficult season for the Quakers ended in relegation to non-league football.*

⇡ *Bournemouth's players celebrate as the club's promotion to League 1 is confirmed following the Cherries' 2–0 victory over Burton on April 24 2010.*

Football League Tables and Awards

Championship table

Team	P	Home W	D	L	F	A	Away W	D	L	F	A	Pts
Newcastle	46	18	5	0	56	13	12	7	4	34	22	102
West Brom	46	16	3	4	48	21	10	10	3	41	27	91
Nottm Forest	46	18	2	3	45	13	4	11	8	20	27	79
Cardiff	46	12	6	5	37	20	10	4	9	36	34	76
Leicester	46	13	6	4	40	18	8	7	8	21	27	76
Blackpool	46	13	6	4	46	22	6	7	10	28	36	70
Swansea	46	10	10	3	21	12	7	8	8	19	25	69
Sheff Utd	46	12	8	3	37	20	5	6	12	25	35	65
Reading	46	10	7	6	39	22	7	5	11	29	41	63
Bristol City	46	10	10	3	38	34	5	8	10	18	31	63
Middlesbrough	46	9	8	6	25	21	7	6	10	33	29	62
Doncaster	46	9	7	7	32	29	6	8	9	27	29	60
QPR	46	8	9	6	36	28	6	6	11	22	37	57
Derby	46	12	3	8	37	32	3	8	12	16	31	56
Ipswich	46	8	11	4	24	23	4	9	10	26	38	56
Watford	46	10	6	7	36	26	4	6	13	25	42	54
Preston	46	9	10	4	35	26	4	5	14	23	47	54
Barnsley	46	8	7	8	25	29	6	5	12	28	40	54
Coventry	46	8	9	6	27	29	5	6	12	20	35	54
Scunthorpe	46	10	7	6	40	32	4	3	16	22	52	52
Crystal Palace	46	8	5	10	24	27	6	12	5	26	26	49
Sheff Wed	46	8	6	9	30	31	3	8	12	19	38	47
Plymouth	46	5	6	12	20	30	6	2	15	23	38	41
Peterborough	46	6	5	12	32	37	2	5	16	14	43	34

League 1 table

Team	P	Home W	D	L	F	A	Away W	D	L	F	A	Pts
Norwich	46	17	3	3	48	22	12	5	6	41	25	95
Leeds	46	14	6	3	41	19	11	5	7	36	25	86
Millwall	46	17	5	1	48	15	7	8	8	28	29	85
Charlton	46	14	6	3	41	22	9	9	5	30	26	84
Swindon	46	13	8	2	42	25	9	8	6	31	32	82
Huddersfield	46	14	8	1	52	22	9	3	11	30	34	80
Southampton	46	15	5	3	48	21	8	9	6	37	26	73
Colchester	46	15	5	3	37	21	5	7	11	27	31	72
Brentford	46	9	12	2	34	21	5	8	10	21	31	62
Walsall	46	10	8	5	36	26	6	6	11	24	37	62
Bristol Rovers	46	13	3	7	32	30	6	2	15	27	40	62
Milton Keynes Dons	46	10	5	8	31	28	7	4	12	29	40	60
Brighton	46	7	4	12	26	30	8	10	5	30	30	59
Carlisle	46	10	4	9	34	28	5	9	9	29	38	58
Yeovil	46	9	7	7	36	26	4	7	12	19	33	53
Oldham	46	7	7	9	23	28	6	6	11	16	29	52
Leyton Orient	46	10	6	7	35	25	3	6	14	18	38	51
Exeter	46	9	10	4	30	20	2	8	13	18	40	51
Tranmere	46	11	3	9	30	32	3	6	14	15	40	51
Hartlepool	46	10	6	7	33	26	4	5	14	26	41	50
Gillingham	46	12	8	3	35	15	0	6	17	13	49	50
Wycombe	46	6	7	10	26	31	4	8	11	30	45	45
Southend	46	7	10	6	29	27	3	3	17	22	45	43
Stockport	46	2	6	15	21	51	3	4	16	14	44	25

League 2 table

Team	P	Home					W	D	L	F	A	Pts
		W	D	L	F	A	Away W	D	L	F	A	
Notts County	46	16	6	1	58	14	11	6	6	38	17	93
Bournemouth	46	16	3	4	33	16	9	5	9	28	28	83
Rochdale	46	14	3	6	45	20	11	4	8	37	28	82
Morecambe	46	14	6	3	44	24	6	7	10	29	40	73
Rotherham	46	10	9	4	29	18	11	1	11	26	34	73
Aldershot	46	12	7	4	43	24	8	5	10	26	32	72
Dag & Red	46	15	2	6	46	27	5	10	8	23	31	72
Chesterfield	46	14	3	6	38	27	7	4	12	23	35	70
Bury	46	11	6	6	29	23	8	6	9	25	36	69
Port Vale	46	8	8	7	32	25	9	9	5	29	25	68
Northampton	46	9	9	5	29	21	9	4	10	33	32	67
Shrewsbury	46	10	6	7	30	20	7	6	10	25	34	63
Burton Albion	46	9	5	9	38	34	8	6	9	33	37	62
Bradford	46	8	8	7	28	27	8	6	9	31	35	62
Accrington Stanley	46	11	1	11	38	39	7	6	10	24	35	61
Hereford	46	12	4	7	32	25	5	4	14	22	40	59
Torquay	46	9	6	8	34	24	5	9	9	30	31	57
Crewe	46	7	4	12	35	36	8	6	9	33	37	55
Macclesfield	46	7	8	8	27	28	5	10	8	22	30	54
Lincoln City	46	9	7	7	25	26	4	4	15	17	39	50
Barnet	46	8	10	5	30	18	4	2	17	17	45	48
Cheltenham	46	5	8	10	34	38	5	10	8	20	33	48
Grimsby	46	4	9	10	25	36	5	8	10	20	35	44
Darlington	46	3	3	17	14	40	5	3	15	19	47	30

PLAYER OF THE YEAR

Championship: Kevin Nolan (Newcastle)
League 1: Jermaine Beckford (Leeds)
League 2: Craig Dawson (Rochdale)

← *Peter Whittingham's league-leading 20 goals did much to guide Cardiff to the 2009/10 Championship Play-Off Final.*

YOUNG PLAYER OF THE YEAR

Nathaniel Clyne (Crystal Palace)

GOLDEN BOOT

Championship:	Nicky Maynard (Bristol City)/ Peter Whittingham (Cardiff)	20 goals
League 1:	Rickie Lambert (Southampton)	30 goals
League 2:	Lee Hughes (Notts County)	30 goals

GOLDEN GLOVE

Championship:	Dorus De Vries (Swansea)	25 clean sheets
League 1:	Fraser Forster (Norwich)	22 clean sheets
League 2:	Kasper Schmeichel (Notts County)	24 clean sheets

↑ *Kevin Nolan played a crucial role as Newcastle marched to the 2009/10 Championship crown in emphatic style to secure an immediate return to the Barclays Premier League.*

English Cups Review

The cup competitions once again provided plenty of drama in 2009/10, with Chelsea and Manchester United retaining the FA Cup and Carling Cup respectively and Southampton securing the Johnstone's Paint Trophy after a goal-fest at Wembley.

Two of the biggest shocks in recent years saw Leeds triumph at Old Trafford and then Reading win at Anfield to send Manchester United and Liverpool, who have won the FA Cup a combined total of 18 times between them, out in the third round of the competition. The Royals also ousted top-flight opposition in Burnley before exiting in the quarter-finals. Meanwhile, Notts County defeated Wigan in a fourth-round replay.

Portsmouth made light of their problems off the field to reach their second FA Cup final in three seasons. However, it was a case of what might have been for Pompey. Kevin-Prince Boateng missed a penalty against Chelsea before Didier Drogba continued his incredible scoring streak at Wembley to net the only goal for the Blues, who could afford a spot-kick miss of their own when Frank Lampard blazed wide.

An inability to convert from 12 yards cost Chelsea dear in the Carling Cup, however. Carlo Ancelotti's side were beaten 4–3 on penalties by Blackburn after the scores had ended level at 3–3 following a thrilling quarter-final tie at Ewood Park. Rovers went on to lose 7–4 on aggregate to Aston Villa in the last four.

Manchester United and Manchester City, who had cruised past Arsenal in round five, renewed rivalries in the other semi-final in a game that more than lived up to the hype. Carlos Tevez's brace against his former club meant it was advantage City after the first leg at Eastlands. The Argentina international was on target again in the return clash at Old Trafford to haul the sides level at 3–3 on aggregate after Paul Scholes and Michael Carrick had added to Ryan Giggs' effort in the first encounter. Wayne Rooney then took centre stage with a last-gasp winner, and he also headed the decisive goal in United's 2–1 final success over Aston Villa.

In the Johnstone's Paint Trophy, Barnet stunned Millwall in the first round and Chesterfield and Stockport enjoyed emphatic victories over Burton and Crewe respectively. Southampton needed penalties to see off Torquay and progress to the regional quarter-finals, where Saints boss Alan Pardew plotted the downfall of his former club, Charlton.

Adam Collin kept his cool to save the decisive spot-kick as Carlisle beat Leeds in a penalty shootout to reach Wembley, while Southampton secured their place in the final with a 4–1 aggregate win over MK Dons.

The Saints got off to the perfect start in the showpiece final when Rickie Lambert tucked away an early penalty and Adam Lallana doubled his side's advantage before the half-time interval. Further goals from Papa Waigo and Michail Antonio put the result beyond any doubt before Gary Madine pulled one back for Carlisle late on. The 4–1 victory earned Southampton their first piece of silverware in 34 years.

FA CUP

Winners: Chelsea
Runners-up: Portsmouth
Top scorer: John Carew (Aston Villa) 6

←·· *Portsmouth's Jamie O'Hara and Frederic Piquionne console Kevin-Prince Boateng after the Ghana international missed a penalty in the 54th minute of the 2010 FA Cup final.*

↓ *Carlos Tevez was in riotous goalscoring form for Manchester City in the 2009/10 Carling Cup. Cross-city rivals United ended City's run in the semi-finals.*

←·· *The Reading players swamp Shane Long after the striker netted the Royals' second extra-time goal to dump Liverpool out of the 2009/10 FA Cup.*

CARLING CUP

Winners: Manchester United
Runners-up: Aston Villa
Top scorer: Carlos Tevez (Manchester City) 6

JOHNSTONE'S PAINT TROPHY

Winners: Southampton
Runners-up: Carlisle
Top scorer: Papa Waigo (Southampton) 5

←·· *Southampton's Rickie Lambert celebrates with the Johnstone's Paint Trophy after the Saints beat Carlisle 4–1 in the final.*

European Cups Review

Fulham were left to fly the flag for English clubs in Europe. Arsenal, Chelsea, Liverpool and Manchester United had all been knocked out of the Champions League by the time the Cottagers took on Atletico Madrid in the final of the inaugural Europa League in May. The Londoners were eventually beaten 2–1 by the Spanish side after extra time, but they enjoyed some memorable moments along the way.

Goals from Zoltan Gera and Bobby Zamora secured a crucial 2–1 victory in the first leg of the Cottagers' last-32 clash against Shakhtar Donetsk, with a 1–1 draw in the Ukraine seeing them through to a two-legged tie against Italian giants Juventus. It turned out to be one of the great European encounters of all time. Fulham's dream appeared to be over when they slipped to a 3–1 defeat in Turin, but on an incredible night in the return leg at Craven Cottage, Roy Hodgson's men recovered from going a goal down to win 4–1 on the evening and 5–4 on aggregate. Fabio Cannavaro's dismissal helped their cause, but they still had it all to do, and Clint Dempsey's sublime late chip was worthy of winning any game.

Hard-fought victories against German duo Wolfsburg and Hamburg earned Fulham a passage to the final, where Simon Davies' goal cancelled out Diego Forlan's strike, only for the former Manchester United ace to snatch a fortuitous winner with four minutes of extra time remaining.

Of England's four representatives in the Champions League, Arsenal and Manchester United went the furthest, reaching the quarter-final stage. Lionel Messi then scored four goals in an awesome one-man display at the Nou Camp to give Barcelona a 6–3 aggregate victory over the Gunners, while United went out on away goals to Bayern Munich, who won courtesy of a strike from former Chelsea winger Arjen Robben.

The Blues exited the competition at the last-16 stage, losing 3–1 on aggregate to former coach Jose Mourinho and his Inter Milan side, while Liverpool, following a hugely disappointing campaign, failed to make it out of their group. The Reds finished third in Group E, six points behind Lyon and a further two behind Fiorentina, to slip into the Europa League.

The Merseysiders would have gone on to play Fulham in the final of the second-tier competition had they been able to hold on against Atletico Madrid, but Forlan was again the scourge of the English sides. The Uruguay international made it 2–1 on the night against the Reds and 2–2 overall, meaning the Primera Division outfit eventually edged through on away goals.

Aston Villa failed to get through the qualifying rounds after losing to Rapid Vienna, while Everton squeezed through Group I, despite losing 5–0 away to Benfica, but were then knocked out by another Portuguese side, Sporting Lisbon, in the last 32.

↓ Jose Mourinho made a happy return to Stamford Bridge when he master-minded Inter Milan's 3–1 aggregate win over his former side, Chelsea, in the last 16 of the 2009/10 Champions League.

EUROPA LEAGUE

Winners: Atletico Madrid
Runners-up: Fulham
Top scorer: Oscar Cardozo (Benfica)/   9
Claudio Pizarro (Werder Bremen)

↑ Goalscorer Clint Dempsey and Paul Konchesky celebrate Fulham's fourth goal during the Cottagers' remarkable come-from-behind victory over Juventus in the Europa League.

CHAMPIONS LEAGUE

Winners: Inter Milan
Runners-up: Bayern Munich
Top scorer: Lionel Messi (Barcelona) 8

⇢ Manchester United's Patrice Evra (right) outjumps Bayern Munich's Arjen Robben in the second leg of the two sides' Champions League quarter-final at Old Trafford in April 2010.

↑ Arsenal's Abou Diaby (left) and Barcelona's Lionel Messi battle for the ball during the Champions League quarter-final second-leg match at the Nou Camp.

English League Records

The Football League has changed dramatically since the first ball was kicked back in 1888.

In that inaugural season, the competition was made up of just one division, consisting of 12 teams. Now, almost 125 years on, there are four divisions, with 92 clubs competing in total.

The top flight is the pinnacle of the English game. It is revered and respected right around the world and attracts some of the best players on the planet. It has always been held up as a shining example of how football should be organised, and over the years it has gone from strength to strength.

The arrival of the Premier League in particular has helped to take the game to new heights. The competition was formed in May 1992 as part of a restructuring designed to help football in England grow and flourish. Initially, the league was composed of 22 teams, but it was always the intention to reduce that number to 20 to promote development and excellence at club and international level, and this was achieved in 1995.

Throughout its history, the top flight has been the setting for some amazing matches and feats of individual and collective brilliance – from the first title winners, Preston, and their top scorer, John Goodall, right through to the 2009/10 Barclays Premier League champions, Chelsea, whose team is packed with world-class stars.

Further down the pyramid, the action is just as enthralling. The second tier – which came into being in 1892 – was rebranded as the Championship in 2004, with the third tier, formed in 1920, and the fourth tier – a relatively new addition, having first been introduced in 1958 – becoming known as League 1 and League 2 at the same time. Throughout all the divisions, fans have got used to seeing edge-of-the-seat drama and superb individual skill week in, week out.

The expanded number of teams and structure of the competition is just one of many changes to have affected The Football League down the years. In 1981, for example, following a proposal by television pundit and former Coventry chairman Jimmy Hill, the decision was taken to award three points for a win, rather than two as had previously been the case. The idea was that this would encourage greater attacking play, with more at stake for clubs involved in promotion and relegation battles.

The play-offs were another exciting introduction in 1986, offering teams who finished in the top six or seven places in their respective divisions the chance to compete in an end-of-season play-off for promotion. The play-offs now mean that even long after the titles have been handed out, supporters are guaranteed a nail-biting climax to the campaign.

It all adds up to a fast-paced, modern and exciting game that makes English football the envy of the world.

It's all too much to bear for Liverpool players and fans alike as another chance goes begging during the Reds' 3–2 home defeat to arch-rivals Manchester United on September 11 1999.

Barclays Premier League All-Time Records

The Premier League was formed in 1992 and originally consisted of 22 teams, although that was cut to 20 for the start of the 1995/96 season. The competition is now the most watched, and the most lucrative, league in world football. Blackpool are the 44th different team to compete in the division, but only four have won the title, with Manchester United leading the way as the most successful club.

Tottenham's Jermain Defoe scores the first of his record-equalling five goals in a match in the Barclays Premier League clash with Wigan at White Hart Lane on November 22 2009.

Manchester United's John O'Shea and Liverpool's Fernando Torres battle for the ball during the Barclays Premier League giants' clash at Anfield in October 2009. Liverpool won the match 2–0, with Torres scoring one of the goals.

Champions and Runners-up

DUO SHARE MARK

Liverpool share the record for the most top-flight titles in English football, but they have yet to win the Premier League. The Merseyside club's last success came in 1989/90, when they finished nine points ahead of Aston Villa. The Reds dominated English football throughout the 1970s and 80s, winning 11 of their 18 titles. Manchester United equalled that overall record when they won the league in 2009. That was the seventh time they had been crowned champions since 1999 and their 11th Premier League title.

The mastermind behind Liverpool's domination of English football in the 1970s and 80s, Bob Paisley celebrates the last of his six league championship titles in 1983.

UNITED UP AND RUNNING

Manchester United were the first winners of the Premier League in 1992/93. Sir Alex Ferguson's men claimed the title in style, finishing 10 points ahead of Aston Villa. The season started badly for the Red Devils, who took just one point from their opening three games. However, they improved dramatically to win 24 games and lose just six times over the course of the campaign. Eric Cantona and Mark Hughes were joint top scorers for the Red Devils that season with 15 goals each.

PREMIER LEAGUE TITLE WINNERS

1992/93	Manchester United
1993/94	Manchester United
1994/95	Blackburn
1995/96	Manchester United
1996/97	Manchester United
1997/98	Arsenal
1998/99	Manchester United
1999/00	Manchester United
2000/01	Manchester United
2001/02	Arsenal
2002/03	Manchester United
2003/04	Arsenal
2004/05	Chelsea
2005/06	Chelsea
2006/07	Manchester United
2007/08	Manchester United
2008/09	Manchester United
2009/10	Chelsea

TITLE DECIDER

The Premier League era has witnessed many memorable title races, but arguably the most exciting and dramatic decider of recent times actually came three years before the league was formed. Arsenal were vying for the championship with Liverpool in 1989, and amazingly the two sides found themselves playing each other in the last game of the season to decide who won the trophy. The Gunners needed a 2–0 win but were only leading through an Alan Smith header going into the last minute. Michael Thomas, who later went on to play for Liverpool, then scored a crucial second right at the end of the game to snatch the trophy for the Londoners.

RUNNER-UP GUNNERS

Arsenal have been runners-up in the Premier League on five occasions. They finished second four times between 1999 and 2003, with Manchester United beating them to the title on each occasion. United have themselves been runners-up four times, with Chelsea missing out three times and Newcastle twice. Aston Villa, Blackburn and Liverpool have all finished second once since the league began.

ROVERS MISS OUT

Blackburn claimed the title in 1994/95 but finished seventh the following season. That is the lowest finish by the defending champions in the competition's history. Kenny Dalglish, who had been in charge for the title-winning campaign, took up a director of football role at Ewood Park at the end of that season and his assistant, Ray Harford, was named as the club's manager.

Thirty-four goals from Alan Shearer, the league's leading scorer, and owner Jack Walker's seemingly limitless funds were major factors in Blackburn's march to the Premier League crown in 1994/95.

⟵ Newcastle manager Kevin Keegan holds his head in his hands as his team draw 1–1 against Nottingham Forest on May 2 1996 to lose further ground to Manchester United in the title race.

⤓ It's celebration time for Chelsea after Didier Drogba (left) scores the only goal of the game in the 2010 FA Cup final against Portsmouth. Victory for the Londoners saw them win the double for the first time in the club's history.

MAGPIES' WINGS CLIPPED

Newcastle threw away a 12-point lead at the top of the table to finish second to Manchester United in 1995/96. The Magpies won many admirers that term for their attacking brand of football, but they struggled to keep it tight at the back and were eventually overtaken by United, who finished four points ahead. Kevin Keegan's side were runners-up to the Red Devils again the following season.

BLUES DOUBLE UP

Chelsea became the third team in Premier League history to win the double in 2009/10. In English football this means winning the Barclays Premier League title and the FA Cup. The Blues finished one point ahead of Manchester United to win the league and then claimed a 1–0 victory in the FA Cup final against Portsmouth, with Didier Drogba scoring the only goal of the game. Manchester United and Arsenal have both done the double twice since the competition was formed – while United also achieved the treble, including the Champions League, in 1999. Going further back, Preston, Aston Villa, Tottenham and Liverpool have also achieved the feat.

DOUBLE AND TREBLE WINNERS

Treble

Manchester United 1998/99

Double

Preston	1888/89
Aston Villa	1896/97
Tottenham	1960/61
Arsenal	1970/71, 1997/98, 2001/02
Liverpool	1985/86
Manchester United	1993/94, 1995/96
Chelsea	2009/10

UNITED'S TREBLE TRIUMPH

Manchester United claimed an amazing treble in 1999, winning the league title, the FA Cup and the Champions League in the same season. They came out on top in one of the closest title races in the competition's history, with both Arsenal and Chelsea pushing them all the way. United then beat Newcastle 2–0 in the FA Cup final, with Teddy Sheringham and Paul Scholes on target, but they saved the best for last when they scored two goals in injury time to snatch a dramatic 2–1 win against Bayern Munich in the Champions League final in Barcelona.

⟵ Huge crowds gathered to honour the treble-winning Manchester United side on their return from victory in the 1999 Champions League final.

Participation, Promotion and Relegation

IMPRESSIVE DEBUTS

Newcastle and Nottingham Forest share the record for the highest Premier League finish by a newly-promoted team. The Magpies claimed the second-tier title in style in 1993/94, with Andrew Cole scoring 12 goals in 11 games and fellow forward David Kelly netting 24. They then took that momentum into the following campaign, finishing third in the top flight. Forest matched that feat in 1994/95, despite having finished as runners-up to Crystal Palace in the second tier. Stan Collymore and Bryan Roy fired the Reds to a UEFA Cup spot.

ONE-SEASON WONDERS

Blackpool are the 44th different team to play in the Premier League since the competition began in 1992, and they will be keen to avoid becoming the fourth one-season wonder. Plenty of teams have been promoted to the top flight then relegated the following term, but Swindon, Barnsley and potentially Burnley are the only clubs who have gone down after one season and have yet to return to the top flight.

↑ *(Left to right) Ian Evatt, Seamus Coleman, Rob Edwards and Billy Clarke celebrate Blackpool's promotion to the Barclays Premier League.*

LONG-SERVING DUO

Aside from the seven clubs who have featured in every Premier League season, Blackburn and Newcastle have spent the most time in the division. Rovers had been promoted to the top flight via the play-offs when the competition started in 1992/93 and finished fourth in their first season. They were relegated in 1998/99 but regained their place in 2001/02 and have stayed there ever since. Newcastle have also featured in 16 of 18 Premier League seasons and are back there in 2010/11 after finishing as second-tier champions in the most recent campaign.

↑ *Bryan Roy (above) with 13 goals and Stan Collymore with 22 combined with deadly effect in 1994/95 to take newly-promoted Nottingham Forest to an unlikely third place.*

BIG FOUR MONOPOLY

Arsenal, Chelsea, Liverpool and Manchester United are known as the 'Big Four'. This stems from the fact that since season 2003/04, these sides have dominated the division, finishing in the first four places, albeit in a different order, in all but two seasons. Everton snatched fourth spot in 2004/05, while Tottenham managed the feat in 2009/10, with Liverpool the side to miss out both times. Manchester United are the only club never to have finished outside of the Premier League's top four.

↓ *Chelsea and Manchester United, two of the Barclays Premier League's big guns, pay homage to the late Sir Bobby Robson before the start of the 2009 FA Community Shield final.*

BEATING THE DROP

There have been a number of dramatic relegation escapes in the competition over the years. In 1992/93, Oldham took nine points in a week, with wins against Aston Villa (1–0), Liverpool (3–2) and then Southampton (4–3) on the last day, to haul themselves out of the drop zone. Harry Redknapp replaced Alain Perrin at Portsmouth midway through the 2005/06 season and led the club to safety with 20 points from nine matches. And West Ham won seven of their last nine games under Alan Curbishley – including 1–0 wins at Arsenal and Manchester United – to stay up in 2006/07.

Oldham's players celebrate a magical week at the end of the 1992/93 season – nine points out of nine secured their Premier League survival.

PREMIER LEAGUE EVER-PRESENTS

Arsenal
Aston Villa
Chelsea
Everton
Liverpool
Manchester United
Tottenham

UPS AND DOWNS

Bolton, Barnsley and Crystal Palace were promoted to the Premier League at the end of the 1996/97 season – and they were relegated in the same order after just one term. It is the only time in the competition's history that all three clubs joining the division have gone down the following season. In 2001/02, Fulham, Blackburn and Bolton all survived – the only time that all three promoted teams have avoided relegation.

THE PRICE OF PROMOTION

Getting a place in the Barclays Premier League brings with it huge financial rewards, while relegation from the division can often make life difficult for a club. The second-tier play-off final is said to be worth tens of millions of pounds to the winners, due in part to added television revenue. A portion of this TV money is given to the three relegated teams in what are known as 'parachute payments'. Clubs now receive these for four seasons, provided they do not gain promotion back to the top flight during that time.

THE GREAT ESCAPE

West Brom are the only team in Premier League history to have avoided relegation having been bottom of the table at Christmas. They pulled off 'The Great Escape' in 2004/05 with a last-day win at home to Portsmouth. Geoff Horsfield and Kieran Richardson, who had impressed on loan from Manchester United, scored the goals in a decisive 2–0 victory. The Baggies finished that season a point ahead of both Crystal Palace and Norwich and two in front of bottom club Southampton, who all failed to win their last match.

RAMS RECORD

Derby hold the record for being relegated from the division with the least amount of points. The Rams endured a difficult campaign in 2007/08, taking just 11 points from 38 matches. They managed just one win – a 1–0 success against Newcastle in September – and suffered 29 defeats. Nottingham Forest went down with the highest points total in the first Premier League season. They took 40 points, although they did play 42 games.

Derby keeper Roy Carroll looks dejected after Arsenal striker Emmanuel Adebayor completes his hat-trick during the Gunners' 6–2 victory at Pride Park in April 2008.

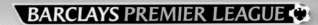

Winning and Losing Streaks and Draws

RECORD DRAWS

Sheffield United and Manchester City both drew 18 games during the 1993/94 season. The duo, who each drew 10 matches at home that year and shared a goalless stalemate at Maine Road, hold the record for the most draws in a single campaign along with Southampton, who managed the same number in 1994/95.

GOALLESS DRAWS SEASON BY SEASON			
1992/93	38	2001/02	46
1993/94	43	2002/03	42
1994/95	51	2003/04	82
1995/96	27	2004/05	60
1996/97	41	2005/06	64
1997/98	33	2006/07	68
1998/99	49	2007/08	52
1999/00	22	2008/09	84
2000/01	28	2009/10	32

ALL-TIME HIGH

The number of goalless draws in a single Premier League season reached a high in 2008/09. There were 84 fixtures that failed to produce a goal – the most since 2003/04. Manchester United drew 0–0 at home to Arsenal that year while the Gunners and Tottenham played out a goalless north London derby at White Hart Lane and Birmingham took a hard-earned point off Chelsea. Liverpool were involved in five 0–0 draws, against Blackburn, Wolves, Manchester City, Fulham and Hull.

RED DEVILS PLAY IT STRAIGHT

Manchester United went on a run of nine straight victories without conceding a goal between Boxing Day 2008 and February 2009. The sequence started with a 1–0 win at Stoke, with Carlos Tevez scoring the only goal, while Paul Scholes, Dimitar Berbatov and Wayne Rooney were on target in a 3–0 victory against Fulham on February 18 – the last game of the streak.

⟶ Dimitar Berbatov nets Manchester United's second goal on the half-hour mark during their routine 3–0 win over Fulham on February 18 2009. It was the Red Devils' ninth straight victory without conceding a goal.

ARSENAL TURN IT AROUND

Arsenal are the most successful team in Premier League history at turning a half-time deficit into a win, managing to come from behind to secure three points 25 times up until the end of the 2009/10 season. Three second-half goals turned the game on its head at Bolton in March 2008 after Matt Taylor had given the home side a 2–0 lead at the break. Arsenal won 3–2. And Robin van Persie scored twice at Stamford Bridge in November of that year as Arsenal recovered from Johan Djourou's first-half own goal to beat Chelsea 2–1.

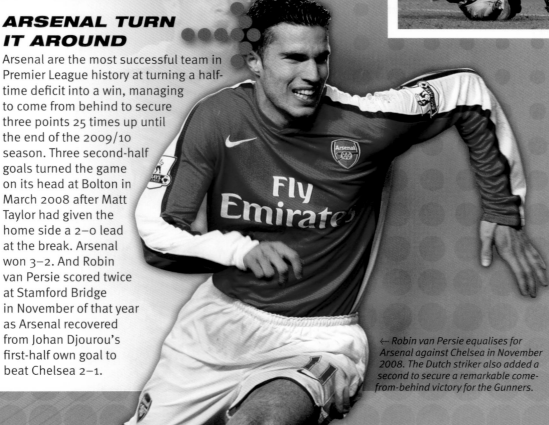

⟵ Robin van Persie equalises for Arsenal against Chelsea in November 2008. The Dutch striker also added a second to secure a remarkable come-from-behind victory for the Gunners.

HOME SWEET HOME

Manchester United went 182 home games without losing by more than one goal between August 1992 and November 2001. The Red Devils rarely lose at Old Trafford, but they were comfortably beaten 3–0 by Everton on August 19 1992, with Peter Beardsley, Robert Warzycha and Mo Johnston scoring for the visitors. However, it wasn't until December 1 2001 that United were made to suffer another defeat thanks to goals from Mario Melchiot, Jimmy Floyd Hasselbaink and Eidur Gudjohnsen that gave Chelsea a 3–0 win.

↑ *Thierry Henry slots home his second goal, and Arsenal's third, during the Gunners' 4–3 win over Everton at Highbury in May 2002.*

GUNNERS ON A ROLL

Arsenal set the record for the most consecutive Barclays Premier League wins in 2002. The Gunners managed 14 over two seasons, with the impressive run starting with a 1–0 victory at Everton in February and continuing until the end of the 2001/02 campaign when Thierry Henry bagged a brace to help beat the Toffees 4–3 at Highbury. Arsene Wenger's side won the opening game of the 2002/03 season at home to Birmingham, but the sequence was ended on August 24 with a 2–2 draw at West Ham.

UNLUCKY RUN FOR BLACK CATS

Sunderland endured 15 straight defeats on their way to suffering relegation in 2002/03. That record number of consecutive losses started with a 2–1 loss at Everton on January 18 2003, despite the Black Cats having taken the lead through Kevin Kilbane. The miserable sequence continued until the end of the season – they were thumped 4–0 at home by a Freddie Ljungberg-inspired Arsenal on the last day. The Wearsiders went down with 19 points that term.

⇢ *Sunderland's Gavin McCann experiences that sinking feeling after 15 straight defeats in the 2002/03 season condemned the Black Cats to relegation.*

STALEMATE FOR CITY

Manchester City became the third team in the competition's history to draw seven consecutive matches when they were held to a string of stalemates in 2009/10. Craig Bellamy earned City a point in a 1–1 draw at Aston Villa in October 2009 to start the sequence. It continued against Wigan (1–1), Fulham (2–2) and Birmingham (0–0) before Burnley snatched a point in a 3–3 draw at Eastlands. A 2–2 draw at Anfield followed, with Hull scoring a late penalty to take a point in the last game of the run.

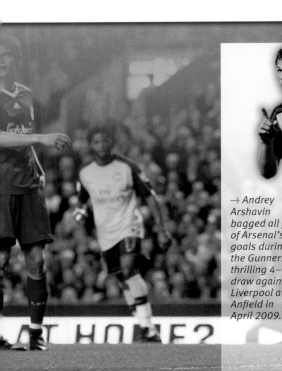

⇢ *Andrey Arshavin bagged all four of Arsenal's goals during the Gunners' thrilling 4–4 draw against Liverpool at Anfield in April 2009.*

HIGH-SCORING DRAWS

There have been some thrilling draws during the Premier League years, with 11 matches finishing 4–4. The most recent came at Anfield in April 2009 when Andrey Arshavin scored all of Arsenal's goals against Liverpool, while the first was in February 1995 between Aston Villa and Leicester. A ding-dong battle between Charlton and West Ham ended 4–4 in November 2001, with both teams leading twice. Paul Kitson grabbed a hat-trick for the visitors.

Scorelines, Scoring Streaks and Clean Sheets

SEVEN-UP POMPEY

Portsmouth and Reading were involved in the highest-scoring match in Premier League history on September 29 2007. There were 11 goals scored as the game finished 7–4 to the home side. Pompey were leading 2–1 at the break, with Benjani Mwaruwari scoring both of their goals. Dave Kitson levelled for the Royals, who then found themselves 5–2 behind – Benjani completing his hat-trick. There were two goals in injury time, with Sulley Muntari scoring a penalty and Sol Campbell putting through his own net.

⟵ Sean Davis celebrates after scoring the sixth of Portsmouth's goals in their 7–4 victory over Reading in September 2007.

CASE FOR THE DEFENCE

Up to the end of the 2009/10 season, Manchester United had kept a total of 311 clean sheets – the most in the league's history. The competition was four games old when the Red Devils managed their first shut-out – a 1–0 win at Southampton on August 24 1992. Sir Alex Ferguson's side kept 19 clean sheets in 2009/10 as they finished as runners-up to Chelsea.

CLARETS DROWN THEIR SORROWS

Burnley managed just three clean sheets during their season-long stay in the Barclays Premier League. All three came at Turf Moor, with two of them coming against Manchester United and Everton in successive matches at the start of the campaign. Swindon hold the record for the least home clean sheets, managing just two in season 1993/94.

⟶ Steve Gohouri (left) and Titus Bramble (right) celebrate Wigan's remarkable come-from-behind victory over Arsenal in April 2010.

BIGGEST PREMIER LEAGUE WINS

Manchester United	9–0	Ipswich	(04/03/1995)
Tottenham	9–1	Wigan	(22/11/2009)
Newcastle	8–0	Sheff Wed	(19/09/1999)
Chelsea	8–0	Wigan	(09/05/2010)
Nottingham Forest	1–8	Manchester United	(06/02/1999)
Middlesbrough	8–1	Manchester City	(11/05/2008)

COMEBACK KINGS

Wigan produced one of the most amazing comebacks in top-flight history against Arsenal in April 2010. Trailing 2–0 with 10 minutes left, the relegation-threatened Latics turned the match around, scoring three times through Ben Watson, Titus Bramble and Charles N'Zogbia to snatch a 3–2 win. Other memorable comebacks down the years include Manchester United's 5–3 win at Tottenham after being three goals down at half-time in September 2001 and Fulham's last-gasp 3–2 victory after finding themselves 2–0 down at Manchester City in April 2008.

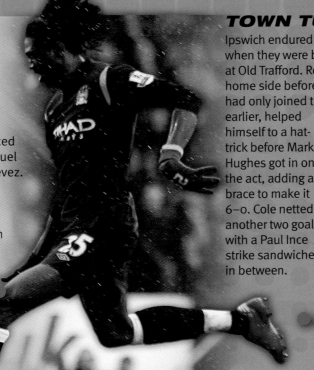

HALF-TIME HIGH

Manchester City scored five first-half goals at Burnley in April 2010 to equal Sheffield Wednesday's record for the biggest half-time lead in the competition's history. The rain was pouring at Turf Moor as the visitors raced into a three-goal lead through Emmanuel Adebayor, Craig Bellamy and Carlos Tevez. Patrick Vieira and Adebayor's second made it five, and the game finished 6–1. Wednesday were 5–0 up at the interval against Bolton at Hillsborough in November 1997, with Andy Booth scoring a 15-minute hat-trick.

⇢ *It took Emmanuel Adebayor just four minutes to open Manchester City's account against Burnley in April 2010; the Togolese scored his second – and City's fifth – on 45 minutes.*

TOWN TUMBLE

Ipswich endured an afternoon to forget in March 1995 when they were beaten 9–0 by Manchester United at Old Trafford. Roy Keane opened the scoring for the home side before Andrew Cole took over. Cole, who had only joined the club from Newcastle two months earlier, helped himself to a hat-trick before Mark Hughes got in on the act, adding a brace to make it 6–0. Cole netted another two goals, with a Paul Ince strike sandwiched in between.

⇠ *Stan Collymore nets the winner in Liverpool's dramatic 4–3 victory over Newcastle in April 1996. Many consider this to be the greatest Premier League match ever played.*

⇡ *Andrew Cole became the first player in Premier League history to score five goals in a match during Manchester United's 9–0 demolition of Ipswich in March 1995.*

UNITED KEEP IT TIGHT

Manchester United set a new record when they went 14 consecutive games without conceding a goal during the 2008/09 season. The run started on November 15 2008 with a 5–0 win against Stoke, with Cristiano Ronaldo opening the scoring early and sealing the rout late on. United were also 5–0 winners at West Brom at the end of January, with the Portuguese winger again bagging a brace. Roque Santa Cruz ended the sequence when he scored for Blackburn after 32 minutes of a 2–1 United win at Old Trafford on February 21.

COLLYMORE CLOSING IN

Liverpool's 4–3 win over Newcastle on April 3 1996 is regarded by many as the greatest Premier League game of all time. The Magpies' title challenge had faltered going into the match, and the night started badly when Robbie Fowler scored after two minutes. They hit back to lead 2–1 through Les Ferdinand and David Ginola, only for Fowler to level. Faustino Asprilla restored Newcastle's lead but Stan Collymore broke their hearts, equalising in the 68th minute before netting a dramatic injury-time winner.

UNITED'S CLEAN SHEET RECORD

Manchester United	5–0	Stoke	(15/11/2008)
Aston Villa	0–0	Manchester United	(22/11/2008)
Manchester City	0–0	Manchester United	(30/11/2008)
Manchester United	1–0	Sunderland	(06/12/2008)
Tottenham	0–0	Manchester United	(13/12/2008)
Stoke	0–0	Manchester United	(26/12/2008)
Manchester United	1–0	Middlesbrough	(29/12/2008)
Manchester United	3–0	Chelsea	(11/01/2009)
Manchester United	1–0	Wigan	(14/01/2009)
Bolton	0–1	Manchester United	(17/01/2009)
West Brom	0–5	Manchester United	(27/01/2009)
Manchester United	1–0	Everton	(31/01/2009)
West Ham	0–1	Manchester United	(08/02/2009)
Manchester United	3–0	Fulham	(18/02/2009)

Points Records

↑ (Left to right) Chelsea's Robert Huth, Tiago, Mateja Kezman, Jiri Jarosik, Arjen Robben, Didier Drogba and Ricardo Carvalho celebrate with the Barclays Premier League Trophy in 2004/05.

BLUES ON A HIGH

Chelsea recorded the highest points total in Premier League history when they won the title in 2004/05. The Blues finished the campaign with 95 points, 12 more than second-place Arsenal and three more than Manchester United had managed in 1993/94. They won 29 of their 38 games, drew eight and lost just once that year. Their sole defeat came at Manchester City in October.

SECOND-PLACE SPURS

Tottenham would have finished as runners-up to Chelsea if games during the 2009/10 season had ended at half-time. Arsenal would have been third, Manchester City fourth and Manchester United way off the pace in fifth.

←···· Gareth Bale was one of Tottenham's star players in their rise to fourth place in the Barclays Premier League in 2009/10, but if all the games had ended at half-time, things would have been even better for the north London club.

TITLE-WINNING TOTALS

Season	Team	Points
1992/93	Manchester United	84
1993/94	Manchester United	92
1994/95	Blackburn	89
1995/96	Manchester United	82
1996/97	Manchester United	75
1997/98	Arsenal	78
1998/99	Manchester United	79
1999/00	Manchester United	91
2000/01	Manchester United	80
2001/02	Arsenal	87
2002/03	Manchester United	83
2003/04	Arsenal	90
2004/05	Chelsea	95
2005/06	Chelsea	91
2006/07	Manchester United	89
2007/08	Manchester United	87
2008/09	Manchester United	90
2009/10	Chelsea	86

RED DEVILS MAKE THEIR POINT

Perhaps unsurprisingly, Manchester United have gathered the most points in Premier League history. The Red Devils have only finished outside of the top two in two seasons since the competition began – 2003/04 and 2004/05 – and that is reflected in their total of 1,494 points. Arsenal are second in the list having taken 183 points less, while Chelsea are third with 1,267.

←--- *(Left to right) Ole Gunnar Solskjaer , David Beckham and Phil Neville celebrate Manchester United's Premier League success in 1996/97.*

HOME COMFORTS

Manchester United have taken the most points at home in Premier League history. The 11-time champions had taken 831 points from 348 home games up until the end of the 2009/10 season. Newcastle had played 40 games less than two of the league's ever-presents, Aston Villa and Everton, but had taken two more points at home than Villa and 22 more than the Toffees. United also top the table for the most away points, having collected 663.

BAGGIES BEAT THE DROP

West Brom took just 34 points during the 2004/05 season but managed to avoid relegation. That was the lowest points total to beat the drop in Premier League history. The battle for survival went to the last day of the season, with Crystal Palace and Norwich relegated with 33 points and Southampton finishing bottom with 32. Hull stayed up with 35 points in 2008/09.

TIGERS ARE TOO TAME

Had Hull kept it tight in the last five minutes of games, they would have collected eight more points and finished 16th in 2009/10, rather than suffering relegation. The Tigers conceded 16 goals between 85 and 90 minutes, with five of those significantly affecting the outcome. Didier Drogba and Nicklas Bendtner scored injury-time winners for Chelsea and Arsenal respectively, while Hull threw away a 2–1 lead in the last three minutes to lose 3–2 at Portsmouth. Steve Gohouri equalised at the death to earn Wigan a point in the penultimate game of the season.

POINTS DEDUCTIONS

A number of Premier League clubs have had points deducted for different reasons. Portsmouth lost nine for entering administration in 2010, while Middlesbrough had three points taken away for failing to fulfil a fixture against Blackburn due to injury and illness in 1996/97. Arsenal and Manchester United also had points deducted following an on-pitch scuffle in 1990.

COMPETITION LOW

Manchester United claimed the 1996/97 title with a competition-low total of 75 points. Sir Alex Ferguson's side recorded 21 victories – the least amount of wins of any Premier League champions – drew 12 games and lost five, including a 5–0 thumping at Newcastle and 3–2 defeat at home to Derby. They still scooped the trophy by seven points from Newcastle, Arsenal and Liverpool, who all finished that season with 68 points.

↑ *United goalkeeper Peter Schmeichel looks downcast after Alan Shearer scores Newcastle's fourth during the Magpies' 5–0 win at St James' Park in October 1996.*

←--- *Nicklas Bendtner scores in the 90th minute to condemn Hull to a last-gasp 2–1 defeat against Arsenal on March 13 2010.*

SIX-POINTERS

The term 'six-pointer' is often heard when the football season enters its final few weeks. Teams obviously still only get three points for a win, but if they are struggling at the bottom of the table or battling it out for promotion at the top and come up against one of their rivals, getting those points can significantly boost a team's hopes of beating the drop or going up.

Top Scorers

THE BOOT FITS

Thierry Henry has won the Premier League Golden Boot a record four times. Arsenal legend Henry first scooped the award in season 2001/02 when he netted 24 goals, edging out Jimmy Floyd Hasselbaink, Alan Shearer and Ruud van Nistelrooy, who all scored 23 times. The Frenchman finished second to Van Nistelrooy the following season but claimed the accolade for the next three terms. Henry hit 30 goals in 2003/04 – eight more than his nearest rival. He bagged 25 in 2004/05 and 27 the season after that.

DEFOE EARNS HIS SPURS

Jermain Defoe became the third player in the league's history to score five goals in one game in November 2009. The England striker equalled the record during Tottenham's incredible 9–1 win against Wigan. Goalscoring hot-shots Andrew Cole and Alan Shearer are the other two members of the unique club. Cole was first to achieve the feat, netting five of Manchester United's nine goals against Ipswich in March 1995. Shearer managed his impressive haul for Newcastle in an 8–0 victory against Sheffield Wednesday in September 1999.

↑ *Jermain Defoe bags his fifth goal of the match and Tottenham's seventh during Spurs' sensational 9–1 win over Wigan in November 2009.*

⇐ *Thierry Henry was a goalscoring king for the Gunners, netting 174 goals in 254 Premier League appearances for Arsenal between 1999 and 2007.*

PREMIER LEAGUE GOALSCORERS

Alan Shearer	260
Andrew Cole	187
Thierry Henry	174
Robbie Fowler	163
Les Ferdinand	149
Michael Owen	147
Teddy Sheringham	147
Frank Lampard	129
Jimmy Floyd Hasselbaink	127
Dwight Yorke	123

SUB OF THE DAY

Ole Gunnar Solskjaer holds the record for scoring the most goals in a single Premier League game after coming on as a substitute. The Norwegian striker came off the bench for Manchester United at Nottingham Forest on February 6 1999 to score four goals in the last 10 minutes as the Red Devils won 8–1 at the City Ground.

DUO SHARE LANDMARK

Andrew Cole and Alan Shearer share the landmark for the most goals scored in a Premier League season. Cole was first to set the record when he netted 34 in 42 games for Newcastle in 1993/94. Shearer equalled that haul the following season to help fire Blackburn to the title.

RAMPANT ROONEY

Wayne Rooney is the only Englishman to have scored more than 25 goals in a Premier League season since 1999/00. Kevin Phillips had been the last player to achieve the feat, scoring 30 for Sunderland at the turn of the millennium, before Rooney hit 26 in 2009/10 as Manchester United finished runners-up in the title race.

RED-HOT BLUES

Chelsea scored 68 times at Stamford Bridge during their title-winning season of 2009/10 – a record for the most home goals in a single Premier League campaign. The Blues went goal crazy, enjoying big wins against Blackburn (5–0), Wolves (4–0), Sunderland (7–2), Aston Villa (7–1), Stoke (7–0) and Wigan (8–0). Manchester United netted a record 47 goals away from home in 2001/02 but had to settle for third place.

SHEAR CLASS

Alan Shearer is the Premier League's leading all-time goalscorer, having netted 260 times in 441 appearances from the league's first season in 1992/93 until the end of the 2005/06 campaign. The former Blackburn and Newcastle striker tops the chart by 73 goals from Andrew Cole, who scored 187 overall. Shearer bagged his first Premier League goals for Rovers in a 3–3 draw at Crystal Palace on August 15 1992, while his last came for the Magpies – a penalty in a 4–1 win against fierce rivals Sunderland at the Stadium of Light on April 17 2006.

IMPRESSIVE GIG FOR RYAN

Ryan Giggs has scored in all 18 Premier League seasons since the competition began in 1992. The winger has spent his entire career at Manchester United, and he scored his first goal in the competition in September 1992 to put his side ahead in a 1–1 draw at Tottenham. Welshman Giggs netted five top-flight goals in 2009/10, with his last coming on the final day of the season against Stoke.

←··· A winger with sublime talent, Ryan Giggs has been a constant feature of the Manchester United squad since the 1991/92 season.

THE KING OF SPAIN

Fernando Torres scored 24 times for Liverpool in his first season with the club in 2007/08 – the most by any player in a debut Premier League campaign. The Spaniard finished joint second in the goalscoring charts alongside Arsenal's Emmanuel Adebayor. Torres scored his first top-flight goal in only his second game – a 1–1 draw against Chelsea at Anfield. He netted two league hat-tricks later that term, with the first coming in a 3–2 win against Middlesbrough and the second in a 4–0 victory against West Ham.

↑ A legend at both Blackburn and Newcastle, Alan Shearer scored an all-time Premier League record 260 goals in only 441 appearances – at a rate of a goal every 1.7 matches.

···→ Signed for a club-record fee of nearly £20million in July 2007, Fernando Torres proved an instant hit with Liverpool fans, scoring 24 times in his first season.

Goals

SINCLAIR OWNS UP

Frank Sinclair scored two own goals in as many weeks for Leicester in 1999. Unfortunately for the defender, both goals came in injury time at the end of games and cost the Foxes points. He sent an unchallenged header past his own goalkeeper, Tim Flowers, at Highbury to gift Arsenal a 2–1 win in August, and the following weekend he handed his former club Chelsea a point when he headed the ball into his own net under pressure from Tore Andre Flo. Sinclair also scored a bizarre own goal in 2002, coolly slotting the ball past Ian Walker to give Middlesbrough a 1–0 win.

THE HUMAN SLING

Stoke unleashed their secret weapon on the Barclays Premier League in 2008 courtesy of Rory Delap's incredible long throw-ins. The midfielder's missiles are said to be more accurate than a corner, and they set up nine goals in his debut season in the league – including both of his side's efforts in a 3–2 defeat at home to Everton in September and another brace in a 2–1 win against Arsenal two months later.

THROW-IN WOE

Aston Villa goalkeeper Peter Enckelman saw a throw-in roll under his foot and into the back of the net during a derby clash with Birmingham at St Andrew's in 2002. Villa defender Olof Mellberg threw the ball back to the shot-stopper, who missed it completely. A goal was given, although rules actually state that if the ball is not touched by another player from a throw-in before going into the net then a corner kick should be awarded.

↑ Aston Villa goalkeeper Peter Enckelman had a night to forget on September 16 2002, conceding a bizarre own-goal as Birmingham ran out 3–0 winners in the first Birmingham derby for 16 years.

AJ IS PENALTY KING

Andrew Johnson scored 11 penalties for Crystal Palace during the 2004/05 campaign – a Premier League record for the most in a single season. Johnson scored three from the spot in January 2005 and a brace of penalties in one game to earn the Eagles a 2–0 win against Birmingham a month later. The prolific striker netted 21 league goals in total that term – four less than Golden Boot winner Thierry Henry. Chelsea's Frank Lampard was one penalty away from equalling Johnson's record in 2009/10.

KING OF THE GOALSCORERS

Ledley King scored after just 10.2 seconds of a Premier League game at Bradford in December 2000. King tried his luck with a shot from outside the area that deflected off a defender and found the bottom corner. It was the England centre-back's first goal for Tottenham. The game ended 3–3.

THIRD TIME LUCKY FOR LAMPS

Frank Lampard was forced to re-take a penalty twice during a game against West Ham in 2009. Chelsea were trailing to Alessandro Diamanti's spot-kick when Matthew Upson brought down Daniel Sturridge in the box. Lampard stepped up to score, but referee Mike Dean ruled that several players had encroached into the area as he took his kick. The England midfielder tried a second time, but Dean once again pulled him back for the same offence. Fortunately for the Blues, Lampard kept his nerve to despatch the penalty at the third time of asking.

↑ Pace and a low, flat trajectory are the key ingredients of Rory Delap's headline-grabbing throw-in technique.

FOWLER ON FIRE

Robbie Fowler scored the fastest hat-trick in Premier League history in August 1994. Fowler, playing for Liverpool in a home clash against Arsenal, bagged a treble in just four minutes and 33 seconds. The ball fell kindly in the box for his opener, with the prolific forward adding a second with a neat finish into the bottom corner. Fowler practically walked in his third following a fortunate rebound. Liverpool won the game 3–0.

† Goals in the 26th, 29th and 31st minutes for Liverpool against Arsenal on August 28 1994 secured Robbie Fowler a place in the record books. It remains the fastest hat-trick in Premier League history.

LONG-RANGERS

Goalkeeper Paul Robinson scored a free-kick from almost 90 yards for Tottenham against Watford in March 2007. The former England shot-stopper launched his kick upfield, with the bounce deceiving his opposite number, Ben Foster, before the ball flew over his head and into the net. Earlier that same season, Matthew Taylor had scored a long-range volley from more than 40 yards for Portsmouth against Everton and Xabi Alonso had netted from 65 yards in Liverpool's 2–0 win at home to Newcastle.

⤳ Ben Foster (left) and Paul Robinson swap stories at the end of a game in which the latter had fortuitously beaten the former with a 90-yard free-kick.

FIVE STAR

Five players have scored in the Premier League for six different clubs. Nick Barmby, Craig Bellamy, Marcus Bent, Andrew Cole and Les Ferdinand have all managed the feat. Bellamy, who is now a regular for Manchester City, has also scored top-flight goals for Liverpool, Newcastle, West Ham, Coventry and Blackburn. He netted his first Premier League goal for Coventry in a 2–1 win at Southampton in August 2000.

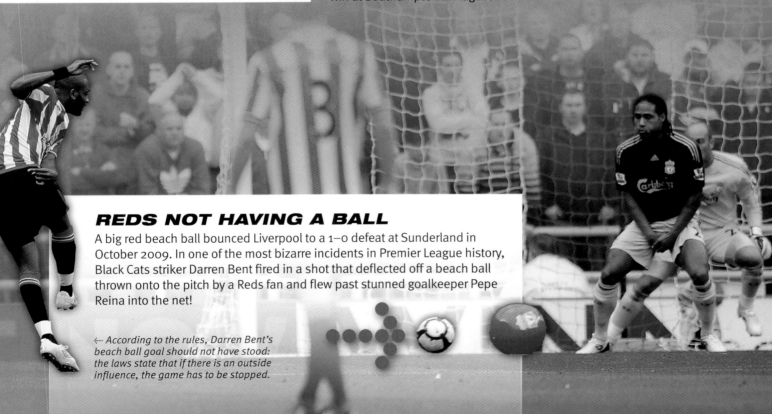

REDS NOT HAVING A BALL

A big red beach ball bounced Liverpool to a 1–0 defeat at Sunderland in October 2009. In one of the most bizarre incidents in Premier League history, Black Cats striker Darren Bent fired in a shot that deflected off a beach ball thrown onto the pitch by a Reds fan and flew past stunned goalkeeper Pepe Reina into the net!

⟵ According to the rules, Darren Bent's beach ball goal should not have stood: the laws state that if there is an outside influence, the game has to be stopped.

Goalkeepers

FRIEDEL'S A FIXTURE

Aston Villa goalkeeper Brad Friedel holds the record for the most consecutive Premier League appearances. At the end of season 2009/10, the American shot-stopper had featured in 228 unbroken games. He set the record on November 30 2008 when he played for the 167th time against Fulham and made his 200th straight appearance on October 31 2009. Friedel thought his run had been ended when was sent off at Liverpool in a 5–0 defeat in March 2009, but the red card was overturned, allowing him to play in Villa's next game.

⟶ *Brad Friedel has been a permanent feature in the Barclays Premier League since August 2004, making an all-time record 228 consecutive appearances.*

SPOT OF BOTHER

Craig Gordon and Shay Given share the record for having the most penalties scored past them in a single Premier League season. Sunderland goalkeeper Gordon was beaten eight times during the 2007/08 campaign, including two in one game against Wigan. Given matched that feat in 2008/09, with Xabi Alonso on target from the spot in a 5–1 win for Liverpool. Dean Kiely had seven penalties put past him while playing for Charlton in 2002/03 and was sent off conceding one against Fulham on the last day.

↓ *Wigan's Denny Landzaat successfully slots a penalty past Sunderland's Craig Gordon. The Scotland keeper conceded a record eight penalties during the course of the 2007/08 season.*

GOLDEN GLOVE WINNERS

2004/05	Petr Cech	(Chelsea)
2005/06	Pepe Reina	(Liverpool)
2006/07	Pepe Reina	(Liverpool)
2007/08	Pepe Reina	(Liverpool)
2008/09	Edwin van der Sar	(Manchester United)
2009/10	Petr Cech	(Chelsea)

BLUNDERFUL GOALS

Goalkeeping blunders are pretty common in football, and the Premier League has seen its fair share over the years. Manchester United shot-stopper Massimo Taibi allowed a Matt Le Tissier shot to trickle through his legs in September 1999, while Tim Flowers was deceived by a divot on the pitch as a Stan Collymore strike looped over him and into the net in February 1996. Shay Given was left red-faced by Dion Dublin in November 1997 when he didn't realise the striker was behind him and put the ball down, allowing Dublin to nip in and score.

SCHMEICHEL LANDS AWARD

Peter Schmeichel was awarded the Premier League's Save of the Decade award in April 2003. The Danish shot-stopper, who was also named in the Team of the Decade, landed the prize for a stunning reflex stop to keep out a John Barnes header in a game against Newcastle in December 1997. Schmeichel is also one of only three goalkeepers to have scored in the Premier League. He pulled a goal back for Aston Villa in a 3–2 defeat at Everton in October 2001.

RISKY BUSINESS

Petr Cech wears a protective headguard in goal following an incident during a match with Reading in October 2006 that saw him fracture his skull. He came off worst as he challenged for the ball with Stephen Hunt. The midfielder's knee hit the goalkeeper's head. Cech was immediately taken to hospital, where he underwent surgery. Thankfully, he was able to make a comeback against Liverpool in January 2007.

⚹⋯ *Petr Cech's collision with Stephen Hunt during Chelsea's match against Reading on October 14 2006 left the Czech keeper with serious head injuries.*

SAVES OF THE SEASON

Burnley's Brian Jensen made more saves than any other top-flight goalkeeper in 2009/10. Jensen's total of 241 stops was seven more than Joe Hart, who spent the season at Birmingham on loan from Manchester City. Chelsea's Petr Cech made 164 saves.

METHOD IN THE MADNESS?

Most goalkeepers claim to have a technique for trying to save penalties. Former Arsenal stopper David Seaman famously claimed to have a system, although he refused to reveal what it was! David James, who played for Portsmouth during the 2009/10 campaign, said: 'Sometimes it's just instinctive. There have been a couple times when I have known which way the ball was going as soon as the guy put it on the spot. Then the only thing you have to do is stand up long enough to save it.'

⋯⋫ *Flamboyant, erratic and brilliant in equal measure, 1998 World Cup winner Fabien Barthez never quite managed to establish himself as Peter Schmeichel's long-term successor at Manchester United.*

BURRIDGE IS GOLDEN OLDIE

Goalkeeper John Burridge is the oldest player to have featured in the Premier League. Burridge was at Manchester City when he claimed the record, coming on to replace the injured Tony Coton at half-time against Newcastle in April 1995 aged 43 years, four months and 26 days. He kept a clean sheet as the game ended goalless. Keepers hold the top five positions in the oldest player chart, with Alec Chamberlain, Steve Ogrizovic, Neville Southall and Kevin Poole completing the quintet.

† *Golden oldie John Burridge made the last of his appearances in English football's top flight in April 1995, 26 years after he made his debut as a professional footballer, with Workington.*

ECCENTRIC KEEPERS

Goalkeepers are often seen as eccentric characters, and the Premier League has witnessed some of the most colourful. Fabien Barthez, formerly of Manchester United, was known to attempt step-overs or dribble past opposing strikers. And Liverpool's Bruce Grobbelaar was once involved in a disagreement with his own team-mate, Steve McManaman, in a clash against Everton in 1993/94.

Appearances

PREMIER LEAGUE APPEARANCES

David James	573
Ryan Giggs	548
Gary Speed	535
Sol Campbell	496
Emile Heskey	469
Frank Lampard	467
Paul Scholes	443
Alan Shearer	441
Jamie Carragher	435
Phil Neville	429

2009/10 EVER-PRESENTS

Brad Friedel	(Aston Villa)
Roger Johnson	(Birmingham)
Jussi Jaaskelainen	(Bolton)
Wade Elliott	(Burnley)
Brian Jensen	(Burnley)
Tyrone Mears	(Burnley)
Tim Howard	(Everton)
Pepe Reina	(Liverpool)
Patrice Evra	(Manchester United)
Darren Bent	(Sunderland)
Peter Crouch	(Tottenham)
Robert Green	(West Ham)
Hugo Rodallega	(Wigan)
Paul Scharner	(Wigan)

ALI'S ONE GAME

Ali Dia is one of the Premier League's most memorable figures, despite making just one appearance in the competition back in 1996. The story goes that Dia's agent phoned Southampton's manager at the time, Graeme Souness, and convinced him that he was speaking to legendary striker George Weah. He claimed Dia was his cousin, who had played for Paris St Germain in France and was a regular for his country. Souness subsequently signed Dia on a one-month contract to give him a chance to show his skills, and the forward was thrown into action after 32 minutes of a home game against Leeds. He lasted less than an hour before being hauled off, and he was released soon afterwards!

↑ *David James' record haul of 573 Premier League appearances appeared to come to an abrupt halt with Portsmouth's relegation in 2009/10.*

JAMES IS TOP DOG

David James is the Premier League's record appearance holder. When the 2009/10 season came to an end, the veteran shot-stopper had featured in 573 matches for five clubs – Liverpool, Aston Villa, West Ham, Manchester City and Portsmouth. James, who turned 40 in August 2010, made his first appearance in the competition in Liverpool's 1–0 defeat to Nottingham Forest on August 16 1992.

⋯➤ *Marcus Bent has appeared for more Premier League clubs than any other player – a remarkable seven since he first appeared for Crystal Palace in the 1997/98 season.*

BENT MAKES HIS MARC

Much-travelled striker Marcus Bent has turned out in the Premier League for seven different clubs. Since making his bow for Crystal Palace in January 1998, Bent has also played for Blackburn, Ipswich, Leicester, Everton, Charlton and Wigan. He enjoyed his best top-flight goalscoring seasons in 2001/02 and 2003/04, netting nine times for Ipswich and then Leicester.

VAN IN RUUD HEALTH

Ruud van Nistelrooy scored in a record 10 consecutive Premier League matches in 2003. The Dutch striker, who netted 95 top-flight goals for Manchester United in five seasons at the club, started the run with a hat-trick in a 3–0 win against Fulham at Old Trafford on March 22. He scored twice in a 4–0 win against Liverpool and grabbed another treble in a 4–1 success against Charlton before the end of the 2002/03 campaign. Van Nistelrooy then netted in United's opening game of season 2003/04 against Bolton and at Newcastle in August before the sequence came to an end.

┈┈▷ *A huge hit at Old Trafford, where he averaged an impressive 19 Premier League goals a season, Ruud van Nistelrooy hit heady heights in 2003 when he scored in 10 consecutive matches.*

TAKING THE MIKAEL

Mikael Forssell is one of four players to have been substituted in nine consecutive Premier League matches. He was taken off in nine straight games for Birmingham in 2008, although in one match against Tottenham he received a standing ovation, having scored a hat-trick. Elano also took the plaudits in three of the games in which he was taken off by Manchester City, leaving the action in the closing stages having scored each time. Former Everton striker Tomasz Radzinski (2002) and Sheffield Wednesday midfielder Mark Pembridge (1998) also share the record.

RYAN WINGS IT

Ryan Giggs has made the most Premier League appearances for the same club, featuring 548 times for Manchester United between 1992 and 2010. The veteran winger is the most successful player in the competition's history, having claimed 11 title-winners' medals. He was named the PFA Player of the Year in 2009 at the age of 36 after two incredibly successful decades at Old Trafford.

◁┈┈ *Hat-trick hero Mikael Forssell acknowledges the applause of a happy home crowd as he leaves the pitch during Birmingham's 4–1 victory over Tottenham on March 1 2008.*

⬇ *A surprise mid-season return to Arsenal in January 2010 kept alive Sol Campbell's impressive record of having appeared in every one of the Premier League's 18 seasons.*

OLE, OLE, OLE!

Ole Gunnar Solskjaer scored a record 17 Premier League goals as a substitute during his 11-year spell at Manchester United. The Norwegian striker famously netted four times after coming off the bench in a game against Nottingham Forest in 1999, while he also made an impact as a sub in the Champions League, snatching a late winner in the final against Bayern Munich that same year.

TRIO REACH 18 NOT OUT

Ryan Giggs, Sol Campbell and David James are the only players to have featured in all 18 Premier League seasons. Giggs' first appearance in the competition came in Manchester United's 3–0 defeat at home to Everton in August 1992, where he played 81 minutes before being substituted for Dion Dublin. Campbell looked set to lose his proud record in 2009/10 when he left Portsmouth and joined fourth-tier Notts County. However, he later re-joined former club Arsenal and returned to the top flight. James suffered relegation with Portsmouth in 2009/10.

Other Player Records

HAIR-RAISING STORIES

Everton ace Marouane Fellaini is undoubtedly one of the most recognisable players in the Barclays Premier League due to his stand-out hairstyle. Toffees' assistant manager Steve Round once even claimed that the midfielder's afro was contributing to the Belgian picking up more bookings. 'He's put it down to inexperience, but we've also put it down to the fact that he's quite recognisable,' Round said. Other bizarre hairstyles to crop up in the top flight over the years have included Djibril Cisse's variety of patterned cuts and Javier Margas, who dyed his hair claret and blue – the same colour as his West Ham shirt.

⇢ *Marouane Fellaini joined Everton for £12million (rising to £15million) from Standard Liege in September 2008 and has achieved cult status with the Goodison Park faithful.*

↑ *Gary Neville (Manchester United, right) and younger brother Phil (Everton) lead out their teams prior to the north-west rivals' top-flight clash at Old Trafford on January 31 2009.*

WHAT'S IN A NAME?

Getting the name and number of your favourite player on the back of your shirt can be expensive – especially if your idol is Jan Vennegoor of Hesselink, Diniyar Bilyaletdinov or Zurab Khizanishvili! There have been lots of long-named stars who have graced the top flight, although former Bolton favourite Stelios Giannakopoulos chose to make life easier for everybody by having his first name on the back of his shirt!

⇢ *Jan Vennegoor of Hesselink's name is the Dutch equivalent of an English double-barrelled surname. At 20 letters, it was also the longest surname in the Barclays Premier League in 2009/10.*

SIBLING RIVALRY

During the 2009/10 season, there were five sets of brothers playing in the top flight. Gary and Phil Neville are arguably the most famous, with Phil leaving Manchester United – and his sibling – for Everton in August 2005. Twin brothers Rafael and Fabio Da Silva are following in the Nevilles' footsteps at Old Trafford, while Manchester United team-mate Rio Ferdinand has a brother, Anton, who plays for Sunderland. Michael and Andy Dawson turned out for Tottenham and Hull respectively, while Gary and Steven Caldwell were brought together in the top flight when Steven's Burnley were promoted and Wigan signed Gary in January 2010.

FOREIGN DIGNITARIES

During the 2009/10 season, players from 69 different countries featured in Barclays Premier League matches. There have been many memorable foreigners who have graced the top flight over the years, and at the end of the 2001/02 season, to help mark the 10th anniversary of the competition, a vote was taken to decide the best overseas players. A star-studded list included Arsenal's French duo Thierry Henry and Patrick Vieira, Danish goalkeeping legend Peter Schmeichel and his former Manchester United team-mate, French hero Eric Cantona.

JOBS FOR THE BOYS

Football is, or can be, a relatively short-lived career, meaning that some players need to find alternative employment after hanging up their boots. Former Sweden international Tomas Brolin played for Leeds and Crystal Palace in the Premier League and starred at World Cup USA 1994, but after retiring from football aged 32, he reportedly started selling nozzles for vacuum cleaners! Other unusual career choices include that of ex-Nottingham Forest midfielder Neil Webb, who became a postman, and Wimbledon legend Vinnie Jones, who has featured in a number of Hollywood movies.

MOST REPRESENTED NATIONALITIES 2009/10 (number of players from each country)

England	223
France	39
Ireland	32
Scotland	21
Wales	16
Brazil	15
Spain	15
Netherlands	14
Northern Ireland	13
United States	10
Nigeria	9
Senegal	8
Portugal	8
Italy	8
Belgium	7
Norway	7
Argentina	6
Australia	6
Croatia	6
Ivory Coast	6

⇢ *Measuring a mighty 6ft 7½in (202cm), Wolves' Stefan Maierhofer is the Premier League's tallest-ever player.*

A TOAST TO SHERI

Former England striker Teddy Sheringham holds the record as the oldest player, other than goalkeepers, to have featured in the Premier League. Sheringham was 40 years and 272 days old when he made his last top-flight appearance – a 1–0 defeat for West Ham against Manchester City at Upton Park on December 30 2006.

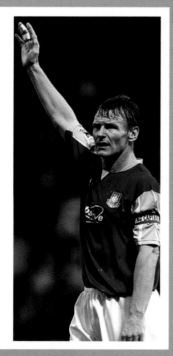

LAND OF THE GIANTS

Stefan Maierhofer is the tallest player to have played in the competition. The giant Austria international, who signed for Wolves from Rapid Vienna in August 2009, is 202 centimetres tall. That's two centimetres taller than former West Ham goalkeeper Ian Feuer, who previously held the record. Maierhofer made an instant impact after joining Wanderers, scoring on his debut at Blackburn. However, he spent the back end of 2009/10 on loan at Bristol City.

⇠ *The oldest outfield player ever to appear in the Premier League, Teddy Sheringham made his final top-flight appearance 18 years after he had made his first.*

WELCOME MATT

Matthew Briggs became the youngest player to appear in the division when he came off the bench for Fulham in their clash with Middlesbrough in May 2007. Briggs was 16 years and 65 days old when he came on for Moritz Volz in the 77th minute of a 3–1 defeat at the Riverside Stadium. It remains Briggs' only top-flight appearance.

ALL THE SMALL THINGS

They say that great things come in small packages, but pint-sized players have traditionally struggled to make an impact in the Premier League. Since the league began in 1992, six players have measured up at 163 centimetres. Left-back Alan Wright was the most prominent of those – he made 260 appearances for Aston Villa in an eight-year spell between 1995 and 2003. The remaining five players – Danny Wallace, Paul Brayson, Andres D'Alessandro, Andrew Ducros and Clint Marcelle – only made 43 appearances between them. Liverpool defender Emiliano Insua and Tottenham winger Aaron Lennon were the smallest players playing in the top flight in 2009/10, measuring up at 165cm.

Attendances

TABLE TWIST

Wigan, Portsmouth and Burnley would have been the three teams relegated from the top flight in 2009/10 if the table had been decided on average attendances alone. Only 14,323 fans turned up to watch the Latics' goalless draw with Pompey at the DW Stadium – the smallest crowd of the campaign. Portsmouth's lowest attendance was 16,207, when they drew 0–0 with Blackburn, while 18,397 witnessed Burnley's 1–1 draw with Fulham in December.

MAINE VENUE

The record attendance for any top-flight game came at Maine Road – Manchester City's old stadium – on January 17 1948. City's derby rivals, Manchester United, took on Arsenal, with Old Trafford being rebuilt after sustaining damage during the Second World War. Reported figures range from 81,962 to 83,260, and although the total number of spectators cannot be confirmed, the 1–1 draw has gone down in history as having the highest attendance of any Football League match.

↑ Be it by plane, bus or car, Addicks fans descended en masse to Ewood Park to cheer on Charlton in their crucial relegation encounter against Blackburn in April 2007.

OPERATION EWOOD

Charlton launched 'Operation Ewood' to get as many fans as possible to Blackburn for a crucial relegation clash in April 2007. The club put on 79 free coaches to transport almost 4,000 fans to Lancashire, while other supporters opted to fly from London Gatwick to Liverpool. It turned out to be the Addicks' biggest away following since the 1998 Play-Off Final at Wembley, but they failed to produce the goods on the pitch, losing 4–1!

↳ A revamped Old Trafford was fully opened for the first time on March 31 2007, when a crowd of 76,098 saw Manchester United beat Blackburn 4–1.

DRAWING A CROWD

Manchester United set a Premier League attendance record when 76,098 spectators watched them ease to a 4–1 win against Blackburn at Old Trafford on March 31 2007. There were just 214 empty seats as second-half goals from Paul Scholes, Michael Carrick, Park Ji-Sung and Ole Gunnar Solskjaer earned United victory. Matt Derbyshire had fired Rovers ahead in the 29th minute. There has since been a reduction in capacity at the stadium.

TOP HOME ATTENDANCES 2009/10

Manchester United (v Stoke)	75,316
Arsenal (v Tottenham)	60,103
Sunderland (v Manchester United)	47,641
Manchester City (v Tottenham)	47,370
Liverpool (v Hull)	44,392

⇡ *A crowd of 52,181 turned out at St James' Park to watch Newcastle's final home game of a successful championship-winning 2009/10 season. The match against Ipswich ended in a 2–2 draw.*

LOYAL FOLLOWING

Newcastle's St James' Park has a capacity of 52,387, making it the third largest club stadium in English football. The Magpies were relegated from the top flight at the end of the 2008/09 season, but they still played in front of crowds of over 40,000 in 16 of their 23 home games in the second tier.

RISE AND SHINE

The earliest kick-off ever in the competition's history was on October 2 2005 when a clash between Manchester City and Everton started at 11.15am. The game had been moved from its original Saturday afternoon slot due to the Toffees' UEFA Cup commitments. Two fixtures had already been scheduled for the Sunday, so the game started early. A crowd of 42,681 were in attendance – one fan turning up in pyjamas as a joke – as a stunning 25-yard strike from Danny Mills and an injury-time goal from Darius Vassell secured City a 2–0 win.

HOME AND AWAY

A survey commissioned in 2009 by the body who runs the Barclays Premier League found that those fans who watched their team play away from home felt that the atmosphere at these games was often even more intense and enjoyable than home games. The day-trip to new grounds and cities plus the comaraderie of travelling with like-minded supporters makes away games the best for those who go.

RECORD LOW FOR DONS

Wimbledon attracted the lowest attendance in Barclays Premier League history, with only 3,039 spectators turning up for a game against Everton in January 1993. The record-low crowd witnessed a 3–1 win for the visitors, with Tony Cottee scoring twice and Ian Snodin adding a third before the Dons pulled a goal back through John Fashanu. Wimbledon were sharing Selhurst Park with Crystal Palace at the time.

⇣ *Empty terraces for Wimbledon's home match against Everton in the 1992/93 season – it was the lowest attendance in Barclays Premier League history.*

AVERAGE ATTENDANCES 2009/10

Manchester United	74,864
Arsenal	59,927
Manchester City	45,513
Liverpool	42,864
Chelsea	41,423
Sunderland	40,355
Aston Villa	38,573
Everton	36,725
Tottenham	35,794
West Ham	33,683
Wolves	28,366
Stoke City	27,162
Blackburn	25,428
Birmingham	25,246
Hull	24,390
Fulham	23,909
Bolton	21,881
Burnley	20,654
Portsmouth	18,249
Wigan	17,998

Managers

MANAGER OF THE YEAR SINCE 2001

2000/01	George Burley	(Ipswich)
2001/02	Arsene Wenger	(Arsenal)
2002/03	Sir Alex Ferguson	(Manchester United)
2003/04	Arsene Wenger	(Arsenal)
2004/05	Jose Mourinho	(Chelsea)
2005/06	Jose Mourinho	(Chelsea)
2006/07	Sir Alex Ferguson	(Manchester United)
2007/08	Sir Alex Ferguson	(Manchester United)
2008/09	Sir Alex Ferguson	(Manchester United)
2009/10	Harry Redknapp	(Tottenham)

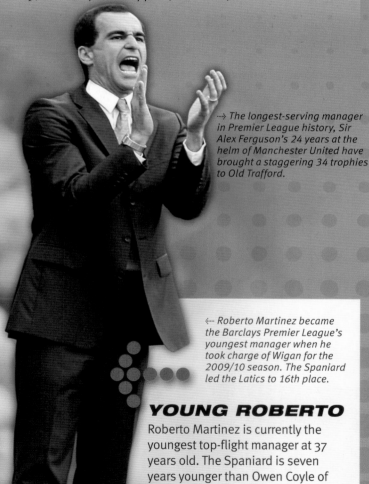

⋯▷ *The longest-serving manager in Premier League history, Sir Alex Ferguson's 24 years at the helm of Manchester United have brought a staggering 34 trophies to Old Trafford.*

◁⋯ *Roberto Martinez became the Barclays Premier League's youngest manager when he took charge of Wigan for the 2009/10 season. The Spaniard led the Latics to 16th place.*

YOUNG ROBERTO

Roberto Martinez is currently the youngest top-flight manager at 37 years old. The Spaniard is seven years younger than Owen Coyle of Bolton. There are four managers in their 60s. Sir Alex Ferguson is the oldest top-flight manager at 68, while Tottenham boss Harry Redknapp is five years younger. Roy Hodgson is 63 and Arsenal's Arsene Wenger turned 60 in October 2009.

FERGIE IS PART OF THE FURNITURE

Sir Alex Ferguson is currently the longest-serving manager, as well as the most successful, in English football. He was appointed boss of Manchester United in November 1986, meaning the 2010/11 season marks the Scot's 25th in the Old Trafford dugout. Arsene Wenger has just completed his 14th season at Arsenal, putting him second in the list, with Everton's David Moyes fourth overall throughout the divisions after spending the last nine campaigns at Goodison Park.

THE NAME GAME

Jose Mourinho was dubbed 'The Special One' by the media on his arrival at Chelsea in June 2004, but he is not the only boss to have been given a nickname by fans and the press. Another former Chelsea coach, Claudio Ranieri, earned the tag of 'The Tinkerman' for his constant experimentation with the Blues' line-up, while Sam Allardyce is affectionately known as 'Big Sam', Alex McLeish is 'Big Eck' and Sir Alex Ferguson is 'Fergie'.

MULTI-NATIONAL MANAGERS

Managers from nine different countries were in charge of top-flight clubs at the end of the 2009/10 campaign. Of the 20 teams, England had five bosses, Scotland and Italy had three, while there were two from Spain and two from the Republic of Ireland – Owen Coyle and Mick McCarthy. Coyle was born in Paisley, Scotland, and McCarthy hails from Barnsley, but both represented Ireland during their playing careers. Frenchman Arsene Wenger, Tony Pulis from Wales, Northern Irishmen Martin O'Neill and Iain Dowie (the latter played for the country 59 times) along with Avram Grant of Israel completed the multi-national line-up.

SHORT AND NOT SO SWEET

Les Reed was in charge of Charlton for just six weeks in late 2006. Reed had been Iain Dowie's assistant at The Valley but was promoted to manager on November 14 when Dowie left the club. He managed just one victory and saw his side knocked out of the Carling Cup by fourth-tier outfit Wycombe before leaving his post on Christmas Eve. Sammy Lee is another boss whose appearance in the division was fleeting. He spent 11 games in charge of Bolton between April and October 2007, while Colin Todd lasted 17 matches as boss of Derby County in 2001/02.

⬊ Kevin Keegan watches on as Newcastle's faint Premier League title hopes fade following their 1–1 draw against Nottingham Forest on May 2 1996.

KEEGAN LOSES HIS COOL

Top-flight bosses are always good for a memorable soundbite, but perhaps the most famous is Kevin Keegan's emotional outburst following Newcastle's 1–0 win at Leeds in April 1996. The Magpies had seen a significant lead at the top of the Premier League overturned by Manchester United, meaning that the title race was really hotting up. Keegan, hitting back at a comment made by United boss Sir Alex Ferguson, ended his televised rant with the now immortal line: 'I would love it if we beat them, love it!'

BROWN'S DRESSING DOWN

A manager's half-time team-talk can play a big part in how a side performs in the second half of a game. Normally, it's held in the dressing room, but on Boxing Day 2008, Hull boss Phil Brown took the unusual step of telling his players his thoughts on the pitch in front of the club's travelling fans. The Tigers were 4–0 down at the time against Manchester City, but they improved after the break to go down 5–1.

⋯⟩ Already 4–0 down in the match against Manchester City in December 2008, Phil Brown reads the half-time riot act to his Hull players.

PORTERFIELD WINS SACK RACE

Ian Porterfield was the first managerial casualty of the Premier League era. He left his job at Chelsea in February 1993 and was replaced on a temporary basis by David Webb. However, chairman Ken Bates opted to bring in Glenn Hoddle for the start of the 1993/94 campaign. Three more managers left their jobs at the end of that inaugural season, with Steve Coppell resigning at Crystal Palace, Brian Clough retiring at Nottingham Forest and Doug Livermore being replaced by Ossie Ardiles at Tottenham.

⋯⟩ On February 15 1993, Ian Porterfield paid the price for Chelsea's dramatic slump in form by becoming the first managerial casualty of the Premier League era.

MOYES MAKES HIS MARK

David Moyes became an instant hit with Everton fans when he labelled the Toffees 'The People's Club' on his arrival in March 2002. Glasgow-born Moyes said: 'I am from a city that is not unlike Liverpool. I am joining the people's football club. The majority of people you meet on the street are Everton fans.' That statement went down well with the blue half of Merseyside, although not so much with Liverpool fans!

Stadiums

THEATRE OF DREAMS

Manchester United's Old Trafford home is the largest stadium in the top flight. The 'Theatre of Dreams', as it is commonly known, has a capacity of 75,769, which is over 15,000 more than Arsenal's Emirates Stadium can hold. The capacity had been just over 76,000 until the seating was reorganised in 2009. Wembley, which plays host to all the major domestic cup finals and also the England national team, has a capacity of 90,000. Both stadiums have been given a five-star rating by UEFA.

↑ George Armstrong (with his arms raised) celebrates after handing Arsenal the lead in their FA Cup semi-final clash against Stoke at Villa Park on April 15 1972. The match ended in a 1–1 draw.

A LONG JOURNEY

Sunderland's trip to Portsmouth and vice versa was the longest journey undertaken in the Barclays Premier League in 2009/10. The Black Cats' Stadium of Light home is 336 miles away from Fratton Park, a trek of around six hours! Both games between the two sides finished 1–1, while the teams were also paired together in the FA Cup. Pompey came out on top in that game, securing a 2–1 victory in Hampshire.

PARK LIFE

Villa Park has hosted a record 55 FA Cup semi-finals. Tottenham beat West Brom 4–0 in the first tie to be played there in 1901, while Manchester United were 4–1 winners against Watford the last time it was used in 2007. Its central location makes it the ideal venue if teams from the north are drawn against teams from the south. Hillsborough, the home of Sheffield Wednesday, has been used for 34 semi-final matches and Old Trafford for 23.

STANLEY PARK DIVIDE

The stadiums of Merseyside rivals Liverpool and Everton are only separated by Stanley Park. Anfield, the home of the Reds, and Everton's Goodison Park are the closest two grounds in the top flight, although Nottingham Forest and Notts County's stadiums are actually the closest in English football.

↓ Separated by Stanley Park, Merseyside's two great football arenas, Goodison Park (left) and Anfield (right), are only 0.586 miles (0.944km) apart.

TOP 10 PREMIER LEAGUE CAPACITIES

Stadium	Club	Capacity
Old Trafford	(Manchester United)	75,769
Emirates Stadium	(Arsenal)	60,432
Stadium of Light	(Sunderland)	48,707
City of Manchester Stadium	(Manchester City)	47,405
Anfield	(Liverpool)	45,362
Villa Park	(Aston Villa)	42,783
Stamford Bridge	(Chelsea)	42,449
Goodison Park	(Everton)	40,157
White Hart Lane	(Tottenham)	36,230
Upton Park	(West Ham)	35,303

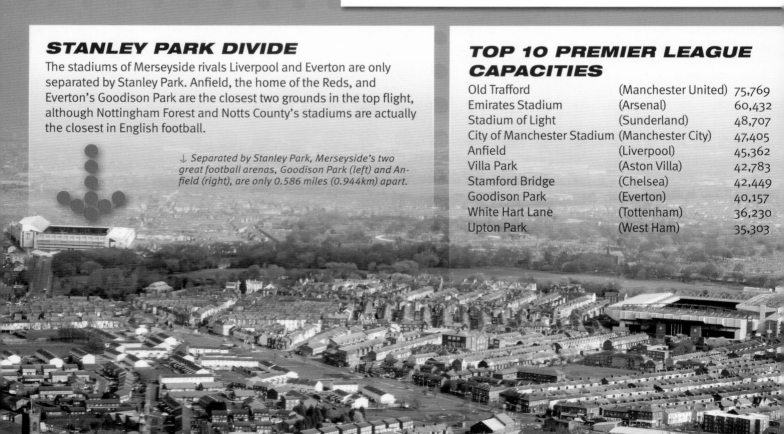

↑ *Burnley have played at Turf Moor for 127 years. The ground was the oldest of any in the top flight in the 2009/10 season.*

TURF TIMES

Burnley have been playing their home games at Turf Moor since 1883, making it the oldest stadium in the top flight in 2009/10. The first grandstand was built in 1885, while the stadium was refurbished during the 1990s. The Clarets played their first match at the ground on February 17 1883, losing 6–3 to Rawtensall, while the first Football League game to take place there was on October 6 1888.

NEW HOME FOR GUNNERS

Arsenal's Emirates Stadium is the newest stadium in the Barclays Premier League, having been officially opened in July 2006. It is the third biggest stadium in London after Wembley and Twickenham – the home of England's rugby union team. The ground was initially known as Ashburton Grove until a multi-million pound sponsorship deal was struck. It has a capacity of 60,432 spectators, although the highest attendance currently stands at 60,161. That was for a 2–2 draw against Manchester United in November 2007.

FULL TO CAPACITY

Eight of the 20 stadiums used in the top flight in 2009/10 can hold over 40,000 people. That is the second highest amount of any division in Europe, with Germany leading the way. The Bundesliga boasts 12 grounds capable of holding 40,000 or more spectators, with seven over the 50,000 mark. There are seven Italian clubs, six in the top flight of Spain and four in France with capacities of over 40,000.

QUINTET ON THE MOVE

Middlesbrough were the first of five teams to move into a new stadium while playing Premier League football. Goals from Craig Hignett and Jan Age Fjortoft earned the Teessiders a 2–0 win the first time they played at their new home in the league, against Chelsea on August 26 1995. Derby swapped the Baseball Ground for Pride Park in 1997, with Bolton moving to the Reebok Stadium in the same year. Manchester City opened the City of Manchester Stadium with a 1–1 draw against Portsmouth in August 2003, while Arsenal played their first league game at the Emirates Stadium against Aston Villa on August 19 2006.

⇢ *Middlesbrough's Jan Age Fjortoft (left) keeps the ball from Chelsea's Ruud Gullit during the first league match at the Riverside Stadium on August 26 1995.*

⇠ *Michael Ballack (right) challenges Samir Nasri (left) during Chelsea's 2–0 victory over London rivals Arsenal at Stamford Bridge on February 7 2010.*

LONDON LIFE

There were 20 London derbies in the Barclays Premier League in 2009/10, with champions Chelsea coming out on top overall. The Blues took 19 points from eight games, winning all of their matches against their local rivals at Stamford Bridge. Fulham and Chelsea are both based in west London, Arsenal and Tottenham are situated in the north, while West Ham are actually based in the east of the capital. The Hammers managed just three points in their eight derby games, drawing at Upton Park against Fulham, Arsenal and Chelsea.

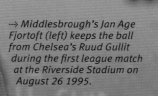

Transfers

GROVES STARTS A TREND

Big-money transfers may be commonplace in English football nowadays, but Willie Groves was actually the first player to be transferred for over £100. The Scottish forward moved from Celtic to West Brom in 1890, but it was his switch from the Baggies to rivals Aston Villa three years later that set the record. Groves went on to help the Villans to the First Division title in 1894.

COLE IS OUT OF TOON

Andrew Cole broke the British transfer record in January 1995 when he swapped Newcastle for Manchester United. It was the first record-breaking move since the introduction of the Premier League. Cole had scored 34 top-flight goals for the Magpies in season 1993/94 and added nine more in 18 games in 1994/95 before making the move to Old Trafford. The Red Devils paid £6.25million cash for Cole and also sent Keith Gillespie in the opposite direction.

⟶ *A crowd of 15,000 diehard fans braved the rain to salute Alan Shearer's world-record transfer to Newcastle in 1996.*

⟵ *Wayne Rooney became the most expensive teenager in British football history when he signed for Manchester United in August 2004.*

SHEAR MAGIC FOR MAGPIES

Newcastle broke the world transfer record to land Alan Shearer from Blackburn in July 1996. The Magpies paid Rovers £15million to sign the prolific England striker, who had finished the 1995/96 campaign with 31 league goals. Shearer netted 25 times in the Premier League in his first season with his boyhood club to top the goalscoring charts for the third consecutive term. He also scooped the PFA Player of the Year award for the second time.

LAST-GASP DEALS

Transfer deadline day always creates a buzz, with clubs attempting to push through deals at the last minute. Manchester United have left it late to complete moves for both Wayne Rooney and Dimitar Berbatov in recent years. Rooney became the world's most expensive teenager when he swapped Everton for Old Trafford on August 31 2004 for a fee of around £27million. And Berbatov's signature was still drying on the contract taking him from Tottenham when the transfer window closed on September 1 2008.

BRITISH TRANSFER RECORDS SINCE 1995*

Player	Transfer	Fee	Date
Andrew Cole	(Newcastle to Manchester United)	£6.25million	Jan 1995
Dennis Bergkamp	(Inter Milan to Arsenal)	£7.5million	June 1995
Stan Collymore	(Nottingham Forest to Liverpool)	£8.5million	June 1995
Alan Shearer	(Blackburn to Newcastle)	£15million	July 1996
Nicolas Anelka	(Arsenal to Real Madrid)	£22.5million	Aug 1999
Juan Sebastian Veron	(Lazio to Manchester United)	£28.1million	July 2001
Rio Ferdinand	(Leeds to Manchester United)	£29.1million	July 2002
Andriy Shevchenko	(AC Milan to Chelsea)	£30.8million	July 2002
Robinho	(Real Madrid to Manchester City)	£32.5million	Sept 2008
Cristiano Ronaldo	(Manchester United to Real Madrid)	£80million	June 2009

* Reported fees

RECORD-BREAKING RONALDO

Cristiano Ronaldo holds the world transfer record following his incredible £80million move from Manchester United to Real Madrid in June 2009. The Portugal winger enjoyed a stunning season at Old Trafford in 2007/08, scoring 42 goals in all competitions – 31 of those in the league – but United rejected Madrid's advances that summer. However, Ronaldo expressed his desire to leave the club after another impressive campaign in 2008/09 – he scored 18 top-flight goals and 25 in total – and the record-breaking deal was sealed that summer.

⟵ It took a world-record transfer fee of £80million for Real Madrid to prise Cristiano Ronaldo away from Old Trafford.

FIRMANI'S ITALIAN JOB

The cosmopolitan nature of the English game frequently sees players come and go from overseas, but Eddie Firmani was the first player to move abroad from a British club. He set a British transfer record when he left Charlton for Italian side Sampdoria in July 1955.

SWITCHING SIDES

Transfers between derby rivals have caused a few stirs over the years. Sol Campbell's move from Tottenham to Arsenal in July 2001 didn't go down well with the White Hart Lane faithful, while Ashley Cole was given a tough time by Gunners fans following his switch to Chelsea in August 2006. Nick Barmby moved from Everton to Liverpool in a £6million deal in July 2000 – the highest fee the Reds have ever paid to their Merseyside rivals.

⟵ Eric Cantona's arrival galvanised Manchester United, who won the Premier League title in four of the Frenchman's five seasons at the club.

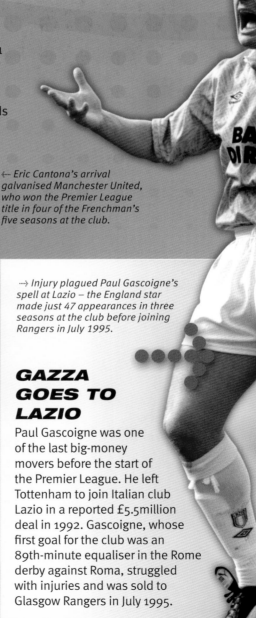

⟶ Injury plagued Paul Gascoigne's spell at Lazio – the England star made just 47 appearances in three seasons at the club before joining Rangers in July 1995.

BARGAIN BUYS

Everybody loves a bargain, and that's what Manchester United got when they signed Eric Cantona from Leeds for £1.2million in November 1992. The Frenchman had helped the Yorkshire club to the First Division title before leaving for Old Trafford. Cantona went on to become a United legend, scoring 64 Premier League goals. Fellow Frenchman Christophe Dugarry also proved to be a steal for Birmingham in 2003 when he scored five goals in as many games during a loan spell from Bordeaux to help the club avoid relegation.

GAZZA GOES TO LAZIO

Paul Gascoigne was one of the last big-money movers before the start of the Premier League. He left Tottenham to join Italian club Lazio in a reported £5.5million deal in 1992. Gascoigne, whose first goal for the club was an 89th-minute equaliser in the Rome derby against Roma, struggled with injuries and was sold to Glasgow Rangers in July 1995.

Owners and Chairmen

CITY SLICKERS

Manchester City are one of the biggest buyers of players in the Barclays Premier League. They are owned by billionaire Sheikh Mansour bin Zayed Al Nahyan, who is a member of the Abu Dhabi royal family. In Sheikh Mansour's first summer in charge of the club in 2009, City spent over £90million on Roque Santa Cruz, Gareth Barry, Emmanuel Adebayor, Kolo Toure and Joleon Lescott, while also splashing out an undisclosed amount on Carlos Tevez.

SMITH COOKS UP A HALF-TIME TREAT

Celebrity chef Delia Smith memorably made an impassioned plea for support from Norwich fans on the Carrow Road pitch at half-time of a game against Manchester City in February 2005. The Canaries were leading 2–0 when Smith, the club's joint majority shareholder, grabbed a microphone and came onto the field. After praising the Norwich fans as the best in the division, she then urged them to be more vocal in the second half, asking: 'Where are you? Let's be having you!' City went on to lose the game 3–2.

⇂ *A former season-ticket holder at Norwich, Delia Smith (along with husband Michael Wynn-Jones) became the club's joint majority shareholder in 1996.*

↑ *Carlos Tevez signed for Manchester City in July 2009 and his performances quickly made him a hit with the home fans.*

SULLIVAN AND GOLD

David Sullivan and David Gold have been joint chairmen at two Barclays Premier League clubs. The pair bought Birmingham in 1993, helping them to avoid relegation to the third tier. Blues reached the competition for the first time at the end of season 2001/02. Sullivan and Gold sold the club to Carson Yeung in the autumn of 2009 and at the start of 2010 they bought a stake in West Ham – the team that they both support.

↑ *Long-time supporters of West Ham, David Sullivan (left) and David Gold (right) completed their takeover of the Upton Park club in January 2010.*

YOU'RE FIRED!

Lord Alan Sugar, star of the television show *The Apprentice*, was chairman of Tottenham between 1991 and 2001. Spurs won just one trophy during his reign – the League Cup in 1999 – but he did break the club's transfer record to bring Les Ferdinand to White Hart Lane in 1997. Lord Sugar sacked several bosses during his time in charge – presumably giving him an early chance to perfect his now famous 'You're fired' catchphrase!

Lord Alan Sugar's 10-year reign as Tottenham chairman saw seven different managers at the White Hart Lane club.

DIRECTORS IN THE PICTURE

The role of director of football may be a common one on the continent, but it is relatively new to the English game. Those in the job are normally seen as a go-between from the manager to the club's board and the owner, and they rarely get involved in the coaching of players. Avram Grant has held the position at both Chelsea and Portsmouth, going on to take over as manager of the club on both occasions.

THE AMERICAN DREAM

There has been an influx of American businessmen into the Barclays Premier League over the last few years. Three of the perceived 'Big Four' – Manchester United, Arsenal and Liverpool – have either an American owner or a large shareholder from the USA. The Glazer family own United, George Gillett and Tom Hicks run Liverpool and Stan Kroenke has a large shareholding in the Gunners. Missouri-born Ellis Short is the majority shareholder at Sunderland, while Randy Lerner – who also owns the Cleveland Browns American football team – has been in charge at Aston Villa since 2006.

A VOTE OF CONFIDENCE

It's nice to have the support of the powers-that-be, but getting a vote of confidence from your chairman is not always a sign that things are going well as a manager. That normally happens if a team is under pressure due to poor results or performances. Burnley chairman Barry Kilby felt the need to go public and give his backing to Brian Laws in March 2010, just 10 games into his spell as the Clarets' boss. Gianfranco Zola, meanwhile, was also given a vote of confidence by new West Ham owner David Sullivan in 2009/10, only to be released in the summer.

A FAN WITH A PLAN

Steve Gibson helped his boyhood club to reach new heights in the Premier League. The Middlesbrough chairman took over the Teessiders in 1994 having become a director at just 26. He raised the club's profile by building a brand new all-seater stadium and bringing in big-name players such as Juninho and Fabrizio Ravanelli, and he guided them to a seventh-place finish in the top flight in 2004/05.

A self-made millionnaire and a lifelong Boro fan, Steve Gibson is one of the most respected chairmen in English football.

ROMAN'S EMPIRE

Roman Abramovich took English football to a new level when he bought Chelsea in July 2003. That summer, the Russian billionaire immediately brought in world-class players such as Claude Makelele and Arjen Robben. In May 2006, he smashed the British transfer record to sign Andriy Shevchenko. Since Abramovich took over, Chelsea have won the Barclays Premier League title three times, the FA Cup three times, the Carling Cup twice and have been beaten finalists in the Champions League.

Russian billionaire Roman Abramovich has invested heavily in Chelsea since buying the west London club in July 2003.

Supporters

↑ Everton fan Sylvester Stallone acknowledges the Goodison Park fans before the Toffees' match against Reading in January 2007.

SONGS OF PRAISE

Some of the league's top stars have been immortalised in song by supporters down the years. 'Ooh-Ahh, Cantona' could regularly be heard ringing around Old Trafford when 'King Eric' turned out for Manchester United, while Fernando Torres can boast his own chant at Liverpool. To the tune of 'The Animals Went In Two By Two', the fans on the Kop sing: 'His armband proved he was a red – Torres, Torres. You'll never walk alone, it said – Torres, Torres. We bought the lad from sunny Spain, he gets the ball, he scores again. Fernando Torres, Liverpool's number nine'!

↓ Liverpool's ground, Anfield, has long been known as one of the great cathedrals of British football and its Kop stand (below) is famous around the world.

PREMIER LEAGUE A-LISTERS

Some of Hollywood's biggest stars support Barclays Premier League clubs. Tom Hanks is an Aston Villa fan, Samuel L. Jackson fell in love with Liverpool while shooting a film there, and Sylvester Stallone – star of Rocky and Rambo – watched Everton draw 1–1 with Reading in January 2007. Brad Pitt is said to be a Manchester United fan, while pop star Justin Timberlake was once photographed at Old Trafford. Funnyman Will Ferrell wore a Chelsea shirt when he watched the Blues beat Inter Milan in a pre-season friendly in America.

FULHAM FANS FEELING GOOD

Fulham fans were more pleased by their team's performances than any other supporters in the top flight in 2009/10. In a national newspaper survey of over 5,000 supporters, followers of the Cottagers gave their team a 92 per cent approval rating when asked to rate the performance of their club's players. The Londoners enjoyed impressive home wins against Manchester United (3–0) and Liverpool (3–1), as well as reaching the final of the Europa League.

BLUE-NOSE CARRAGHER

Jamie Carragher may turn out for Liverpool every week, but he was an Everton fan growing up. He revealed: 'Everton controlled my life and dominated my thoughts 24/7. I went to the away games, followed them across Europe and in the mid-80s went to Wembley so often it began to feel like Alton Towers!' The Reds defender is not the only player to reveal his boyhood idols. Robbie Keane grew up as a Liverpool supporter, Manchester City's Adam Johnson is a Sunderland fan and Joleon Lescott, who used to play for Wolves, apparently has a soft spot for Aston Villa!

THE LOUDEST TOP-FLIGHT FANS*

Stoke	101.80 decibels
Tottenham	97.58 decibels
Liverpool	95.40 decibels
Portsmouth	94.30 decibels
Newcastle	94.06 decibels
Aston Villa	92.20 decibels
Chelsea	92.06 decibels
Middlesbrough	91.30 decibels
Arsenal	90.80 decibels
West Brom	90.26 decibels

* Figures recorded in 2008/09

↑ Officially the top flight's most vociferous supporters, Stoke fans cheer on their team in the home match against Chelsea in September 2009.

ASIA AND BEYOND

The Barclays Premier League is the most popular and most watched league in the world, and it has a particularly strong following in Asia. The Barclays Asia Trophy was introduced in 2003 as a way of giving fans across the continent the chance to catch a glimpse of their heroes in action. It has taken place in a different country once every two years since, with Chelsea, Bolton, Portsmouth and Tottenham all having won the title. Malaysia, Thailand, Hong Kong and China have all staged the event.

↓ Tottenham's Wilson Palacios (left) and Hull's Geovanni (right) battle for the ball during the two sides' Barclays Asia Trophy clash in Beijing in July 2009.

BRITANNIA RULES THE SOUNDWAVES

Stoke fans are officially the loudest in the top flight. The Potters were the only club to exceed 100 decibels when crowd noise was measured up and down the country at the start of the 2008/09 season. The noise generated by the Britannia Stadium faithful is equal to that of an aeroplane taking off! Tottenham fans were second in the table, reaching 97.5 decibels.

MR PORTSMOUTH

The Barclays Premier League waved goodbye to one of its most recognisable fans when Portsmouth were relegated at the end of the 2009/10 season. John Anthony Portsmouth Football Club Westwood – or 'Mr Portsmouth' as he is more commonly known – attends matches wearing an unmistakable tall hat and blue wig. He has around 60 Pompey tattoos, the club crest shaved onto his head and 'PFC' engraved on his teeth. Now that's commitment!

⋯→ Ardent fan John 'Portsmouth Football Club' Westwood can barely contain his emotions as his beloved team win the FA Cup final against Cardiff in 2008.

QUALITY COUNTS

Supporters watch their favourite team for a variety of reasons, but the quality of football on offer is the main draw for followers of top-flight clubs. The chance to see some of the world's best players came second in an official survey of just under 40,000 fans, which was conducted by the Premier League in 2009, while the passion of the crowd was a close third.

LATICS GIVE BACK

Wigan's players showed solidarity with the club's supporters when they refunded fans who had bought tickets for the 9–1 defeat at Tottenham in November 2009. The total pay-out came to around £15,000, with Latics skipper Mario Melchiot saying at the time: 'We feel that as a group of players we badly let down our supporters. This is a gesture we have to make and pay them back for their loyalty.'

Disciplinary Records

CAMEO APPEARANCES

Three players have been sent off in the Premier League era without even touching a ball! Swedish defender Andreas Johansson's first act after coming on for Wigan on the last day of the 2005/06 season was to bring down Freddie Ljungberg in the penalty area. His second was to walk off the pitch after being shown a red card! Keith Gillespie was playing for Sheffield United when he was dismissed for elbowing Reading's Stephen Hunt in January 2007, just a few seconds after entering the action. And Dave Kitson lasted less than a minute of Reading's clash with Manchester United in August of that same year before he was sent off for a late challenge on Patrice Evra.

⇢ Reading's Dave Kitson sees red less than a minute after coming on as a substitute during the Royals' 0–0 draw against Manchester United in August 2007.

CLEAN COTTAGERS

Fulham were shown just 46 yellow cards as a team during the 2009/10 season – six less than nearest rivals Manchester City. In contrast, Sunderland were shown nearly twice that many, with 82 bookings to their name. Kagisho Dikgacoi was the only Fulham player to be sent off. He was given his marching orders following an off-the-ball incident with West Ham's Scott Parker in the first half of a 2–2 draw at Upton Park.

⇠ Fulham's Kagisho Dikgacoi is sent off in the 40th minute of his side's match against West Ham on October 4 2009. It was the Cottagers' only red card of the season.

REDS HAVE BEST RECORD

Liverpool have the best disciplinary record of the seven clubs who have been involved in the Premier League since the start. At the end of season 2009/10, the Reds had totalled 815 bookings and 39 red cards from 696 matches. Aston Villa have only had 38 players sent off since 1992, but they recorded 84 more yellow cards than the Merseysiders.

TEVEZ IS A HAMMERS HERO

Carlos Tevez remains a hero to West Ham fans, despite scoring two goals against them during the 2009/10 campaign. The Argentina international refused to celebrate his brace in Manchester City's 3–1 victory against his former club in September 2009. Explaining his act of sportsmanship, Tevez said: 'They were my first club in England and, in my heart, part of me will always be a Hammer. Personally, I would have preferred to beat another club.'

NOTE OF CAUTION

Four players share the record for the most yellow cards received in a single Premier League season. Mark Hughes was playing for Southampton and Olivier Dacourt turned out for Everton when they were both cautioned 14 times during the 1998/99 campaign. Robbie Savage equalled that total in 2001/02 while at Leicester, and Paul Ince repeated the feat in season 2003/04 when he was bossing the Wolves midfield. Eric Cantona was sent off four times during Manchester United's title-winning season of 1993/94 – the most by any player in a single Premier League campaign.

⤓ *It's yet another yellow card for Everton's Olivier Dacourt, this time against Leeds on September 12 1998.*

DUNNE AND DUSTED

Richard Dunne joined Duncan Ferguson and Patrick Vieira on eight top-flight red cards when he was sent off in Manchester City's 1–0 win against Wigan in January 2009. The Republic of Ireland international was dismissed shortly after Pablo Zabaleta had put City ahead. That was Dunne's second league dismissal of the 2008/09 season, and he was sent off for a third time in the UEFA Cup clash against Hamburg the following April.

⤏ *Manchester City defender Richard Dunne has his head in his hands after being shown a red card in the final moments of his side's 2–1 defeat to Tottenham in November 2008.*

GUNNERS TOP FAIR PLAY TABLE

Arsenal topped the Fair Play table at the end of season 2009/10, holding off stiff competition from north London rivals Tottenham. The table is decided via a points system, with various aspects of a club's performance being assessed after every game. The amount of bookings and red cards, as well as positive play and respect towards referees, are taken into consideration. The top three national associations in UEFA's Fair Play League are given an extra Europa League place, although England missed out in the most recent campaign.

FAIR PLAY TABLE 2009/10

Arsenal	1303 points
Tottenham	1300 points
Fulham	1282 points
Manchester United	1275 points
Chelsea	1272 points
Burnley	1254 points
Aston Villa	1253 points
Manchester City	1249 points
Everton	1241 points
West Ham	1240 points

⤏ *A record 94 yellow cards and five red cards make Lee Bowyer, now with Birmingham, perhaps the most combative player in Premier League history.*

BOWYER IS BOOKED UP

Lee Bowyer is the most booked player in Premier League history. Bowyer, who is known for his tough-tackling approach, was shown a yellow card on eight occasions while playing for Birmingham in 2009/10 to take his overall total to 94. That figure is five more than fellow midfielder Robbie Savage, who comes second on the all-time list.

Referee Records

RESPECT CAMPAIGN

The Football Association launched the Respect campaign in the summer of 2008 aimed at improving the behaviour of players and coaches towards referees and officials. Guidelines were set out that now mean only the team captain is allowed to approach the referee, while all players are asked to adhere to a basic code of conduct governing their behaviour on the pitch.

REFEREE RECORD 2009/10

Name	Games	Yellow	Red
Martin Atkinson	31	127	5
Stuart Attwell	15	58	2
Steve Bennett	29	109	5
Mark Clattenburg	31	84	5
Mike Dean	30	116	6
Phil Dowd	29	88	5
Chris Foy	26	69	2
Kevin Friend	13	41	4
Mark Halsey	1	0	0
Mike Jones	20	64	1
Andre Marriner	28	97	9
Lee Mason	22	60	6
Lee Probert	22	75	6
Anthony Taylor	2	5	0
Peter Walton	27	67	4
Howard Webb	28	101	3
Alan Wiley	26	81	5

GRAHAM TOPS POLL

Graham Poll brandished a joint record 10 red cards during the 1997/98 and 2000/01 Premier League campaigns. He sent off Leeds duo Gary Kelly and Alf-Inge Haaland before half-time in a goalless draw at Chelsea in December 1997 – both for second bookable offences. Poll showed three red cards in Sunderland's 1–0 defeat at home to Manchester United in January 2001, with Michael Gray the first to go and Alex Rae and Andrew Cole following after the break. Rob Styles sent 10 players off during season 2003/04 and Steve Bennett did the same in 2005/06.

⟶ Graham Poll is the only referee in Premier League history to have issued 10 red cards in a season on two occasions.

OLDEST AND YOUNGEST

Peter Walton is the top flight's oldest referee, while Stuart Attwell is the youngest. Walton, who turned 51 in October 2010, took charge of his first game in the competition in 2003 – a 4–3 win for Wolves against Leicester. Attwell, who celebrated his 28th birthday in October 2010, became the youngest person ever to officiate in the Premier League when he took charge of Blackburn's 1–1 draw with Hull aged just 25 in August 2008.

↓ Burnley's Brian Jensen looks on in disbelief as Mike Dean points to the spot following a foul on Blackburn's Martin Olsson in March 2010. Blackburn scored from the spot-kick and won 1–0.

DEAN'S DECISIONS

Mike Dean awarded 17 penalties in the 30 top-flight games he officiated during the 2009/10 season. Wayne Rooney converted three of them, scoring one to help Manchester United to a 2–1 win against Arsenal at Old Trafford and two in a 4–1 victory at Portsmouth. Pompey's Kevin-Prince Boateng also scored from the spot in that game. Dean gave a penalty apiece as West Ham drew 1–1 with Chelsea in December, although he made Frank Lampard re-take his twice!

CARROLL'S LUCKY ESCAPE

Goalkeeper Roy Carroll enjoyed a lucky escape when he spilled a 50-yard effort from Pedro Mendes over the line in the closing seconds of an Old Trafford clash between Manchester United and Tottenham in January 2005. Referee Mark Clattenburg and his assistant Rob Lewis were too far away from the incident to judge whether the Portuguese midfielder's first-time shot had gone in or not. Television replays showed that the ball had crossed the line, but the goal was not given.

JOB SWAP

Second jobs are not uncommon for referees. David Elleray was a school teacher as well as a top-flight referee, with Elleray apparently unable to officiate at the World Cup finals in France in 1998 due to commitments at Harrow School, where he was a geography teacher. Howard Webb, who took charge of the Champions League and World Cup finals in 2010, is a police officer back home in South Yorkshire, while Mike Riley is a qualified accountant.

⟶ *David Elleray combined Premier League refereeing duties with his job as a teacher at Harrow School.*

MARRINER DIVES IN

Andre Marriner dished out nine red cards in the top flight in 2009/10 – the most by any referee. He sent off two players in a single game on two occasions. The first was in October when Liverpool claimed a 2–0 win against Manchester United at Anfield, with Nemanja Vidic and Javier Mascherano both dismissed. Marriner then sent off Kenwyne Jones and Radoslav Kovac in Sunderland's 2–2 draw with West Ham later that month.

⇡ *Dermot Gallagher was on the Premier League's referee roster for 15 years before his retirement in 2007.*

GALLAGHER IS A HIT

Dermot Gallagher spent a record 15 years refereeing in the Premier League between 1992 and 2007. Gallagher's first game in the competition was a 2–0 win for Coventry at Tottenham on August 19 1992, while his final fixture was a 2–2 draw between Liverpool and Charlton at Anfield on May 13 2007. He didn't dish out a single yellow or red card during that match. Graham Poll officiated in the Premier League for 14 years, while Mike Riley managed 13.

⟶ *Martin Atkinson shows Everton's Steven Pienaar a yellow card during the Merseyside derby at Anfield on February 6 2010. The match, which Liverpool won 1–0, saw six yellow and two red cards.*

YELLOW PERIL

Martin Atkinson has handed out the most yellow cards in a single Premier League season. The Yorkshire official booked 127 players during the 2009/10 campaign. That figure is four more than Mike Dean showed in 2008/09.

Championship All-Time Records

The second tier was first introduced in 1892, starting out with 12 clubs. That number has doubled under the current format, with the npower Championship – as it is now known – continuing to go from strength to strength. Over the years, big guns such as Manchester United and Liverpool have competed in the division, alongside smaller teams like Darwen and Loughborough – both of whom left their mark, albeit for the wrong reasons!

Reading captain Graeme Murty lifts what was, until 1992, the trophy awarded to the champions of England's top tier. Since the advent of the Premier League, it has gone to the champions of the second tier, and in 2005/06, Reading won the title with a record points total of 106.

Champions, Participation, Promotion and Relegation

LOUGHBOROUGH LAND RECORD

Loughborough managed just one victory during the 1899/00 season – a second-tier record. The Leicestershire club were elected to The Football League for the start of the 1895/96 campaign but lasted just five seasons before dropping out. Loughborough's sole win that term came with a 2–1 victory at home to Burton United. They finished rock bottom with eight points and having scored just 18 times – also a Football League landmark for the fewest goals scored in a season.

BLACK CATS POUNCE

Sunderland romped to the league title in 1998/99, finishing a massive 18 points ahead of runners-up Bradford. Peter Reid was in charge as the Black Cats lost just three games – against Barnsley, Tranmere and Watford – to end the campaign with a then-record 105 points. Reading broke that when they went a point better in 2005/06.

↓ Peter Reid won The Football League championship as a player at Everton in the top flight in 1985, and then was boss of Sunderland when they finished top of the second tier 14 years later.

SMALL HEATH STAY PUT

Small Heath, or Birmingham as they are now known, finished top of the very first second-tier table in 1892/93 – but they missed out on promotion. Before automatic promotion was introduced, the bottom three teams in the top flight took on the top three from the second tier each season to determine who went up. Small Heath played Division One's bottom club, Newton Heath (now Manchester United), and were beaten 5–2 in a replay after the initial clash had finished 1–1. Bizarrely, both the runners-up, Sheffield United, and Darwen, who finished third, did win promotion.

DONNY DOWN AND OUT

The 1904/05 season ended in disappointment for Doncaster, with their eight-point total equalling Loughborough's record for the lowest ever. However, Rovers managed treble the amount of wins, beating Barnsley, Leicester and Glossop and drawing with Blackpool and Port Vale in a league that also included Manchester United and Liverpool. Cambridge hold the record for the lowest total since three points for a win was introduced, taking just 24 in 1983/84.

SECOND BEST

West Brom finished second to Newcastle with 91 points in 2009/10, but that is not the highest total for a runner-up in the division. Leicester went one better in the 2002/03 campaign, finishing six points behind champions Portsmouth to gain automatic promotion with an impressive 92-point haul.

↑ Roman Bednar (one from right) sprays the bubbly after West Brom finished runners-up in the Championship in 2010.

LOSING LIONS

Millwall lost a record 12 games during the 1987/88 season but still managed to win the league. Runners-up Aston Villa, Middlesbrough, who finished third, Bradford in fourth and even fifth-place Blackburn all lost fewer matches than the Lions. However, John Docherty's side won 25 games – three more than their closest rivals – to win the title by four points and earn a place in the top flight for the first time in the club's history.

→ Under manager John Docherty, Millwall took the policy of win some, lose some to new levels in 1987/88. They lost more games than four other rivals, but still won the second-tier title.

TOON ARMY MARCH ON

St James' Park was a fortress for Newcastle during their 2009/10 Championship title-winning campaign. Chris Hughton's side were unbeaten in their 23 home games, winning 18 and drawing the other five. The Magpies' first home match back in the second tier was a 3–0 success against Reading, with Shola Ameobi scoring a hat-trick. Other notable results included a 5–1 win against Cardiff and a 6–1 victory against Barnsley. Newcastle finished the season with 102 points.

→ Chris Hughton worked with 10 bosses at Tottenham and three at Newcastle before being given the top job in 2009. He won the second-tier title in his first season.

SECOND TIER FOUNDER MEMBERS

Ardwick
Bootle
Burslem Port Vale
Burton Swifts
Crewe
Darwen
Grimsby
Lincoln
Northwich Victoria
Sheffield United
Small Heath
Walsall Town Swifts

EAGLES SOAR DESPITE DRAWS

Crystal Palace set a new landmark in 1978/79 when they claimed the championship despite drawing 19 games. The Eagles drew more matches than any other team in the division that term, but they clinched the league crown by a point from runners-up Brighton and Stoke in third.

DOWN TO THE WIRE

Leeds' dramatic final-day League 1 promotion success in 2009/10 was nothing new for the Yorkshire club – back in 1989/90 they snatched the second-tier title on goal difference from Sheffield United. Lee Chapman's strike was enough to earn Leeds a 1–0 win at Bournemouth on the last day, while the Blades claimed an emphatic 5–2 success at Leicester. However, it was the Elland Road side who took the championship thanks to a goal difference of +27 – seven better than their rivals.

→ Leeds signed Lee Chapman in January 1990 to score the goals to take them back to the top flight. The move paid off as United took the second-tier title and Chapman was their last-day match-winner.

Team Records

SCORING BLUES FOR CITY

Birmingham failed to score in a record 24 of their 46 matches in 1988/89. Blues got the season off to a losing start when they were beaten 1–0 at Watford, and that set the tone as they went on to suffer relegation. The longest run of consecutive games they went without hitting the net was six.

↓ Derby's only win of the 2007/08 Barclays Premier League season came against Newcastle in September. Rob Hulse was the Rams' match-winner when they ended their 36-game winless run against Sheffield United almost 12 months later.

SWANS MAKE IT THREE

Swansea became the third team in the league's history to draw eight games in a row following a run of stalemates in 2008/09. The sequence started with a 1–1 draw at Coventry, although the home side needed a late leveller from Daniel Fox to snatch a point. A goalless draw at Birmingham on December 28 was the last game of the run. Middlesbrough first set the record at the end of season 1970/71. Southampton also achieved the feat in 2005/06.

LONGEST UNBEATEN RUNS

33 games	Reading	2005/06
28 games	Liverpool	1893/94
27 games	Chelsea	1988/89

↑ Leon Britton missed part of Swansea's run of eight consecutive draws after he was red-carded against Cardiff on November 30 2008.

REDS ROMP TO TITLE

Liverpool managed to go through the whole of the 1893/94 season without losing a game. The Reds claimed the title by eight points from Small Heath – or Birmingham City as they are known today – with an impressive record of 22 wins and six draws. Two points were awarded for a victory in those days, with the Merseysiders collecting 50 from 28 games.

ROTTEN RUN FOR RAMS

Derby went 36 matches without a victory from September 22 2007 to September 13 2008, although the run actually started in the Premier League and ended in the second tier. The sequence began with a heavy 5–0 loss at Arsenal, with Emmanuel Adebayor scoring a hat-trick, and continued for the remaining 31 league games until their relegation was confirmed. Four more second-tier games followed in 2008/09 before goals from Paul Green and Rob Hulse finally secured a 2–1 win against Sheffield United.

UNITED FALL SHORT

Mighty Manchester United were a second-tier team back in 1904/05 when they set a record for the most consecutive wins at that level. The Red Devils clocked up 14 straight victories, although that was still not enough to win them the title, as they finished third. Bristol City and Preston subsequently matched that record run, and unlike the Manchester giants, they went on to claim the championship. The Robins were almost unbeatable in season 1905/06, while North End achieved the feat in 1950/51.

HOME SWEET HOME

Liverpool and Sheffield Wednesday are the only teams to have won every home game during a second-tier season. The Reds completed that remarkable achievement during 1893/94, winning all 14 of their matches at Anfield as part of an unbeaten league campaign. Six years later, the Owls won all 17 of their home games on their way to clinching the championship by two points.

DONS DOWN AND OUT

Wimbledon suffered a record 33 defeats during the 2003/04 campaign on their way to finishing bottom of the second tier. The Londoners, who moved to Milton Keynes and reformed as MK Dons the following season, won just eight times all campaign and drew their other five games. They were beaten 4–0 by Watford, 5–0 by West Ham and 6–0 at Nottingham Forest during a season to forget.

FOREST CHOP SQUAD

Nottingham Forest used just 25 different players during 2009/10 – the lowest number of any club in the division. Manager Billy Davies worked wonders with his small squad to guide the Reds to a third-place finish and a play-off place. Derby and Peterborough had the least settled line-ups, both fielding 39 different players in the league.

⇥ *Nottingham Forest, managed by Billy Davies, used only 25 players as they improved 16 places from 2008/09 to 2009/10. Despite finishing third in the table, Forest lost to sixth-place Blackpool in the play-off semi-final.*

AWAY FORM COSTLY FOR POSH

Peterborough managed just two wins away from home during the 2009/10 campaign – the worst record in the second tier. Their victories came at Watford in March, when Liam Dickinson scored the only goal of the game, and on the last day of the season at Plymouth, where Craig Mackail-Smith scored a brace in a 2–1 victory.

⇥ *Peterborough's seven-month wait for a league victory away from London Road in 2009/10 came courtesy of an effort from Liam Dickinson. Posh had to wait another seven weeks to double their away wins total, by which time their relegation had been confirmed.*

Player Records

MAGPIES STEAL GOALS

Kevin Nolan and Andy Carroll shared top spot in the goalscoring stakes for Newcastle as the Magpies netted 90 times on their way to the Championship title in 2009/10. The goals were spread throughout the team, with midfielder Nolan and striker Carroll both grabbing 17 apiece in the league and fellow forward Peter Lovenkrands hitting 13. Runners-up West Brom found the back of the net 89 times – with Chris Brunt and Graham Dorrans scoring 26 of those between them.

PAIR ARE HOT SHOTS

Bristol City striker Nicky Maynard had the highest number of shots on target by any player in 2009/10 as he shared the division's Golden Boot with Cardiff midfielder Peter Whittingham. Both players scored 20 league goals, with Maynard's return coming from 74 efforts on target, compared to 55 from the Bluebirds ace.

DUO ARE ALL BOOKED UP

Blackpool midfielder Charlie Adam and Preston's Ross Wallace were both shown 13 yellow cards in 2009/10 – the highest total for any player in the second tier since 2006/07. Cardiff striker Jay Bothroyd committed the most fouls in the Championship with 103. He received 12 yellow cards.

FRAZER'S FIRST

Frazer Richardson was the first player to score a goal in the newly-named Championship in 2004. Leeds, who had been relegated from the Premier League at the end of 2003/04, played Derby in an early kick-off on August 7, and full-back Richardson netted the game's only goal in the 72nd minute with a well-struck left-footed drive.

↑ Frazer Richardson's goal made Leeds the first leaders of the newly-named Championship in 2004. United, however, won only 13 of their remaining 45 matches and ended the 2004/05 campaign in mid-table.

↖ Nicky Maynard of Bristol City scored a goal almost every other game in 2009/10, netting 20 in 42 appearances. He averaged 1.76 shots on target per match and had a success rate of one in 3.7 shots on target.

BIG-MONEY MOVERS

A number of players have made the jump from Championship level to the Premier League in recent seasons. Everton in particular have been quick to identify the talent available in the second tier, having signed Joleon Lescott, Phil Jagielka and Andrew Johnson from Wolves, Sheffield United and Crystal Palace respectively. Tim Cahill also proved a shrewd buy for the Toffees when he joined the club for around £2million from Millwall in the summer of 2004. Other recent big-money moves between the two divisions include Theo Walcott and Aaron Ramsey joining Arsenal from Southampton and Cardiff and Gareth Bale moving to Tottenham from the Saints.

STALWARTS ARE EVER READY

Sheffield Wednesday and Watford both had three players who were involved in all 46 league games during the 2009/10 season. Owls trio Lee Grant, Tommy Spurr and Darren Potter and the Hornets' Scott Loach, Adrian Mariappa and Danny Graham were six of 13 ever-presents in the Championship, although nine of Graham's tally were substitute appearances. Swansea pair Dorus De Vries and Ashley Williams also featured in every match, as did Crystal Palace's Darren Ambrose and Shaun Derry. Adam Federici of Reading, Derby's Robbie Savage and Clinton Morrison of Coventry complete the list.

↑ *Sheffield Wednesday goalkeeper Lee Grant started all 46 Championship matches for the Owls in 2009/10, but he was on the winning side only 11 times as his team suffered relegation.*

RICH FUTURE FOR LAZARUS

Reuben Noble-Lazarus is the youngest player ever to have featured in a Football League match. He made his debut for Barnsley aged 15 years and 45 days in a 3–0 Championship defeat at Ipswich on September 30 2008. Noble-Lazarus came off the bench in the 84th minute as a replacement for Martin Devaney.

LEAGUE OF NATIONS

The Championship's reputation as one of the most popular leagues in Europe is backed up by the fact that 60 different nationalities played in the division at some point during the 2009/10 campaign. Apart from the home nations, France had the most representatives (15), with Holland not far behind (13). There were 10 Spaniards and eight Argentinians, two of whom – Jonas Gutierrez and Fabricio Coloccini – featured for title-winners Newcastle. Countries such as Benin, Lithuania and Sierra Leone were also represented.

FORD MOTORS TO RECORD

Tony Ford made 931 league appearances – a Football League record for an outfield player – during a 26-year career that saw him play for eight different clubs. Grimsby-born Ford spent the most time with his home-town club in the second tier, featuring 355 times in his first spell with the Mariners between 1975 and 1986 and 68 on his return to Blundell Park from 1991 to 1994. Ford made over 100 league appearances for three other clubs – Stoke, West Brom and Mansfield.

⇢ *Tony Ford was the epitome of an 'unsung hero', playing more than 1,000 matches in senior football. Originally a winger, he also scored more than 100 league goals.*

STARS ON SHOW

The 2010 World Cup in South Africa featured 10 players who had spent the previous campaign playing in the Championship. Title-winners Newcastle had Jonas Gutierrez in Argentina's 23, while four of West Brom's squad were at the tournament – Gonzalo Jara (Chile), Marek Cech (Slovakia), Robert Koren (Slovenia) and Chris Wood (New Zealand). The All Whites also had Chris Killen (Middlesbrough), Rory Fallon (Plymouth) and Tommy Smith (Ipswich) in their party. Jay DeMerit of Watford started for the USA against England, but Reading goalkeeper Adam Federici was back-up to Fulham's Mark Schwarzer in the Australia squad.

← *Jonas Gutierrez was yellow-carded in both of Argentina's first two matches at the 2010 World Cup and played only 11 minutes in the two games after completing his suspension.*

Goals

GOALS MAKE BIG DIFFERENCE

Reading's romp to the Championship title in 2005/06 saw the club break a host of records, including the second-tier mark for the best goal difference. The Royals scored a massive 99 goals and conceded only 32, giving them an incredible difference of +67. They won the title that year by 16 points from Sheffield United, who netted 76 times and let in 46 at the other end.

┈┈> *Prolific goalscorers and points-winners Reading celebrate their Championship title in May 2006. The Royals took their great form into their debut season in the top flight.*

BIGGEST WINS

Newcastle	13–0	Newport County	(1946)
Darwen	12–0	Walsall	(1896)
Arsenal	12–0	Loughborough	(1900)
Birmingham	12–0	Walsall	(1892)
Birmingham	12–0	Doncaster	(1903)
Port Vale	0–10	Sheffield United	(1892)

HAMMOND HITS TOP GEAR

Sheffield United recorded the biggest away win in the league's history when they hit 10 goals without reply past Port Vale in December 1892. Prolific forward Harry Hammond netted four times for the Blades as the South Yorkshire side ran riot.

DARWEN FAIL TO EVOLVE

Darwen hold the record for conceding the most league goals in a single season, having shipped 141 during the 1898/99 campaign. The Lancashire-based club were elected to The Football League in 1891 and lasted eight seasons. During their last term, Darwen suffered a record 18 consecutive defeats. Sunderland came close to equalling that run in 2003 when they lost 15 Premier League and two second-tier matches in a row.

⟵ *Dean Ashton scored early and often for Crewe during the first half of the 2004/05 season. It earned him a move to Norwich in the January transfer window.*

ASHTON QUICK OFF THE MARK

Dean Ashton was forced to retire through injury in December 2009 aged just 26, but he briefly held the distinction of having scored the fastest goal since the league became known as the Championship. The former England forward took 10 seconds to open the scoring against Millwall in a 2–1 win for Crewe in 2004. Matt Fryatt shaved a second off that time when scoring for Leicester against Preston in 2006.

HORNETS LACK GOALSCORING SPARK

Watford found the back of the net just 24 times in 42 matches during the 1971/72 season to establish an unwanted league landmark for the fewest goals scored in a single campaign. The Hornets lost 28 times in total and finished the term at the bottom of the table with 19 points – 14 less than Charlton, who finished in 21st place and scored 31 more goals than their London rivals.

ADDICTED TO GOALS

Charlton and Middlesbrough played out an amazing 6–6 draw at The Valley in October 1960 – the highest-scoring draw ever seen in the division. Dennis Edwards scored a hat-trick for the Addicks, while Brian Clough also hit a treble for the visitors. It was 4–4 at half-time, with the free-scoring duo both bagging a brace. Middlesbrough took a 6–4 lead in the 63rd minute, but they were pegged back by Edwards' third and a last-gasp equaliser from Johnny Summers.

⁌⋯ *A young Brian Clough. He netted a hat-trick for Middlesbrough at Charlton, but both teams had to settle for a share of the points.*

GHOST GOALS GALORE!

The second tier has witnessed two bizarre 'ghost goals' over the past few seasons – one that was given when it shouldn't have been and one that went in but was chalked off! Reading were awarded a goal in a clash at Watford in September 2008 by referee Stuart Atwell, despite the ball going four yards wide of the near post. And in August 2009, Crystal Palace striker Freddie Sears thumped a shot into the bottom corner of Bristol City's net that bounced out off the stanchion and was subsequently awarded as a goal-kick!

OLD PROBLEMS FOR NEWPORT

Newport County endured a miserable campaign in 1946/47, conceding 133 goals and scoring 61 on their way to relegation to the third tier. They ended the season with a goal difference of -72, which still stands as the worst in the league's history. The South Wales club, who spent 68 years in The Football League, were hammered 13–0 by Newcastle, conceded seven against West Brom and were hit for six on three occasions that term.

LUCKY 13 FOR MAGPIES

Newcastle's 13–0 win against Newport County in October 1946 remains the biggest margin of victory in a second-tier game. Goalscoring legend Jackie Milburn scored twice for the Magpies, but he was outdone by Len Shackleton, who netted six times on his debut after signing from Bradford Park Avenue. Charlie Wayman added four more goals, with Roy Bentley also on target.

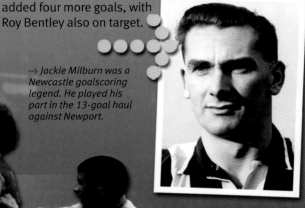

⋯⟶ *Jackie Milburn was a Newcastle goalscoring legend. He played his part in the 13-goal haul against Newport.*

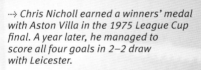

⋯⟶ *Chris Nicholl earned a winners' medal with Aston Villa in the 1975 League Cup final. A year later, he managed to score all four goals in 2–2 draw with Leicester.*

YOU WYNNE SOME...

Samuel Wynne scored four of the five goals in Oldham's 3–2 victory over Manchester United in October 1923. Wynne was the first player to score two for each side, with his goals at the right end coming from a free-kick and a penalty. Chris Nicholl equalled the feat for Aston Villa in a top-flight match at Leicester in March 1976, scoring all four in a 2–2 draw.

League 1 All-Time Records

The third tier – currently known as npower League 1 – came into being in 1920 and was originally split into two leagues – north and south. That format remained in place until 1958 when one combined league replaced regionalisation. Some big clubs have found themselves playing at this level, while the division has also provided the stage for some remarkable individual feats.

A shower of green and yellow confetti marks the moment that Norwich are confirmed as winners of the League 1 championship in May 2010.

Southampton's Dean
Hammond (left) and Adam
Lallana (20) celebrate with
goalscorer Rickie Lambert
during the 2009/10 season.

Champions, Participation, Promotion and Relegation

A VALIANT EFFORT

Port Vale kept an impressive 30 clean sheets in 46 matches on their way to the title in 1953/54. The Valiants only conceded five goals at home during the whole campaign and 21 in total – another divisional record, which they share with Southampton. The Saints achieved the feat in 1921/22.

DOUBLE FOR DALE

Rochdale suffered relegation after managing just two wins from 46 matches during the 1973/74 campaign – the fewest ever recorded at this level. The Lancashire club unsurprisingly finished bottom of the table, seven points behind nearest rivals Southport and having conceded 94 goals. Dale's only wins came against Southend – 2–1 in September 1973 – and Shrewsbury – 3–2 the following January.

BEES SOUNDLY BEATEN

Barnet suffered 10 straight defeats from the start of the 1993/94 season – the worst run by any third-tier side. The Bees went down that term after winning just five and losing 28 of their 46 matches.

↑ Having suffered the loss of key players following their 1993 promotion, it was little surprise that Brian Marwood and Barnet made an awful start to their first season in the third tier. They finished 25 points from safety.

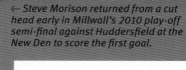

← Steve Morison returned from a cut head early in Millwall's 2010 play-off semi-final against Huddersfield at the New Den to score the first goal.

DEN OF INVINCIBILITY

Play-off winners Millwall lost just once at home during the whole of the 2009/10 season. The Lions, who beat Swindon 1–0 at Wembley in May to secure their promotion, slipped to a 2–0 defeat against Wycombe – a side who were eventually relegated – at the New Den in November. Huddersfield, who Millwall beat in the semi-finals of the play-offs, also tasted defeat just once on home turf – against champions Norwich.

THIRD TIER TITLE WINS

Plymouth	4
Portsmouth	3
Swansea	3
Grimsby	3
Reading	3
Millwall	3
Lincoln	3
Hull	3

ROVERS WIN BIG

Doncaster hold the league record for the most wins in a season. Rovers claimed 33 victories out of 42 matches on their way to the title in 1946/47. They drew six and lost the other three games. The South Yorkshire side posted some impressive wins along the way, putting nine past Carlisle and scoring eight goals without reply against Barrow.

BARNET'S RELEGATION RUN

v Hull	lost 2–1	(h)	14/08/1993
v Port Vale	lost 6–0	(a)	21/08/1993
v Swansea	lost 1–0	(h)	28/08/1993
v Reading	lost 4–1	(a)	01/09/1993
v Blackpool	lost 3–1	(a)	04/09/1993
v Bournemouth	lost 2–1	(h)	11/09/1993
v Fulham	lost 2–0	(h)	14/09/1993
v Leyton Orient	lost 4–2	(a)	18/09/1993
v Wrexham	lost 4–0	(a)	25/09/1993
v Bristol Rovers	lost 2–1	(h)	02/10/1993

READING ON A ROLL

Reading won the title in 1985/86 after making an incredible start to the season that saw them win their first 13 games – a record for the most consecutive victories at the beginning of a campaign. They started that term with 1–0 wins against Blackpool and Plymouth, who went on to finish as runners-up, before really hitting their stride. A narrow victory at Lincoln in October 1985 proved to be the last game of the winning sequence, with Wolves holding the Royals to a 2–2 draw at Elm Park a few days later.

SPOT THE DIFFERENCE

Relegated Stockport ended 2009/10 with the worst goal difference in The Football League. The Hatters were sent down from the third tier having scored 35 goals home and away. County conceded 95, leaving them with a goal difference of –60. Millwall contributed to that statistic by scoring nine goals in two games against Gary Ablett's side (4–0 and 5–0), while Huddersfield hit six without reply at Edgeley Park in April.

RELEGATION ACADEMIC FOR CAMBRIDGE

Cambridge hold the unenviable record of having collected the least points in a third-tier season. The Us claimed just 21 on their way to relegation in 1984/85. They finished 25 points adrift of second-from-bottom Preston and a further point from safety. Cambridge were heavily beaten by eventual champions Bradford (4–0), Walsall (5–0) and York (4–0) during a campaign to forget.

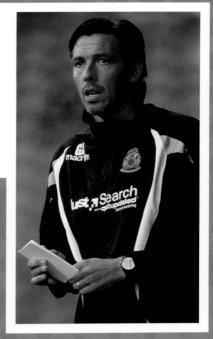

↑ Gary Ablett's notes didn't help him too much as he tried to stem the tide of goals going in against his Stockport team in 2009/10.

LATICS LOVE LIFE ON THE ROAD

Wigan only conceded nine goals in 23 matches away from home during the 2002/03 campaign. The Latics' defence was breached just 25 times in total that term as they romped to the title with a 100-point haul – 14 more than second-place Crewe. Paul Jewell's side lost just two games on their travels and won 15 times.

↓ Wigan's rise up England's football ladder gained pace with their third-tier title in 2003.

Team Records

LONG ROAD FOR ROVERS

Doncaster hold the league landmark for the most consecutive away wins, but it took them seven years to complete that achievement! Their impressive feat started with a 2–1 victory at Stockport on April 22 1939, with Rovers going on to win the last two away games of that season. The league was then interrupted by the Second World War, but on its resumption in 1946, the Yorkshire club claimed six more victories to create an overall record of nine straight wins on their travels.

PALACE STRETCH THEIR POINT

Crystal Palace played out the most home stalemates ever recorded in a row at this level. They made their point seven straight times during a run that spanned across two seasons – 1961/62 and 1962/63. The first game was a goalless draw against Bradford Park Avenue, which was followed by stalemates against Coventry, Port Vale and Bournemouth. The sequence continued into the following term before they finally snatched a 1–0 win against QPR.

POOLS RUN DRY

Hartlepool found goals hard to come by at the start of 1993, with the club failing to score in 11 straight matches. The north-east side had stunned top-flight Crystal Palace with a 1–0 win in the FA Cup on January 2 courtesy of Andy Saville's penalty, but that was the last time they scored for over two months. A goalless draw at Leyton Orient began the run, with Pools losing eight and drawing three games all without hitting the net before Saville was on target again at Blackpool in March to end the hoodoo.

← Andy Saville failed to score at Brisbane Road on January 9 1993, and neither he, nor his Hartlepool team-mates, had a goal to celebrate for two months.

HORNETS HARD TO BEAT

The overall Football League record for the most successive draws away from home in a single campaign is held by Watford. The Hornets were playing in the third tier when they embarked on a nine-game run during 1996/97. Wayne Andrews opened the scoring in a 1–1 draw at Bury to start the sequence on October 19 1996, with the ninth game coming against Wycombe in February of the following year.

⋯→ Wayne Andrews (right) in action for Watford. This FA Cup tie against Northampton in November 1996 was one of the few games that Watford didn't draw on their travels in 1996/97.

UNBEATABLE BEES

Brentford enjoyed a 100 per cent home record during the 1929/30 season. The Bees won all 21 of their games at Griffin Park that term, putting six past Merthyr Town and Walsall and scoring five goals against Brighton, Torquay, Watford and Fulham. It was not enough to win them the third-tier title, though, as they finished seven points behind champions Plymouth.

ELECTRIC AVENUE

Bradford Park Avenue hold the third-tier record for the most consecutive home wins. The 25-game sequence spanned across two seasons – 1926/27 and 1927/28. It began on October 9 1926 with a 2–0 victory against Ashington and continued for the rest of that campaign before a 4–0 win against Durham City kicked off the following season. The run went on until Bradford were finally beaten 2–0 by Doncaster in November 1927.

DRAW SPECIALISTS

Chesterfield equalled a league record when they drew eight consecutive matches during the 2005/06 campaign. The run started with a 1–1 draw against Blackpool at Saltergate in November – in which Sammy Clingan was on target – with the sequence continuing into the new year following a goalless draw against Barnsley on January 2. Birmingham (1990/91) and Torquay (1969/70) also achieved the same feat.

←--- *Future Northern Ireland midfielder Sammy Clingan spent almost two seasons at Chesterfield, on loan from Wolves, during which time he scored three goals.*

DALE'S UNWANTED DOUBLE

Rochdale set two unwanted records during the 1931/32 season. A 4–1 loss at Barrow in November 1931 sparked a poor run of results for the Lancashire club, who went on to suffer 17 consecutive defeats. That streak included 9–1 and 6–3 defeats against Tranmere. Dale also lost 13 home matches in a row that term and then started the following campaign with a 1–0 defeat at home to Carlisle to extend their slump.

PIRATES STEAL RECORD

Bristol Rovers went an amazing 32 games without defeat in the early 1970s. Don Megson's side claimed a 2–0 win over Scunthorpe at Glanford Park on April 7 1973 and then stayed unbeaten for the remaining four games of that campaign. They enjoyed a flying start to 1973/74 and played another 27 matches before finally losing 1–0 at Wrexham.

---> *Don Megson's Bristol Rovers finished a point behind third-tier champions Oldham in 1973/74, despite their amazing unbeaten start to the season.*

MOST CLEAN SHEETS IN A SEASON

30	Port Vale	1953/54
27	Middlesbrough	1986/87
26	Aston Villa	1971/72
26	Southampton	1921/22
26	Rochdale	1923/24

DUO KEEP IT CLEAN

Millwall and York share the honour for the most consecutive clean sheets at third-tier level, with both managing 11. The Lions achieved the feat in 1925/26, drawing 0–0 with Gillingham before winning nine and drawing one of the following 10 matches without conceding. York, led by Scottish goalkeeper Graeme Crawford, equalled that in 1973/74, playing out six goalless draws in their 11 games.

↓ *York City goalkeeper Graeme Crawford bravely dives at the feet of Chelsea's Micky Droy. The Minstermen's run of clean sheets in 1973/74 helped them to win promotion to England's second tier for the first and, to date, only time. They lasted only two seasons at that level.*

Player Records

GOAL MACHINES

Ted Hartson scored a staggering 55 goals in a single season for Mansfield in 1936/37. And amazingly, the same feat was also achieved by Luton goal ace Joe Payne the same term! Hartson scored his hatful in Division Three North, while Payne matched that in the South. Hartson scored seven goals in a single game against Hartlepool on his way to the record.

TROLLOPE TOPS TABLE

John Trollope spent the majority of his career playing in the third tier on the way to establishing the record for the most Football League appearances for a single club. Trollope, whose son Paul is currently the manager of Bristol Rovers, spent 20 years at Swindon between 1960 and 1980 and featured an amazing 770 times for the club. He made his debut aged just 17 against Halifax in August 1960 and broke Jimmy Dickinson's record in 1980/81. Trollope, who received an MBE for his achievements, went on to manage the Robins.

⇢ *The epitome of the one-club man was Swindon left-back John Trollope, whose finest moment came in the 1969 League Cup final when the Robins beat Arsenal.*

OLD-BOY McBAIN

Neil McBain was 51 years and 120 days old when he played for New Brighton against Hartlepool in March 1947 – making him the oldest player ever to feature in a Football League match. The Merseysiders played in the league from 1923 until 1951 and McBain was managing the club when he created the record, pulling on his goalkeeping gloves following an injury crisis. Unfortunately, he could not prevent New Brighton from slipping to a 3–0 defeat.

BELL RINGS TRUE

Harold Bell holds the overall Football League record for the most consecutive appearances, having played 401 games in a row for Tranmere between 1946 and 1955 while the club was in the third tier. Including FA Cup, Liverpool Senior Cup and Cheshire Bowl matches, Bell played in an incredible 459 unbroken games and made a club-record total of 633 appearances for Rovers. His run was finally ended in August 1955 when he was dropped.

HARDMAN HOLT

Grant Holt put himself in where it hurts in 2009/10 on the way to finishing as one of the top scorers in the league. The striker netted 24 goals to help Norwich win the title, but he also committed the most fouls of any player in the division – 86.

← *Grant Holt celebrates a goal for Norwich against Stockport in 2009/10. He was not only a prolific scorer, but also didn't shirk a challenge, becoming the most penalised player in the division.*

ROCKET RONNIE DOWNS CANARIES

Ronnie Dix became the third tier's youngest goalscorer when he netted for Bristol Rovers against Norwich in March 1928 aged just 15 years and 180 days – a record that still stands. Rovers won the game 3–0 and Dix went on to score 33 league goals for the Pirates before moving to Blackburn. Dix won one full international cap for England, grabbing a goal on his debut against Norway.

EVER-PRESENTS 2009/10

Ben Williams   (Colchester)
Matthew Taylor   (Exeter)
Scott Flinders   (Hartlepool)
Alex Smithies   (Huddersfield)
Peter Clarke   (Huddersfield)
David Forde   (Millwall)
Sean Gregan   (Oldham)

↓ Alex Smithies, the Huddersfield goalkeeper, was an ever-present for his side during the 2009/10 season. His team-mate Peter Clarke also played in every match.

QUINTET SEE RED

Five players were sent off when Wigan took on Bristol Rovers in a third-tier clash in December 1997 – a record held jointly with Chesterfield and Plymouth, who had suffered the same fate 10 months previously. Rovers' David Pritchard was the first to go in first-half injury time for two bookable offences, and from the resulting free-kick, a melee broke out in the box that also resulted in Jason Perry, Andy Tillson and Wigan striker Graeme Jones seeing red. The visitors, who lost the game 3–0, were reduced to seven men in the 71st minute when Josh Low was shown a second yellow card.

PAYNE-FUL DAY FOR ROVERS

Joe Payne scored a remarkable 10 goals in a single game for Luton against Bristol Rovers in April 1936. The Hatters won the Division Three South match 12–0, with centre-forward Payne creating a Football League record with his scoring exploits. Robert 'Bunny' Bell had also been playing third-tier football when he bagged nine goals for Tranmere against Oldham a year previously on Boxing Day 1935. He also missed a penalty in his side's 13–4 victory!

↑ Bristol Rovers defender Andy Tillson was one of five players (four of them from Rovers) sent off during a tempestuous match against Wigan in 1997.

← Jon-Paul McGovern's creativity helped Swindon to reach the 2009/10 promotion Play-Off Final, but he couldn't set up a goal for any team-mates as they lost 1–0 to Millwall.

McGOVERN MAKES GOALS

Wingers pride themselves on setting up goals for their team-mates, and Swindon's Jon-Paul McGovern excelled at it in 2009/10. The Scot laid on 16 goals for the Robins – the most assists of any player in League 1. McGovern only managed one league goal himself, though, as Swindon made it to the Play-Off Final, where they were narrowly beaten by Millwall.

Goals

LIONS ON FIRE

Millwall hold the record for the most home league goals scored in a season. The Lions found the back of the net 87 times at The Den during the 1927/28 campaign on their way to the title. Notable results that term included 9–1 wins against Torquay and Coventry, a 7–1 victory against Walsall and putting six past Brighton, QPR and Gillingham.

HATTERS GO GOAL MAD

Stockport recorded the biggest victory in the division's history when they put 13 goals past Halifax without reply on January 6 1934. There were six different County goalscorers that day, with Joe Hill netting a hat-trick and Percy Downes going one better with four. The Hatters were only leading 2–0 at the break, but eight goals in a 16-minute spell early in the second half put the game well beyond their opponents. They went on to add three more in the last 10 minutes of a remarkable game.

TERRIFIC TRANMERE

The highest-scoring game ever played in the third tier came at Prenton Park on Boxing Day 1935 when Tranmere claimed an amazing 13–4 victory over Oldham! Rovers striker Robert 'Bunny' Bell scored nine goals in the game on his way to a total of 40 that season.

KNOCKOUT TOTAL FOR BANTAMS

Bradford scored 128 times during 1928/29 to break the record for the most goals in a third-tier season. The Bantams, who won the title by a point that year, cruised to an 11–1 win against Rotherham in the opening game and were 8–2 winners at Ashington in October. They also managed successive 8–0 victories against Tranmere and Barrow the following March. Millwall had previously held the record, having rattled in 127 goals the year before.

→ *Scunthorpe striker Billy Sharp celebrates after scoring against Hudderfield at Glanford Park, one of 30 goals he netted during the 2006/07 season, helping the Iron to the third-tier title.*

←‑ *Rickie Lambert won a second straight goalscoring title in the third tier with Southampton in 2009/10. Most unusually, neither of his two clubs, Bristol Rovers in 2009 nor Saints, finished in the top six.*

LAMBERT TOPS CHARTS

Rickie Lambert has been League 1's top scorer for the last two seasons. The striker netted 29 times for Bristol Rovers during the 2008/09 campaign, sharing the Golden Boot with Simon Cox of Swindon. That impressive haul earned him a £1million move to Southampton, where he went one better in 2009/10, hitting 30 league goals – four more than another Swindon player, Billy Paynter.

LEADING SCORERS SINCE 2004/05

2004/05	Dean Windass (Bradford)	27
	Stuart Elliott (Hull)	
2005/06	Billy Sharp (Scunthorpe)	23
	Fredy Eastwood (Southend)	
2006/07	Billy Sharp (Scunthorpe)	30
2007/08	Jason Scotland (Swansea)	24
2008/09	Rickie Lambert (Bristol Rovers)	29
	Simon Cox (Swindon)	
2009/10	Rickie Lambert (Southampton)	30

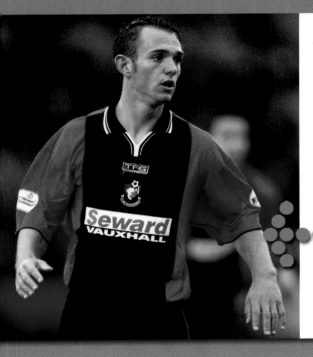

HASTY HAYTER

James Hayter made an instant impact when he scored the fastest hat-trick in Football League history in February 2004. The striker came off the bench for Bournemouth against Wrexham in the 84th minute and scored his first goal in the 86th. Two minutes and 20 seconds later, he was celebrating a treble! The Cherries ran out comfortable 6–0 winners.

← How many goals might James Hayter have scored against Wrexham if he had started the match, rather than come off the bench? As it was, he grabbed three in the final six minutes of the game.

DUO'S FLYING START

Nick Barmby and Matt Fryatt share the distinction of having scored the fastest goals since the division became known as League 1. Barmby was first to achieve the feat, netting after seven seconds of Hull's 3–1 win at home to Walsall in November 2004 with a neat side-footed volley. Fryatt took the same length of time to open the scoring for Walsall in a home match against Bournemouth later that season. Unfortunately, the Saddlers went on to lose the game 2–1.

GOAL-CRAZY CANARIES

Norwich scored 89 goals during their run to the title in 2009/10 – the most of any club in the division. Grant Holt netted 24 and fellow forward Chris Martin bagged 17, while Wes Hoolahan scored 11 times from midfield. The Canaries were 5–0 winners at Colchester and claimed 5–1 and 5–2 victories against Bristol Rovers and Wycombe respectively. Southampton, who finished seventh having started the campaign on –10 points, were the second highest goalscorers with 85, while Huddersfield managed 82.

↓ Norwich were the most prolific team in the third tier in 2009/10. Their 89 goals scored was the division's best and the 136 goals in their 46 matches (for and against) was also the most.

DERBY DELIGHT

Derby rivals Darlington and Hartlepool played out an amazing 5–5 draw at Feethams in November 1936 – the highest-scoring draw in the division's history. In March 2004, Chesterfield and Grimsby played out a 4–4 thriller at Saltergate, with David Reeves completing his hat-trick with a point-saving penalty for the home side.

League 2 All-Time Records

The fourth tier – currently known as npower League 2 – was introduced in time for the start of the 1958/59 season and was first made up of the sides who had finished in the bottom half of the last Division Three North and South tables. This bottom rung of The Football League ladder has featured big names such as David Beckham, Paul Gascoigne and Peter Beardsley.

↓ Rotherham's fans have endured a lot recently, including playing home games in Sheffield since 2008. They turned out in force when the Millers went to Wembley in 2010, but saw them lose 3–2 to Dagenham & Redbridge in the Play-Off Final.

Champions, Participation, Promotion and Relegation

TITANIC TITLE TUSSLE

Wigan and Fulham were involved in the closest title race in fourth-tier history during the 1996/97 campaign. Both teams finished the season on 87 points, but the championship trophy went to Lancashire, despite the Cottagers having a better goal difference. The number of goals scored took precedence that term, and Wigan had netted 12 more than the Londoners.

CHAMPIONS SINCE 2000

1999/00	Swansea	85 points
2000/01	Brighton	92 points
2001/02	Plymouth	102 points
2002/03	Rushden & Diamonds	87 points
2003/04	Doncaster	92 points
2004/05	Yeovil	83 points
2005/06	Carlisle	86 points
2006/07	Walsall	89 points
2007/08	MK Dons	97 points
2008/09	Brentford	85 points
2009/10	Notts County	93 points

↑ John Deehan kisses the trophy after Wigan had seen off Fulham on goals scored to win the fourth-tier championship in 1997.

NO WORRIES FOR NORTH END

Preston drew 17 games but still managed to win the league in 1995/96. North End were held to a thrilling 3–3 draw by Cambridge in September 1995 and played out three consecutive 2–2 stalemates later that month. The Lancashire club won 23 games and lost six matches in all, but they clinched the championship by three points from Gillingham, who also drew 17 times.

⇢ Steve Cotterill spent three months and four days in charge at Notts County in 2010, but he oversaw the Magpies' rise to the top of the fourth tier, and their eventual championship.

COTTERILL HAS MAGPIES FLYING

Steve Cotterill left his role as manager of Notts County at the end of 2009/10 with an incredible record. Having only taken over in February, Cotterill's first match in charge saw the Magpies ease to a 5–0 win against Hereford, with Craig Westcarr scoring a hat-trick. County only lost once in the next 17 games to move steadily up the table and finish the season as champions.

GREEN ARMY MARCH ON

Paul Sturrock led Plymouth to a place in the history books when they equalled a fourth-tier record for the most points in one season under the three-for-a-win system in 2001/02. Argyle claimed 102 points to clinch the championship by five from second-place Luton. Nobody else came close, with Mansfield finishing a massive 23 points behind in third. Swindon had previously managed the same total as Argyle in 1985/86.

←— *Paul Sturrock's Plymouth won 31 matches on their way to claiming the fourth-tier title in 2001/02 with a joint-record 102 points.*

↓ *Jim Stannard enjoyed a great season between the sticks for Gillingham in 1995/96, as they conceded only 20 league goals and won promotion to the third tier.*

ROVERS' POOR RETURN

Doncaster hold the unwanted record for the most losses in a fourth-tier season. Rovers were beaten 34 times during the 1997/98 campaign, winning four games and drawing eight. They managed just 20 points, with a goal difference of -83 – both of which are also records. The Yorkshire side finished 15 points adrift of second-from-bottom Brighton and dropped out of The Football League.

GILLS SET DOUBLE RECORD

Gillingham gained promotion at the end of 1995/96 having kept a record 29 clean sheets. The Gills only conceded 20 goals that term – another fourth-tier landmark – although they also struggled to score, netting just 49 times. That total was less than any other side in the top 12. The Kent club finished as runners-up that year, three points behind champions Preston.

←— *Matt Taylor and Luton had a fine 2001/02 season. In any other year this century, the Hatters' 97 points would have given them at least a share of the title. That season, however, Plymouth gained 102 points.*

RE-ELECTION NOT RELEGATION

The bottom four clubs in the fourth tier had to apply for re-election to The Football League each season from the division's formation in 1958 up until the end of the 1986 campaign. Gateshead were the first club not to be re-elected to that level in 1960. In 1987, The Football League agreed that the team who finished bottom would be replaced by the champions of the Conference – a system that still stands.

ROBINS ARE ROCKING

Swindon won the title by the biggest margin in history in 1985/86. The Robins finished 18 points ahead of second-place Chester, ending the campaign with a joint-record 102 points. The campaign had started badly for the Wiltshire club when they lost 1–0 at home to Wrexham and 4–1 away at Hereford in their first two league matches, but results soon picked up and Lou Macari's side scored four goals on six separate occasions as they cruised to the championship.

LUCKY LOSERS

Two teams share the landmark for the most defeats on the way to winning the division. Exeter lost 13 games – all away from home – during the 1989/90 season, while Brentford equalled that feat in 1998/99. The Grecians didn't lose a game in any competition at St James Park, but their form on their travels almost proved costly. Brentford claimed 26 victories overall in 1998/99 and drew seven games to finish four points ahead of Cambridge.

Team Records

⇢ Jim Bentley and his Morecambe team-mates were thwarted by the goal frame more times than any other team in the fourth tier in 2009/10, but they still managed to finish fourth in the table.

MINSTERMEN DRAW A BLANK

York failed to score in a record 11 of their 23 home matches during the 1990/91 season. The Minstermen's opening game was a 1–0 defeat to Maidstone at Bootham Crescent, and that was a sign of things to come. They ended the campaign in 21st place, with just eight wins to their name at home and only three on their travels.

ROYALS SEAL OF APPROVAL

Reading finished the 1978/79 season strongly, keeping 11 consecutive clean sheets in their final 11 games. A 4–0 victory against Grimsby started the sequence, with the Royals going on to win seven more matches while the other three ended goalless.

IMPS ROMP TO RECORD

Lincoln and Swindon jointly hold the record for the most wins ever recorded in a single season at this level. The Imps cruised to the fourth-tier title in 1975/76 after winning 32 of their 46 matches, drawing 10 and losing just four times. Ten years later, the Robins matched that impressive feat on their way to lifting the championship trophy under the management of Lou Macari.

⬊ Swindon's rise up English football began under the management of Lou Macari and was continued by Glenn Hoddle. Less than 10 years after winning the fourth-tier title, the Robins were in the Premier League.

SHRIMPS FAIL TO FIND THE NET

Morecambe were officially the unluckiest team in the division in 2009/10, striking the woodwork an amazing 25 times – a new high since the competition became known as League 2. The Shrimps finished fourth in the table and were eventually beaten in the play-off semi-final by Dagenham & Redbridge, although they were slightly more fortunate than Championship counterparts Cardiff, who struck the post or the crossbar 27 times – more than any other team in The Football League.

⤑ *After Carlisle's horrendous losing run during 2003/04 – which began after Richie Foran converted a penalty to give his team the lead against Swansea – they couldn't produce enough results to stave off relgation.*

QUICK ON THE DRAW

Hartlepool and Cardiff both drew half of the 46 games they played during the 1997/98 season. Pools finished 17th in the table, despite losing just 11 games, while the Bluebirds were down in 21st place, with nine wins and 14 losses to add to their run of stalemates. Unsurprisingly, the pair played out a 1–1 draw when they met at Ninian Park that term. They share the fourth-tier record with Exeter, who managed the same number of draws back in 1986/87.

POSH'S DATE AT EIGHT

Peterborough hold the divisional record for the number of consecutive draws, having played out eight in a row in 1970/71. Posh's sequence began with a thrilling 3–3 clash against Exeter in December 1970 and ended following an equally watchable 4–4 stalemate against Lincoln at London Road two months later.

NO LET-UP FOR NEWPORT

Newport County set two unfortunate records during the 1970/71 season. The Welsh club went 25 games without a win from the start of the campaign, with the opening 10 all ending in defeat. Their wretched start featured a 6–1 loss to Southport and a 4–1 home defeat against Oldham. They went on to finish the season in 22nd place, having lost 28 of their 46 games.

⤑ *Peter Schmeichel's son, Kasper, has the right genes to be a goalkeeper. In 2009/10, he helped Notts County to keep a division-best 26 clean sheets.*

CARLISLE COME A CROPPER

Carlisle endured a miserable run during the 2003/04 campaign, losing 12 matches in a row on their way to relegation from The Football League. The sequence started with a 2–1 defeat at home to Swansea, despite Richie Foran opening the scoring for the Cumbrians from the penalty spot. Carlisle slipped to 11 more defeats, including a 4–1 loss at home to Scunthorpe, before they finally secured a long-overdue win when they beat Torquay 2–0 thanks to goals from Andy Preece and Paul Arnison.

CLEAN-SHEET KINGS SINCE 2004/05

2004/05	Rochdale	20
2005/06	Northampton	23
2006/07	Bristol Rovers	22
	Hartlepool	
2007/08	Darlington	24
2008/09	Wycombe	21
2009/10	Notts County	26

COUNTY PROVE HARD TO BEAT

Notts County's defence in 2009/10 was one of the meanest ever assembled in the division, with the Magpies setting a new record for the most shut-outs since the competition became League 2. Led by goalkeeper Kasper Schmeichel and captain John Thompson, County kept a total of 26 clean sheets – an achievement only bettered in the whole of fourth-tier history by Gillingham, who recorded 29 in 1995/96.

Player Records

BECKS IN AT THE DEEP END

England ace David Beckham played five games for Preston in the fourth tier during 1994/95. Beckham was on the fringes of the Manchester United first team at the time, and he was loaned to North End to gain some experience. He impressed at Deepdale, scoring two goals – one direct from a corner and the other a typically brilliant free-kick. An injury crisis at Old Trafford saw him recalled by Sir Alex Ferguson, and as a result, Preston's promotion challenge faltered. They were beaten by Bury in the semi-finals of the play-offs that year.

NO-GO FOR TINO

Faustino Asprilla was on the verge of a sensational move to The Football League's basement division with Darlington in the summer of 2002. The former Newcastle and Colombia forward was pictured holding a Quakers shirt alongside the club's chairman at the time, George Reynolds, and he was even presented to the fans. However, he subsequently failed to turn up for a medical and the deal fell through.

⇢ Dagenham & Redbridge's Danny Green didn't just set up goals in 2009/10, he scored them too. He celebrates (right) after netting against Darlington in October 2009.

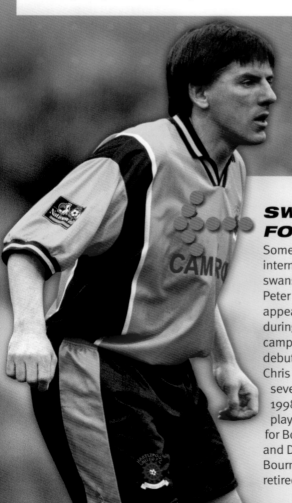

⇠ Peter Beardsley played football for the love of it. At the age of 38 in 1999, he was still playing for Hartlepool in the fourth tier.

SWANSONGS FOR STARS

Some of England's finest internationals have enjoyed swansongs in the fourth tier. Peter Beardsley made 22 appearances for Hartlepool during the 1998/99 campaign, scoring on his debut against Cambridge. Chris Waddle turned out seven times for Torquay in 1998 while Paul Gascoigne played four league games for Boston United in 2004 and Darren Anderton was a Bournemouth player when he retired in December 2008.

MOST ASSISTS 2009/10

Ben Davies (Notts County)	14
Danny Green (Dagenham & Redbridge)	13
Scott Donnelly (Aldershot)	13
Craig Westcarr (Notts County)	12
Chris Dagnall (Rochdale)	12
Chris O'Grady (Rochdale)	12
Adebayo Akinfenwa (Northampton)	10

OPTIONS APLENTY FOR QUAKERS

Darlington used 54 different players in the league in 2009/10 – the highest number of any club in the division. Ian Miller made the most appearances, featuring 40 times, while youngster Jordan Marshall made the least, coming off the bench three times towards the end of the campaign. Accrington used the fewest players, fielding 25.

DID YOU KNOW?

England cricket legend Sir Ian Botham played 11 Football League games for Scunthorpe in the early 1980s. Botham was a household name on the world cricket scene when he initially joined the Iron – at the time a fourth-tier club – apparently in a bid to get fit following an injury. He ended up training with the team during the winter months to maintain his fitness levels, and on occasion he played on a non-contract basis.

SHOCK MOVE FOR SOL

Sol Campbell stunned the footballing world in August 2009 when he signed for League 2 Notts County. However, the former England centre-back played just one game for the Magpies – a 2–1 defeat at Morecambe – before exiting the club. Campbell, who had been a free agent after leaving Portsmouth, moved back to the Barclays Premier League later in the season, rejoining former side Arsenal.

⬆ *Former Scunthorpe players of the 1960s, 1970s and 1980s went on to captain England teams: Ray Clemence and Kevin Keegan at football and Ian Botham at cricket.*

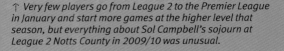

⬆ *Very few players go from League 2 to the Premier League in January and start more games at the higher level that season, but everything about Sol Campbell's sojourn at League 2 Notts County in 2009/10 was unusual.*

CURTIS BOXES CLEVER

Former Grimsby midfielder Curtis Woodhouse quit football to become a professional boxer in 2006. Woodhouse announced that he was hanging up his boots to concentrate on a career in the ring, playing his last match for the Mariners in the League 2 Play-Off Final against Cheltenham in May 2006. However, he returned to football in March 2007 with Conference side Rushden & Diamonds and played for Sheffield FC in 2009/10.

BROTHERLY LOVE

The Boulding brothers, Michael and Rory, played 16 minutes of football together for Bradford in 2009/10. Michael, who can count Aston Villa, Sheffield United, Grimsby and Mansfield among his former clubs, played 21 league games for the Bantams that term, scoring four goals. Sibling Rory made just two appearances, against Bournemouth and Bury. He came on as a 74th-minute substitute against the Shakers to line-up alongside Michael, who scored City's goal in a 2–1 defeat.

GREAT SCOTT!

Scott McGleish was the first player to score in the newly-formed League 2 when he netted for Northampton at Swansea on August 7 2004. Summer signing McGleish didn't take long to open his account for the Cobblers, tapping in after three minutes of his league debut when a David Galbraith cross was deflected off the post and into his path. McGleish also tried to claim Northampton's second goal in the 2–0 win, but it went down as an own goal from Sam Ricketts.

⤏ *Scott McGleish has scored goals everywhere he has played, averaging almost one in every three matches in a professional career that began in 1994. His first goal for Northampton was also the first in the rebranded League 2.*

Goals

QUAKERS KEPT OUT

Darlington scored the fewest goals at home of any team in the division in 2009/10 on their way to relegation to the Conference. The Quakers netted just 14 times and conceded 40 in front of their own fans, winning three games and losing 17 on home soil. They did manage 19 goals on their travels, but that was not enough to keep them up.

⟵ Jamie Chandler was one of 54 players who appeared in league matches for Darlington in 2009/10. The Quakers finished 18 points from safety and were relegated.

HIGHEST-SCORING GAMES

Hull	7–4	Swansea	(1997)
Burton	5–6	Cheltenham	(2010)
Barnet	1–9	Peterborough	(1998)
Rochdale	5–4	York	(2002)
Scunthorpe	6–2	Huddersfield	(2003)

GOAL TREAT FOR POSH

Peterborough fans were almost guaranteed to see goals during the 1960/61 campaign. The club established two notable landmarks on their way to winning the fourth-tier title that season, scoring in 33 consecutive matches and notching up a Football League-best 134 goals overall. Their run of consecutive strikes began on September 20 1960 with a 2–1 victory at Doncaster. Bradford Park Avenue stunned Jimmy Hagan's free-scoring side by claiming a 1–0 win on April 20 1961 to end the impressive sequence.

FRYATT'S FASTEST

Jim Fryatt scored what is believed to be the fastest goal in Football League history while playing for Bradford Park Avenue against Tranmere in April 1964. Fryatt's strike in the penultimate game of the 1963/64 season was recorded at four seconds and set the Yorkshire club on their way to a 4–2 victory. Fryatt made more than 100 appearances for Bradford, one of eight different English clubs he played for.

EARLY GOAL MAKES EASTWOOD'S DAY

Freddy Eastwood scored after just seven seconds of his Football League debut for Southend in a fourth-tier match against Swansea in October 2004. The Essex-born striker went on to mark the occasion with a hat-trick in a 4–2 victory at Roots Hall – one of three trebles he managed for the Shrimpers during his three-year stay at the club.

⟵ Freddy Eastwood (left) scored after seven seconds of his Football League debut for Southend against Swansea, and he finished with a hat-trick. His first season ended with a goal in the 2005 Play-Off Final victory over Lincoln.

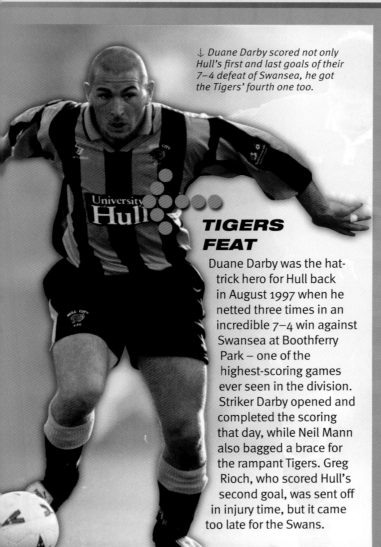

↓ *Duane Darby scored not only Hull's first and last goals of their 7–4 defeat of Swansea, he got the Tigers' fourth one too.*

TIGERS FEAT

Duane Darby was the hat-trick hero for Hull back in August 1997 when he netted three times in an incredible 7–4 win against Swansea at Boothferry Park – one of the highest-scoring games ever seen in the division. Striker Darby opened and completed the scoring that day, while Neil Mann also bagged a brace for the rampant Tigers. Greg Rioch, who scored Hull's second goal, was sent off in injury time, but it came too late for the Swans.

KEMPSON BAGS UNFORTUNATE BRACE

February 2010 was a bad month for Accrington's Darran Kempson, with the defender scoring two injury-time winners – both for the wrong team! His first gifted Lincoln a 2–1 victory at Sincil Bank, and he followed that two games later by finding the bottom corner of his own net against Torquay after he had attempted to take the ball away from striker Ashley Barnes. Perhaps the most famous fourth-tier own goal was scored by Bury's Chris Brass at Darlington in April 2006. He attempted an overhead clearance which cannoned off his face and rebounded into the back of the net!

⤑ *Chris Brass' own goal for Bury against Darlington in 2006 was a fine example of a good idea that went horribly wrong.*

BEES ARE SHOT-SHY

Barnet had the fewest shots of any team in the division in 2009/10, but their goal return was enough to see them avoid relegation. The Bees fired in 401 attempts – two less than bottom club Darlington and a massive 91 fewer than Grimsby, who finished 23rd. However, they found the net more times than both of those clubs (47) and they stayed up by four points.

LOOK HUGHES SCORING

Lee Hughes scored three hat-tricks for Notts County on his way to finishing the 2009/10 season as the league's leading marksman. The former West Brom forward ended the campaign with 30 league goals – four more than Bournemouth striker Brett Pitman. Hughes' best run came between November and January, as he bagged nine goals in seven league games. Rotherham's Adam Le Fondre was third in the goalscoring charts with 25 goals.

TORPEY TIMES IT RIGHT

Steve Torpey jointly holds the distinction of having scored the fastest goal since the fourth tier became known as League 2. Striker Torpey netted for Scunthorpe against Swansea with a neat header in December 2004 – a goal recorded at just seven seconds. It turned out to be the only goal of the game, although Iron winger Peter Beagrie had a penalty saved. Freddy Eastwood also scored for Southend after seven seconds.

⤑ *Steve Torpey scored regularly for Scunthorpe, but his goal after seven seconds against Swansea was the joint fastest since League 2 began.*

Club Records

There are 72 Football League clubs and 20 Premier League teams in England, and each one has their own unique story to tell. From Arsenal to Yeovil, every club, big or small, has had magical memories to savour and moments they would rather forget. Whether it's amazing games with incredible scorelines, record-breaking transfers, goalscoring legends or pop-star wannabes, English football has had it all down the years.

From its humble beginnings as a 12-team league in 1888, The Football League has gone through numerous changes to arrive at the format we know and love today. The introduction of the Premier League in 1992 enhanced the reputation of English football. The top-flight was originally a 22-team league, before being reduced to 20 ahead of the start of the 1995/96 campaign.

Since the introduction of the Premier League, there have been four different winners of the competition – Manchester United, Blackburn, Arsenal and Chelsea – and all of those successes went down in the history books.

The lower leagues have much to get excited about, too. One of the most exciting additions came in 1986/87 when the play-offs were introduced to give more teams in the second, third and fourth tiers the chance to achieve their promotion dreams.

Two sides who used the system to perfection in 2009/10 were Blackpool and Dagenham. The Seasiders only secured their spot in the end-of-season shootout on the final day of the campaign, but they went on to beat Nottingham Forest and then Cardiff in the final at Wembley to snatch a coveted place in the Barclays Premier League.

The Daggers capped their campaign off in similar fashion, finishing seventh in League 2 but then going on to beat Rotherham 3–2 in their final to reach the third tier for the first time in the club's history.

Some of the most talented players ever to grace the English leagues – from the likes of Sir Stanley Matthews, Billy Wright, Sir Tom Finney and George Best right through to modern-day greats such as Cristiano Ronaldo and Fernando Torres – are household names and global superstars. Along with a whole host of cult heroes, they make up the thousands of professional footballers who live out their boyhood dreams on a daily basis.

At every club and at every level, English football has always captured the imagination of fans around the world. And the signs are that will continue to be the case for many years to come.

Blackpool and Cardiff faced each other in the 2009/10 Championship Play-Off Final. At stake was a place in the Barclays Premier League. Blackpool took the spoils.

Barclays Premier League Club Records

The Barclays Premier League is widely regarded as one of the most exciting competitions in world football and has gone from strength to strength since the inaugural season in 1992. Attendances continue to grow, as do television viewing figures both in the UK and abroad, and it is easy to see why, with the league boasting some of the world's greatest players and biggest clubs.

Manchester United's Nemanja Vidic (left) beats Didier Drogba of Chelsea to the ball during a 2010 match between the winners of 10 of the past 12 Premier League championships. United claimed seven of those titles and Chelsea three, including in 2009/10.

Fans of the two Manchester clubs stand in tribute before City and United's clash in February 2008. They were remembering the Munich air crash of 1958 which decimated United's 'Busby Babes'.

Arsenal

Arsenal are one of the most successful clubs in English football, having won 13 top-flight titles and 10 FA Cups during their illustrious history. The Gunners are also the only team to have completed a Premier League season without losing a game. That was in 2003/04 – the last time the London club lifted the league title.

HUMBLE BEGINNINGS

The Gunners may be one of the biggest clubs in the world but they have come a long way since they were founded in October 1886. They turned professional five years later and changed their name to Woolwich Arsenal, with their first competitive match taking place in 1893 – a 2–2 draw with Newcastle.

⤳ *In 2003/04, Arsenal emulated the inaugural champions, Preston North End, by going through a league season undefeated. They played 38 games (26 wins, 12 draws) compared to Preston's 22 (18 wins, 4 draws).*

⤵ *Cesc Fabregas moved to England from Barcelona at the age of 16 in 2003 and made his Arsenal debut later that year. He has been a fixture in the Premier League for so long that it is hard to believe he celebrated his 23rd birthday in May 2010.*

THE INVINCIBLES

Arsenal wrote their name into modern football history in 2003/04 when they went through the entire league season unbeaten on their way to winning the Premier League title. 'The Invincibles', as they became known, were simply unstoppable and went on to stretch their streak to a record 49 games without defeat. It was well into the following season before the mammoth unbeaten run was finally brought to an end when, on October 24 2004, they were finally beaten by arch-rivals Manchester United, who triumphed 2–0 at Old Trafford. During that memorable title-winning season, Arsene Wenger's team failed to score on only four occasions, with Birmingham, Newcastle, Fulham and Manchester United the only teams able to hold them to 0–0.

CESC MAGNIFIQUE

Current captain Cesc Fabregas is the youngest player to have pulled on an Arsenal shirt. He set that record in 2003 when he appeared in a League Cup clash with Rotherham aged 16 years and 177 days. Midfielder Jack Wilshere holds the record for being the youngest Gunner to have played in the Premier League, having made his debut aged 16 years and 256 days against Blackburn in September 2008.

RECORD-BREAKING O'LEARY

David O'Leary is the Gunners' record appearance holder, having played 722 games in all competitions and 558 in the league between 1975 and 1993. The former Republic of Ireland international made his debut for the club in a goalless draw at Burnley in August 1975. Ray Parlour holds Arsenal's record for the most Premier League appearances with 333 – eight more than goalkeeper David Seaman.

⤑ *David O'Leary was a more than dependable central defender. He won two league titles, two FA Cups and two League Cups at Highbury.*

⤓ *Any questions about how Andrey Arshavin was settling in London were answered in April 2009 when he scored four times against Liverpool at Anfield in a pulsating 4–4 draw.*

THE PROFESSOR

Arsene Wenger is known as a real student of the game and has earned the nickname 'The Professor'. That reputation also comes in part from the fact that he is seen as one of the more intellectual managers in the Barclays Premier League. The Frenchman has a Masters degree in Economics and is able to speak several languages. He is fluent in English, German, Spanish and Italian, as well as his native French.

⬆ *Arsene Wenger's influence on Arsenal has been huge, both on and off the pitch. The trophies collected by the Gunners under his leadership bear testament to the Frenchman's football ideology.*

ARSENAL APPEARANCES

David O'Leary	722
Tony Adams	669
George Armstrong	621
Lee Dixon	619
Nigel Winterburn	584
David Seaman	564
Pat Rice	528
Peter Storey	501
John Radford	481
Peter Simpson	477

FROM RUSSIA WITH LOVE

Russian playmaker Andrey Arshavin has taken little time to make himself a firm favourite with the club's fans since arriving for around £15million from Zenit St Petersburg in February 2009. He has scored a number of important goals already in his Arsenal career, including all four in an amazing 4–4 draw with Liverpool at Anfield in April 2009. His first top-flight goal had come a month earlier in a 4–0 win against Blackburn.

ARSENAL'S LEADING GOALSCORERS

Thierry Henry	226
Ian Wright	185
Cliff Bastin	178
John Radford	149
Ted Drake	139
Jimmy Brain	139
Doug Lishman	137
Joe Hulme	125
David Jack	124
Dennis Bergkamp	120

Arsenal

BERGKAMP'S HOT SHOT

Dennis Bergkamp's stunning strike in a 2–0 victory at Newcastle in March 2002 is the greatest goal the club have ever scored, according to an official poll. The Dutchman topped the vote for his mesmerising finish against the Magpies when, following neat build-up play involving Patrick Vieira and Robert Pires, he effortlessly flicked the ball one side of defender Nikos Dabizas and went round the other before coolly slotting past Shay Given.

← Dennis Bergkamp's arrival at Arsenal raised a few eyebrows when he was signed from Inter Milan in 1995, but he flourished under Arsene Wenger and became one of the best players in Premier League history.

↓ Thierry Henry came to epitomise the Arsenal flair under Arsene Wenger, scoring more than 200 goals, and most of them were beautiful.

CANARIES TAKE FLIGHT

The Gunners began life in the Premier League with a surprise 4–2 defeat at home to Norwich. Arsenal had finished fourth in season 1991/92 and it was all going according to plan when Steve Bould opened the scoring and Kevin Campbell added a second before half-time. But the Canaries hit back, with Mark Robins scoring twice and David Phillips and Ruel Fox completing the turnaround. Norwich qualified for Europe by finishing third that term, while Arsenal were 10th.

WENGER'S LUCKY 13

Arsene Wenger became the longest-serving manager in the club's history in 2009/10 when he completed 13 years in charge. The Frenchman was largely unknown outside of his homeland when he arrived at the club in October 1996, having previously coached Monaco and Nancy as well as Japanese club Grampus Eight. However, in the years since, he has established himself as the most successful boss in the Gunners' long history and turned himself into a hero with the club's fans.

THE GREATEST GUNNERS*

1   Thierry Henry
2   Dennis Bergkamp
3   Tony Adams
4   Ian Wright
5   Patrick Vieira
6   Robert Pires
7   David Seaman
8   Liam Brady
9   Charlie George
10 Pat Jennings

* As voted by Arsenal fans

KING HENRY

Thierry Henry was named as Arsenal's greatest player in an official poll in 2008. The French forward is the club's all-time leading goalscorer, having netted 226 times in 380 appearances in all competitions between 1999 and 2007. Henry's most memorable strike came against Manchester United in October 2000 when he flicked the ball up, turned and lobbed a shot over Fabien Barthez. That strike came second in a list of Arsenal's top goals. Henry won two Premier League titles and two FA Cup winners' medals with the Gunners before leaving for Barcelona.

SUNDERLAND'S MEMORABLE MOMENT

Arsenal have won the FA Cup 10 times and have been involved in some of the most memorable cup final tussles. Perhaps their most dramatic victory came in 1979 against Manchester United. The Gunners were leading 2–0 at half-time through a Brian Talbot tap-in and Frank Stapleton's header. That was how it stayed until five minutes before the end, when United managed to haul themselves level. However, there was still time for another twist as, with only a few seconds remaining, Graham Rix sent over a cross which was misjudged by goalkeeper Gary Bailey and Alan Sunderland popped up at the far post to make it 3–2 to the Londoners.

⟵ *What had seemed set to be an unremarkable FA Cup final win for Arsenal against Manchester United in 1979 became memorable when United scored twice late on, only for Alan Sunderland (front) to snatch the trophy with a goal in the final seconds.*

TOTTENHAM TUSSLES

Derby games between Arsenal and Tottenham are always good to watch, but there have been a couple of titanic Barclays Premier League tussles between the two sides in recent years. The first came at White Hart Lane in November 2004. The Gunners came from a goal behind to lead 3–1 and then 4–2, before finally winning 5–4. It was a similar story in October 2008, although this time Spurs managed to snatch a point with two goals in the last two minutes making it 4–4 at the Emirates Stadium.

DRAKE'S SEVEN

Legendary striker Ted Drake scored seven goals in a single game for Arsenal in December 1935 – a club record. Aston Villa were the opposition and found themselves 3–0 down at the break, with Drake scoring a hat-trick. He had bagged six by the hour mark and completed his remarkable scoring feat in the last minute, having also hit the crossbar and had another effort well saved. The game finished 7–1 to the Gunners.

↑ *Ted Drake was almost unstoppable against Aston Villa in 1935, scoring all seven goals in a 7–1 win at Villa Park.*

SPIREITES' RECORD SHOT DOWN

Arsenal created an English record when they scored in 55 consecutive Premier League matches between May 19 2001 and December 7 2002. The run began in a 3–2 defeat at Southampton on the last day of the 2000/01 campaign and continued until 2002/03, as Juan Sebastian Veron and Paul Scholes scored the only goals of the game for Manchester United in a 2–0 win at Old Trafford. Chesterfield had previously held the record, scoring in 46 matches in a row in the third tier between 1929 and 1930.

GUNNERS' FA CUP FINAL WINS

1930	2–0 v Huddersfield
1936	1–0 v Sheffield United
1950	2–0 v Liverpool
1971	2–1 v Liverpool
1979	3–2 v Manchester United
1993	2–1 v Sheffield Wednesday
1998	2–0 v Newcastle United
2002	2–0 v Chelsea
2003	1–0 v Southampton
2005	0–0 v Manchester United (5–4 on penalties)

↓ *Jens Lehmann (left) made the vital saves and skipper Patrick Vieira took the final kick as Arsenal won the 2005 FA Cup final in a penalty shootout.*

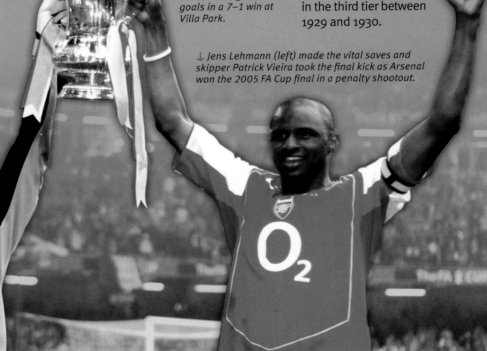

Aston Villa

Aston Villa were top-flight champions and kings of Europe back in the early 1980s, and they have begun to re-emerge as a force under current boss Martin O'Neill. The Irishman led the club to a third consecutive top-six finish in the Barclays Premier League in 2009/10, as well as guiding them to the final of the Carling Cup.

HOME-GROWN TALENT

Aston Villa were the last club to field an all-English starting line-up in a Premier League game. Coventry dampened the occasion by claiming a 4–1 win at Villa Park on February 27 1999. Michael Oakes started the game in goal for Villa, with Alan Wright, Gareth Southgate, Steve Watson and Riccardo Scimeca making up the defence. Ian Taylor, Paul Merson, Simon Grayson and Lee Hendrie were in midfield, while Dion Dublin and Julian Joachim began the game up front. Villa also used three English substitutes – Gareth Barry, Mark Draper and Stan Collymore.

CHAMPIONS OF EUROPE

Villa are one of four English clubs to have won the European Cup. Peter Withe scored the only goal of the game as the midlands side beat German giants Bayern Munich in the final in May 1982. Villa had eased to victory against Valur Reykjavik in the first round and then edged past Dynamo Berlin before seeing off a strong Dynamo Kiev side in the last eight. A single Tony Morley goal separated the Villans and Anderlecht in a two-legged semi-final, and Villa survived the loss of goalkeeper Jimmy Rimmer to injury in the early stages of the final to snatch a 1–0 win.

↑ Left to right: Dwight Yorke, Savo Milosevic and Ian Taylor, the Aston Villa goalscorers in the 3–0 1996 League Cup final victory over Leeds.

VILLANS ARE CUP HEROES

The Villans have won the League Cup five times, with their last success coming in 1996. Savo Milosevic scored a superb opener in a 3–0 win against Leeds, with Ian Taylor adding a second and Dwight Yorke wrapping up the victory late on. Villa, who were the first club to win the competition when they beat Rotherham in 1961, were also victorious against Norwich in 1975, Everton after two replays in 1977 and Manchester United in 1994.

↓ Although experienced England international striker Peter Withe scored Aston Villa's match-winning goal in the 1982 European Cup final, substitute goalkeeper Nigel Spink came on for only his second first-team appearance.

SEVENTH HEAVEN

Villa have won the top-flight title on seven occasions, although six of those successes came between 1894 and 1910. The last time the midlands club tasted championship glory was under Ron Saunders in season 1980/81, as they pipped Ipswich by four points.

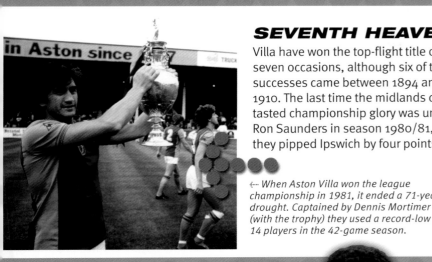

⟵ *When Aston Villa won the league championship in 1981, it ended a 71-year drought. Captained by Dennis Mortimer (with the trophy) they used a record-low 14 players in the 42-game season.*

POINTS MEAN PRIZES

Villa's promotion-winning campaign of 1987/88 brought with it a club-record points haul. Graham Taylor's side finished as runners-up to Millwall in the second tier, having taken 78 points from 42 matches. The Lions topped the table on 82. The club's biggest total when two points were awarded for a win came in the 1971/72 campaign, as they claimed the third-tier title with 70 points and won 32 of their 46 games.

DR WHO?

Foreign bosses are common in English football these days, but Aston Villa were the first top-flight club to appoint a manager from outside Britain or Ireland in July 1990. Slovakian coach Dr Jozef Venglos didn't last long at Villa Park, though, stepping down after the club finished two places above the relegation zone in 1990/91. Venglos remains the only foreigner to have managed the club.

DONS UNDONE BY JOHNSON

Villa's record Premier League victory came against Wimbledon at Villa Park on February 11 1995. An own goal from Dons defender Alan Reeves opened the floodgates and, after Tommy Johnson had helped himself to a hat-trick, Dean Saunders bagged a brace and Dwight Yorke completed a 7–1 victory with seven minutes remaining. Warren Barton netted a consolation for the visitors. The Villans' biggest away victory since the league's inception in 1992 was a 6–0 success at Derby in April 2008.

⬆ *Republic of Ireland defender Paul McGrath battled chronic knee trouble to help Aston Villa finish second in the inaugural Premier League season, and he won the PFA Player of the Year award.*

BIG-TIME CHARLIE

Charlie Aitken holds the record for the most appearances in an Aston Villa shirt. He played 659 times in all competitions in a 16-year spell at the club between 1960 and 1976. Defender Aitken was a member of the Villa side that won the League Cup in 1975, having also been a losing finalist in the competition in 1971. The club were beaten 2–0 by Tottenham in the Wembley showpiece that year, with Martin Chivers scoring both goals for Spurs.

⬇ *Charlie Aitken was the most loyal Villan. His only league winners' medal came when Villa won the Division Three championship in 1972.*

ASTON VILLA APPEARANCES

Charlie Aitken	659
Billy Walker	531
Gordon Cowans	528
Joe Bache	474
Allan Evans	473
Gareth Barry	458
Nigel Spink	454
Tommy Smart	452
Johnny Dixon	430
Dennis Mortimer	405

AWARD-WINNING TRIO

Three Aston Villa players have been named the PFA Player of the Year, with Paul McGrath the last to scoop the prize in 1993. Defender McGrath won the award for his solid performances in a side that finished as runners-up to Manchester United. Andy Gray was the first Villa recipient in 1977, having ended the campaign as the top-flight's leading goalscorer, while David Platt also received the accolade in 1990.

AVFC
PREPARED

Aston Villa

MILNER SHINES

England international James Milner enjoyed an impressive 2009/10 campaign for Villa, setting up 12 goals for his team-mates – the fourth highest number of assists in the top flight – and scoring a career-best seven top-flight goals. Milner first shot to prominence when he became the youngest Premier League goalscorer, netting for Leeds in a 2-1 win against Sunderland on Boxing Day 2002, although that record has since been broken.

↓ James Milner's excellent form for Aston Villa in 2009/10 earned him a trip to South Africa with England for the 2010 FIFA World Cup.

AWAY THE LADS

Only the Barclays Premier League's top two sides won more away games than Aston Villa during the 2009/10 campaign. Martin O'Neill's men claimed nine victories on the road, one less than champions Chelsea and two behind Manchester United. Notable results included a 3–1 win at Liverpool, a 1–0 success at Old Trafford and a derby victory at Birmingham.

↑ Ashley Young tries to get past Lee Bowyer during Aston Villa's 1–0 derby win against Birmingham at Villa Park in April 2010, a result that completed a league double for the Villans.

FLYING START

Villa managed a club-record run of 12 Premier League games unbeaten at the start of the 1998/99 season. The campaign began with a goalless draw at Everton, which was followed by four straight victories. After another stalemate with Leeds at Elland Road, Villa then won four of their next six matches. The run was finally brought to an end when Liverpool claimed a 4–2 victory at Villa Park, helped by a Robbie Fowler hat-trick.

BRAND NEW BADGE

A new club crest was revealed in May 2007, incorporating a star to represent Villa's European Cup success of 1982. The claret and blue stripes used in the previous shield were replaced by an all-blue background, although the traditional lion emblem remained in gold. Aston Villa was shortened to AVFC, but the club's motto, Prepared, remained at the foot of the badge.

A SUPER SHOW

Mighty Barcelona were beaten over two legs as Villa won the European Super Cup in 1982/83. The Catalan giants claimed a 1–0 victory at the Nou Camp in the first game, but a 3–0 extra-time victory in the second leg at Villa Park secured the hosts an aggregate success. Gary Shaw had levelled the tie late on, with a penalty from Gordon Cowans putting Villa ahead before Ken McNaught clinched victory.

MARTIN'S THE MAN

Martin O'Neill has spent the last four years as manager of the club, during which time he has overseen several notable landmarks. Villa went nine top-tier games unbeaten at the start of the Irishman's first season in charge – the best opening run of any club in the top flight that term – and scored 71 goals during the 2007/08 campaign – their highest tally in the Premier League – to finish sixth. They made the top six again in both 2008/09 and 2009/10. O'Neill also led Villa to their first cup final in 10 years in February 2010, but they were beaten 2–1 by Manchester United in the Carling Cup.

PONGO ON SONG

Tom 'Pongo' Waring scored an amazing 49 goals in a single season for Aston Villa during the 1930/31 campaign. The Villans netted a club-record 128 times that term but finished runners-up to Arsenal in the top flight. Waring scored 159 league goals and 167 in total for Villa during a seven-year stay between 1928 and 1935, including 10 hat-tricks. He is the club's sixth highest goalscorer of all time.

⟶ *Tom Waring got his nickname 'Pongo' from a popular cartoon strip of the time. He was not a fan of training, but no one cared, because his goals were so important to the team.*

VILLA'S LEADING GOALSCORERS

Billy Walker	244
Harry Hampton	242
John Devey	186
Joe Bache	184
Eric Houghton	170
Tom Waring	167
Johnny Dixon	144
Peter McParland	120

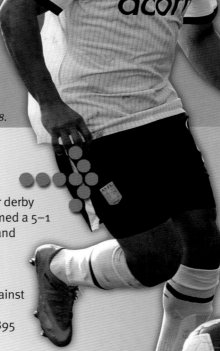

⟵ *Manager Martin O'Neill wears his heart on his sleeve, but there is no doubting his success as boss of Aston Villa.*

⟶ *Gabriel Agbonlahor completed the scoring as Aston Villa equalled their biggest top-division win over Birmingham City, 5–1, in 2008.*

HUNTER GATHERS RECORD

Archie Hunter was the first player to score in every round of the FA Cup when Aston Villa won the competition in 1887. He netted the opener in a 2–0 win against West Brom in the final to complete the feat. Hunter, who was the club's captain at the time, suffered a heart attack during a game against Everton in January 1890 and never played again. He died four years later aged just 35.

BEATING THE BLUES

The club secured their biggest league win over derby rivals Birmingham for 45 years when they claimed a 5–1 victory at Villa Park in April 2008. John Carew and Ashley Young both netted twice, with Gabriel Agbonlahor completing the scoring. Villa had been 4–0 winners in March 1963, while they have also enjoyed some other big victories against Blues over the years. In October 1960 they secured a 6–2 success, while in September 1895 they ran-out 7–3 winners!

Birmingham City

Birmingham have spent the majority of their history in the top flight of English football, with their most successful period coming in the 1950s and early 1960s. They have won just one major trophy, the League Cup in 1963, but there are high hopes that the current side can end that run following a big-money takeover by Carson Yeung in 2009.

TOUGH START AT ARSENAL

Thierry Henry and Sylvain Wiltord were on the scoresheet for Arsenal at Highbury as Birmingham were given a tough baptism of fire in their first Premier League game in August 2002. The 2002/03 season was four games old when Blues finally recorded their first victory. Paul Devlin and Damien Johnson scored the goals as Leeds were beaten 2–1 at St Andrew's. The highlight of City's 13th-place finish that year was a 2–1 success at home to Liverpool.

SHOOTOUT BLUES

Birmingham were a second-tier side when they pushed Liverpool all the way in the 2001 League Cup final. It was the first time in 38 years that the club had reached a major domestic final. Trevor Francis' side forced extra-time when Darren Purse scored from the penalty spot in the dying seconds to cancel out Robbie Fowler's opener. The game went to a penalty shootout, with Andrew Johnson missing the crucial kick. Blues were winners of the competition in 1963, beating midlands rivals Aston Villa 3–1 over two legs.

←··· *Martin Grainger (right) is consoled by Martin O'Connor after Birmingham League Cup final shootout defeat against Liverpool at the Millennium Stadium, Cardiff.*

←··· *Birmingham had to wait until the end of August 2002 before they could celebrate a Premier League win. Damien Johnson (left, with Clinton Morrison), scored the second goal in the 2–1 defeat of Leeds.*

GLOBAL APPEAL

Birmingham's globe crest was adopted by the club in 1972. It was the winning entry in a newspaper competition to design a new badge. It consists of a globe resting on top of a football, with a ribbon draped around it which carries the name of the club and the year of their formation – 1875. The crest was not worn on City's shirts until the 1976/77 campaign.

FORTRESS ST ANDREW'S

Birmingham went 15 home games without defeat during the 2009/10 season. In fact, Blues were only beaten twice at St Andrew's, although one of those losses came in a derby clash against Aston Villa. The impressive sequence began against Sunderland on October 24, with a 2–1 victory against Burnley in the last home game of the season ensuring that the run could continue into the 2010/11 campaign.

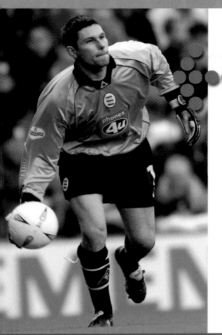

BENNETT WON'T BE BEATEN

Ian Bennett and the title-winning defence of 1994/95 hold the club record for the most clean sheets in a season and also the most consecutive clean sheets in the league. Goalkeeper Bennett made 62 appearances in all competitions that term and didn't concede a goal on 27 occasions. A 2–0 win against Bristol Rovers on October 29 1994 saw Blues embark on a record run of seven league games without the opposition scoring. Bennett also kept 21 clean sheets in 45 league games in season 1997/98, which is another City record.

⟵ Ian Bennett made 287 league appearances for Birmingham in a 12-year career with the Blues.

TRICKY TREV

Trevor Francis was 16 years and 139 days old when he set the record as the youngest player ever to pull on a Birmingham shirt. Francis, who went on to become Britain's first £1million footballer, was sent on as a substitute in a second-tier clash against Cardiff on September 5 1970. He played 328 games for Blues and scored 134 goals before moving to Nottingham Forest in 1979. Francis later returned to St Andrew's as manager, leading the club to the League Cup final in 2001.

⬆ Birmingham's most precocious teenager, Trevor Francis, burst onto the football scene in spectacular fashion.

BLUES' TOP FIVE GOALSCORERS

Joe Bradford	267
Trevor Francis	134
Peter Murphy	127
Freddie Wheldon	118
George Briggs	107

BRADFORD'S GOAL GLUT

Joe Bradford is the club's all-time record goalscorer, having netted 267 times in all competitions between 1920 and 1935. Bradford scored 13 hat-tricks for Blues – 12 in the league and one in the League Cup – and netted 29 times in the top-flight campaign of 1927/28. He was also on target in City's 2–1 FA Cup final defeat to West Brom in 1931. Bradford was capped 12 times for England, netting seven goals.

BRUCE ALMIGHTY

Blues reached the Barclays Premier League for the first time in season 2001/02. Steve Bruce replaced Trevor Francis as manager in December 2001 and turned the club's season around, guiding them to a fifth-place finish and a play-off place. Stern John was the hero in the semi-finals, scoring at Millwall in the 90th minute of the second leg to set up a Millennium Stadium clash with Norwich. A tight contest ended 1–1 after extra-time, with Geoff Horsfield grabbing an equaliser in the 102nd minute. Darren Carter netted the winning penalty in a tense shootout to secure promotion.

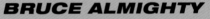

A TRUE BLUE

One of the most famous names in Birmingham's history passed away in 2010. Goalkeeper Gil Merrick was a one-club man, spending 22 years at St Andrew's between 1938 and 1960. That spell makes him the longest-serving Blues player ever, while he also holds the record for the most appearances in a City shirt. Merrick featured in 551 post-war matches, although if you include wartime games that tally is boosted to 713. Merrick went on to manage the club, leading them to the Fairs Cup final in 1961 and League Cup glory in 1963.

⟵ Gil Merrick, saving at the feet of Sunderland's Charlie Fleming (stripes) in 1956, was honoured by Birmingham in 2009 when the Railway Stand at St Andrew's was renamed the Gil Merrick Stand.

Birmingham City

SMALL HEATH GO LARGE

Birmingham were known as Small Heath when they recorded their record league victories. They beat Walsall – or Walsall Town Swifts as they were known at the time – 12–0 in the second tier in December 1892, with Billy Walton and Frank Mobley both scoring hat-tricks. They repeated the feat against Doncaster 11 years later when Freddie Wilcox netted four goals and Arthur Leonard grabbed three in another comfortable win. Blues became known as Birmingham in 1905, adding City to their name in 1945.

ON THE RUN

An 18-game stretch from 1906–1907 represents the club's longest unbeaten home run in all competitions as a top-flight outfit. The likes of Liverpool, Arsenal, Everton and Manchester City were all despatched as Blues gathered momentum, while the run also included draws with Manchester United, Sheffield Wednesday, Sheffield United and Middlesbrough. The latter game was the first to be played at St Andrew's.

---> *Alex McLeish enhanced his reputation as a manager during a very successful season with Birmingham City in 2009/10.*

<--- *Cameron Jerome's 10 goals in the 2009/10 season was his best return for Birmingham and helped them to a mid-table finish in the top flight.*

FAMILIAR FACES

Birmingham boss Alex McLeish named an unchanged line-up for 12 consecutive matches in 2009/10 – a record in the competition. A 1–0 victory against Fulham at St Andrew's on November 21 saw the Scot keep faith with a winning line-up for the next game at Wolves. Another 1–0 win followed, with McLeish then sticking with the same team until Blues' clash with West Ham on February 10, when he opted to make three changes.

CAM'S YOUR MAN

Cameron Jerome ended the 2009/10 campaign as Birmingham's top scorer. Striker Jerome netted 10 goals in total, double that of his nearest rivals, Lee Bowyer and James McFadden. He scored twice against Blackburn and Portsmouth, with Blues winning both games 2–1. Jerome also scooped the club's Goal of the Season award for his spectacular 30-yard strike in the 2–2 draw with Liverpool at Anfield in November.

BLUES' 12-GAME RECORD BREAKERS

GK	Joe Hart
DEF	Liam Ridgewell
DEF	Stephen Carr
DEF	Scott Dann
DEF	Roger Johnson
MID	Lee Bowyer
MID	Sebastian Larsson
MID	Barry Ferguson
ATT	Cameron Jerome
ATT	Christian Benitez
ATT	James McFadden

⤑ *Roger Johnson, who cost Birmingham £5million in the summer of 2009 when he left Cardiff City, was part of the record-breaking Blues line-up that started 12 consecutive games in 2009/10.*

DRAW SPECIALISTS

Blues recorded the most home draws of any team in the Barclays Premier League in 2009/10. They were held nine times in their 19 matches at St Andrew's, drawing with all of the top five teams. Title-winners Chelsea failed to score in a goalless draw in December, while games against Manchester United, Arsenal and Tottenham all finished 1–1. Birmingham's clash with fifth-place Manchester City also ended in stalemate, as did the matches against Liverpool, Everton, Stoke and Hull.

VILLA HAVE DERBY EDGE

Aston Villa are Birmingham's main derby rivals, and they currently have the edge in games between the two sides. In 108 league meetings up to the end of 2009/10, City had managed 36 wins, with Villa having claimed 45. There have been 27 draws. Blues' last derby success came in March 2005, as Emile Heskey and Julian Gray were on target in a 2–0 win.

ITALIAN JOB

Current Champions League holders Inter Milan were humbled in historic fashion as City reached the Fairs Cup final in 1961. Blues won both games 2–1, with Jimmy Harris scoring three goals over the two ties to help secure a 4–2 aggregate victory. Birmingham's feat in beating the Italian giants at the San Siro went unmatched by another English team until Arsenal's 5–1 victory there in the Champions League in 2003. Birmingham reached the Fairs Cup final for two years running in 1960 and 1961, losing both times. They were beaten 4–1 on aggregate by Barcelona and then 4–2 by Roma a year later.

BARREN SPELL FOR BLUES

City went a club-record 17 league games without a win and equalled a sequence of eight straight defeats in season 1985/86. Their winless streak started with a 3–1 defeat at QPR on September 28 1985 and finally ended on February 1 the following year when they snatched a 1–0 victory at Oxford. During that time, they also lost eight games on the spin. Unsurprisingly, they were relegated from the top flight that term.

A FINE FINISH

The 1955/56 season saw Birmingham finish in their highest league position and reach the final of the FA Cup for the second time in their history. They ended the campaign in sixth place in the top flight, just four points behind runners-up Blackpool. Arthur Turner's side were beaten 3–1 by Manchester City in the FA Cup, with Noel Kinsey scoring Birmingham's goal. Blues' only other final appearance came in 1931 when they lost 2–1 to West Brom.

⤑ *Noel Kinsey (left) was one of Birmingham's goalscorers in the 1956 FA Cup semi-final against Sunderland, a match they won 3–0 at Hillsborough to become the first club to reach the FA Cup final without having been drawn at home.*

Blackburn Rovers

Blackburn enjoyed the high life in the early years of the Premier League, with the club following up a second-place finish in 1993/94 by winning the title in thrilling fashion the following season. The Lancashire side also have considerable cup pedigree and won the FA Cup five times in the space of seven years between 1884 and 1891.

SHEARER AND SUTTON

The key to Blackburn's title success in 1994/95 was the strike partnership of Alan Shearer and Chris Sutton, or the 'SAS' as they became known. There were only 12 games during that Premier League campaign in which neither of the lethal duo were on the scoresheet, with Shearer scoring three hat-tricks (against QPR, West Ham and Ipswich) and Sutton one (against Coventry). Shearer ended the season as the league's top scorer with 34, while Sutton netted 15.

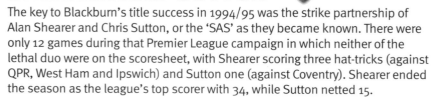

↑ With almost 50 Premier League goals between them, Alan Shearer (left) and Chris Sutton were able to celebrate the title in 1995.

SIMON SAYS SCORE!

Simon Garner is the club's record league goalscorer. Garner netted 168 times in a 14-year spell between 1978 and 1992. Rovers earned promotion to the first-ever Premier League in Garner's final season, beating Leicester 1–0 in the Play-Off Final, with Mike Newell scoring a penalty.

↓ Simon Garner became a legend in Blackburn, helping Rovers climb into the Premier League.

ROVERS MOTOR TO TITLE

Rovers won their first top-flight title since 1914 when they pipped Manchester United to be crowned Premier League champions in 1994/95. The race went down to the final day, but Kenny Dalglish's side were victorious, despite losing 2–1 at Liverpool. United failed to find the winner they needed at West Ham, with a 1–1 draw sending the title to Ewood Park.

WHAT'S THE POINT?

Blackburn's 91-point haul in the 2000/01 season is the highest total they have managed since three points for a win was introduced. Rovers gained promotion back to the Premier League that year, but they still finished the campaign as runners-up to Fulham, who broke the 100-point barrier under the management of Jean Tigana. When two points were awarded for a victory, the Lancashire club posted 60 points in the 1974/75 campaign to claim the third-tier title.

MIMMS KEEPS IT CLEAN

Goalkeeper Bobby Mimms and a Rovers rearguard featuring David May, Colin Hendry, Kevin Moran and Graeme Le Saux equalled a club record of 19 clean sheets in 1992/93. Blackburn had been promoted to the top flight the term before and they defied the critics by finishing fourth in the first-ever Premier League campaign. Jim Arnold was in goal when the club kept the same number of clean sheets in the third-tier campaign of 1979/80.

↑ *Bobby Mimms played behind a solid Blackburn Rovers defence and kept 19 clean sheets in the club's debut season in the Premier League.*

BORO SOUNDLY BEATEN

Middlesbrough were on the receiving end as Blackburn hit nine goals without reply to rack up their record league victory in November 1954. Frank Mooney and Eddie Quigley scored hat-tricks, while Eddie Crossan bagged a brace in the emphatic victory. The club's record cup success came against Rossendale in the first round of the FA Cup in 1884, as they ran out 11–0 winners.

FRIEDEL IN FINE FORM

Rovers were League Cup winners for the one and only time in their history in 2002, beating Tottenham 2–1 at the Millennium Stadium. Matt Jansen opened the scoring for Blackburn in the 25th minute only for Christian Ziege to equalise shortly afterwards. Andrew Cole was the match-winner with just over 20 minutes remaining, taking advantage of hesitant defending to slot home. Rovers had goalkeeper Brad Friedel to thank for preserving their lead, as he pulled off a string of fine saves.

↑ *Brad Friedel's heroics at the Millennium Stadium played a big part in Blackburn's first League Cup success in 2002, as they beat Tottenham 2–1.*

ROVERS' MANAGERS SINCE 1995

Ray Harford	1995–1997
Roy Hodgson	1997–1998
Brian Kidd	1998–1999
Tony Parkes	1999–2000
Graeme Souness	2000–2004
Mark Hughes	2004–2008
Paul Ince	2008
Sam Allardyce	2008–Present

←·· *Andrew Cole repaid Blackburn's faith in him by scoring the winner in the 2002 League Cup final, two months after Rovers had paid Manchester United £8million for his services.*

FANTASTIC FAZ

Derek Fazackerley is Rovers' record appearance holder, having featured in 596 league games for the club between 1970 and 1986. Fazackerley overtook Ronnie Clayton, who played in 529 games for the Ewood Park side. The defender only scored 23 league goals, but he is fondly remembered for his match-winner in a derby clash at Bolton in March 1973. He returned to Blackburn as a first-team coach under Ray Harford and Roy Hodgson.

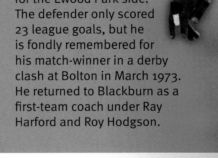

GOAL KING COLE

The Lancashire club broke their transfer record to sign striker Andrew Cole in December 2001. Cole had been a prolific goalscorer at Newcastle and Manchester United, and he scored four goals in his first six appearances for Rovers. He had netted 13 times in all competitions by the end of the 2001/02 campaign, scoring in five consecutive matches during the last two months of the season. He scored 37 goals in total for Blackburn before moving to Fulham.

Blackburn Rovers

ARTE ET LABORE

UNCLE JACK

Jack Walker invested millions of pounds into Blackburn to help the club realise their Premier League dream. Walker made his money in the steel and aviation industries. He took control of Rovers in 1991 and broke the British transfer record twice to sign Alan Shearer and later Chris Sutton. Walker oversaw the redevelopment of Ewood Park and has a stand named after him. 'Uncle Jack' died in August 2000. There is a memorial garden and statue in his honour outside Blackburn's stadium.

HIT FOR SIX

Rovers have won the FA Cup six times, although they last lifted the trophy in 1928. Blackburn were victorious for three years running between 1884 and 1886, and they also won the competition in 1890 and 1891. Rovers last reached the final in 1960, but they were beaten 3–0 by Wolves, with defender Mick McGrath putting through his own net to break the deadlock. They were also runners-up in 1882.

←– Jack Walker's investment in Blackburn was not just on the pitch. He paid for the redevelopment of Ewood Park and his biggest reward came with the 1995 league title.

† Bryan Douglas is denied by Wolves goalkeeper Malcom Finlayson in the 1960 FA Cup final. It is now 50 years since Blackburn have played in the showpiece final.

FOUNDER MEMBERS

Blackburn are one of only three clubs who were founder members of both The Football League and the Premier League. They share the honour with Everton and Aston Villa. Rovers finished fourth out of 12 teams in the first-ever league season of 1888, and they also ended the inaugural Premier League campaign in fourth place – three points behind runners-up Villa.

ROAD TRIP-UP

The club suffered 10 consecutive away defeats over two Barclays Premier League seasons in 2009. The sequence started on March 14 when Arsenal eased to a 4–0 victory, with Liverpool winning by the same margin in their next away fixture. Three more defeats followed that term, meaning that the run continued into 2009/10. In their opening five games of that campaign, Rovers endured tricky trips to Sunderland and Everton and then came up against the eventual top three, Arsenal, Chelsea and Manchester United. They finally secured a win at neighbours Bolton on November 22.

EAGLES LAND AN OPENING POINT

Rovers enjoyed a memorable tussle in their first Premier League match in August 1992. Blackburn were eight minutes away from victory when Simon Osborn rescued Crystal Palace a point in a 3–3 draw at Selhurst Park. Stuart Ripley had cancelled out a Mark Bright opener to make it 1–1 and, after Gareth Southgate had restored the Eagles' advantage, Alan Shearer equalised again. The prolific striker then put Blackburn ahead for the first time in the 82nd minute, but they were denied by Osborn's last-gasp leveller.

← *Alan Shearer's acrobatics couldn't make Blackburn's Premier League debut a winning one, but he did score two of Rovers' goals in their 3–3 draw at Crystal Palace.*

DUNN AND DUSTED

David Dunn was Blackburn's top goalscorer in 2009/10 – but no Rovers player reached double figures. Midfielder Dunn, in his second spell at Ewood Park, netted four times in his first six matches of the campaign, with his goals helping the club to beat Wolves, Aston Villa and Burnley. He was also on target in the 6–2 defeat at Arsenal. Dunn finished the campaign with nine in the league, while Jason Roberts scored five and both Ryan Nelsen and Christopher Samba grabbed four.

BRIGGS SCORES SEVEN

Tommy Briggs scored a club-record seven goals in one game for Rovers in February 1955. Bristol Rovers were on the receiving end when Blackburn claimed an 8–3 victory at Ewood Park. Briggs was a prolific scorer for the Lancashire club between 1952 and 1957, netting 140 league goals in just 194 games.

ROVERS' TOP PREMIER LEAGUE GOALSCORERS SINCE 2001

Season	Player	Goals
2001/02	Andrew Cole	13
2002/03	Damien Duff	9
2003/04	Andrew Cole	11
2004/05	Paul Dickov	9
2005/06	Craig Bellamy	13
2006/07	Benni McCarthy	18
2007/08	Roque Santa Cruz	19
2008/09	Benni McCarthy	10
2009/10	David Dunn	9

← *David Dunn celebrates his goal in the 3–2 defeat of Burnley at Ewood Park in October 2010.*

FREE-SCORING ROVERS

Blackburn netted 114 goals during the 1954/55 season, but it was not enough to win them the title, or even gain them promotion. Rovers were the highest scorers in the second tier by some distance that term, netting 22 more than champions Birmingham. City claimed the title on goal difference from both Luton and Rotherham after all three had finished with 54 points. Rovers finished sixth.

↓ *Striker Jason Roberts continued a proud family tradition when he received an MBE at Buckingham Palace in 2010.*

A SPORTING FAMILY

Jason Roberts is the third member of his family to be given an MBE. Two of the Blackburn striker's uncles – Ken Roberts and former West Brom and Coventry forward Cyrille Regis – had already received recognition from the Queen when Jason was awarded the honour for his services to sport in both Grenada and the UK in 2010. Roberts is also related to Olympic medallist John Regis, while David and Otis Roberts – both uncles – also played professional football.

Bolton Wanderers

Bolton are now firmly established as a Barclays Premier League club, with the Lancashire side rejoining the top flight in 2001, having first gained promotion back in 1995. Wanderers have continued to build in recent years. They played in Europe for the first time in 2005/06, as well as qualifying again for the 2007/08 season.

ROYALS RUMBLED

The 1995/96 season saw Bolton play in the Premier League for the first time. They secured their place with a thrilling play-off success against Reading at Wembley. Wanderers were 2–0 down after 15 minutes and things looked bleak when Reading were awarded a penalty before half-time. However, goalkeeper Keith Branagan saved the spot-kick and, after Owen Coyle and Fabian de Freitas had levelled, Mixu Paatelainen and De Freitas' second made it 4–2 in extra time. The Royals netted a consolation late on to make it 4–3.

↑ *Bolton's players celebrate at Wembley in 1995 after their pulsating 4–3 victory over Reading, which gave the Trotters promotion to the Premier League for the first time.*

THE WHITE HORSE FINAL

Bolton played in, and won, the first-ever game at Wembley Stadium – the 1923 FA Cup final. It is remembered as the 'White Horse Final' after mounted policemen, one on a light-coloured horse, had to be brought in to clear a huge crowd off the pitch. It was the defining image of the day. The official attendance for the game is recorded as 126,047, but it is estimated that close to 300,000 spectators turned up! People were lined up around the side of the pitch when the game began 45 minutes late, with goals from David Jack and Jack Smith earning Bolton a 2–0 win over West Ham.

↓ *The only time a Wembley FA Cup final was not all-ticket was the first one, in 1923, when Bolton beat West Ham 2–0 in front of a crowd that has been estimated at 300,000.*

BIG SAM HAS BOLTON SOARING

Sam Allardyce helped to make Bolton an established Premier League club. Allardyce, who now manages Blackburn, led Wanderers back into the top flight in 2000/01 when they beat Preston 3–0 in the Play-Off Final. The club battled successfully against relegation for the next two terms before an eighth-place finish in 2003/04. A first-ever place in Europe was secured via a top-six finish in 2004/05 and, having narrowly missed out the following season, Bolton repeated the feat again in 2006/07, as they ended the campaign in seventh place.

↓ *Sam Allardyce was a tough-tackling centre-half who played 198 league matches for Bolton in two spells before becoming the club's manager.*

GOODBYE TO BURNDEN PARK

Bolton ended their 102-year association with Burnden Park to move into the Reebok Stadium in 1997. The 27,879-capacity ground, named after the club's main sponsor, opened with two goalless draws. The first came against Everton on September 1 and the second against Manchester United later that month. Alan Thompson scored the first goal at the stadium – a penalty in a 1–1 draw with Tottenham.

FINAL WOE FOR WANDERERS

The Trotters have reached the final of the League Cup twice, but they were beaten 2–1 on both occasions. Steve McManaman had already scored twice for Liverpool when Alan Thompson's stunner gave Wanderers hope in 1995, while Middlesbrough were two goals up after seven minutes of the 2004 showpiece before Kevin Davies pulled one back for the Lancashire club.

NAT HITS LOFTY HEIGHTS

Nat Lofthouse is arguably the most famous name in Bolton's history, having spent his entire 15-year career at the club. He is Wanderers' record goalscorer with 285 in all competitions – 255 of those coming in the league – and has a stand named after him at the Reebok Stadium. Lofthouse, who played for the club between 1946 and 1961, scored both goals as the Trotters beat Manchester United to win the FA Cup in 1958. He also netted 30 goals in 33 appearances for England, putting him sixth in the all-time goalscorers' list for his country.

⤳ *Nat Lofthouse (with trophy) scored both goals in the 1958 FA Cup final, but his second is unlikely to have been allowed to stand in the modern game; he shoulder-charged Manchester United goalkeeper Harry Gregg into the net.*

BOLTON'S LEADING GOALSCORERS

Nat Lofthouse	285
Joe Smith	277
David Jack	161
Jack Milsom	153
Ray Westwood	144
Willie Moir	134
John Byrom	130
Harold Blackmore	122
Neil Whatmore	121
John McGinlay	118

CHELSEA LAND ANELKA

Nicolas Anelka spent two seasons at Bolton before Chelsea paid £11.5million to lure him to Stamford Bridge in January 2008 – a club-record transfer fee received. The Frenchman netted 21 goals in 53 league appearances for Wanderers after signing for £8million from Turkish side Fenerbahce. Swedish striker Johan Elmander cost the club a record £10million from Toulouse in July 2008, with Daniel Braaten moving to France as part of the deal.

WANDERER RETURNS

Current manager Owen Coyle played 78 times for Bolton between 1993 and 1995. Wanderers were the only English club Coyle played for, with the Republic of Ireland striker spending most of his career in Scotland. He was signed by the Trotters from Airdrie for £250,000 in the summer of 1993 and went on to score 23 goals in all competitions.

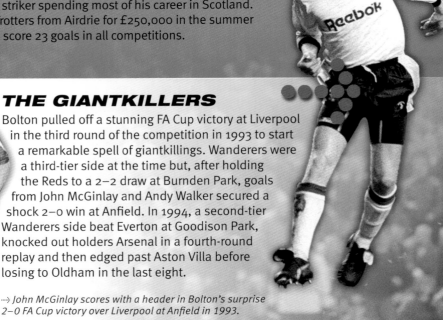

THE GIANTKILLERS

Bolton pulled off a stunning FA Cup victory at Liverpool in the third round of the competition in 1993 to start a remarkable spell of giantkillings. Wanderers were a third-tier side at the time but, after holding the Reds to a 2–2 draw at Burnden Park, goals from John McGinlay and Andy Walker secured a shock 2–0 win at Anfield. In 1994, a second-tier Wanderers side beat Everton at Goodison Park, knocked out holders Arsenal in a fourth-round replay and then edged past Aston Villa before losing to Oldham in the last eight.

⤳ *John McGinlay scores with a header in Bolton's surprise 2–0 FA Cup victory over Liverpool at Anfield in 1993.*

Bolton Wanderers

REMEMBER RICKETTS?

Michael Ricketts was a revelation in his first season with Bolton, scoring 24 goals and sealing promotion in the second tier Play-Off Final of 2001. His Premier League form – he scored 15 before the turn of the year – earned him an England call-up under Sven-Goran Eriksson, and he played 45 minutes of a friendly against the Netherlands in February 2002. It was his one and only appearance for his country and Ricketts left for Middlesbrough in January 2003.

↑ Michael Ricketts takes the ball around Manchester United goalkeeper Fabien Barthez on his way to snatching the Bolton winner at Old Trafford in October 2001.

TROPHY SUCCESS

Wanderers were Football League Trophy winners in 1989. Skipper Phil Brown lifted the cup following a 4–1 win against Torquay at Wembley. Julian Darby, Dean Crombie, Trevor Morgan and Jeff Chandler were the goalscorers that day. Bolton had suffered heartache in the same competition three years previously, losing 3–0 to Bristol City.

FREE-KICKS

Statistics show that Kevin Davies has conceded the most free-kicks since the Premier League began. The Bolton striker was penalised by referees 103 times during the 2009/10 campaign and had been hauled back 766 times in total up to the end of that term.

NEW RECORD AT OLD TRAFFORD

Bolton were the first club in Premier League history to come from behind to beat Manchester United at Old Trafford. The famous victory was achieved in 2001. Juan Sebastian Veron had curled home a stunning free-kick to put United ahead, but Kevin Nolan equalised with a thunderous drive. Goalkeeper Jussi Jaaskelainen played his part with a superb double save to deny Paul Scholes and then Andrew Cole before the break, with a fortunate ricochet allowing Michael Ricketts to snatch a 2–1 win six minutes from time.

↑ Bolton brought Nigerian glamour to the Premier League when they signed 'Jay-Jay' Okocha to partner French World Cup winner Youri Djorkaeff in attack.

WORLD-CLASS ARRIVALS

Bolton made the rest of the Premier League sit up and take notice when they signed internationally-renowned stars Jay-Jay Okocha and Youri Djorkaeff on free transfers in 2002. The duo enhanced Wanderers' top-flight reputation, while also helping them to avoid relegation in 2002/03. Both Nigeria ace Okocha, who later captained Wanderers, and Frenchman Djorkaeff scored seven Premier League goals that term. The club finished eighth the following season.

TROTTER THEORIES

It is not known exactly why Bolton are nicknamed the Trotters, although there are a couple of interesting theories to explain the name. In the early 1900s, Wanderers adopted a club mascot called Tommy Trotter, and around the same time the town became renowned for selling the delicacy of pigs feet – otherwise known as trotters.

FISH LEFT BATTERED

Mark Fish earned 34 caps for South Africa during his time at Bolton, making him the club's most capped player. Fish was a mainstay of the Wanderers defence between 1997 and 2000, making over 100 Premier League appearances. A combative centre-half, Fish once needed 39 stitches after falling through a glass coffee table while playing at home with his son when he was at Charlton!

←··· The fact that Mark Fish played 34 times for South Africa in four seasons at Bolton says much about the number of games on the modern international calendar.

STEADY EDDIE

Eddie Hopkinson is Bolton's record appearance holder, having turned out 578 times for the club in a 13-year spell between 1956 and 1969. Goalkeeper Hopkinson earned 14 caps for England from 1957 to 1959 and was part of the 1958 World Cup squad. Hopkinson, who made 519 league appearances, played his part in helping Wanderers to lift the FA Cup in 1958 – their last major piece of silverware.

BOLTON APPEARANCES

Eddie Hopkinson	578
Roy Greaves	575
Alex Finney	530
Warwick Rimmer	528
Bryan Edwards	518
Ted Vizard	512
Paul Jones	506
Nat Lofthouse	503
Roy Hartle	499
Joe Smith	492

↑ Eddie Hopkinson was a Bolton regular for 13 years between 1956 and 1969, making a club-record 578 appearances.

WANDERING AROUND EUROPE

Wanderers have been involved in two European campaigns, making it past the group stages of the UEFA Cup on both occasions. In 2005/06 they qualified behind eventual winners Sevilla and Zenit St Petersburg, before losing in the last 32 to Marseille. They fared better in 2007/08, progressing from a tough group having already drawn 2–2 with Bayern Munich in Germany. They then beat Atletico Madrid 1–0 on aggregate to make it to the round of 16, where they were knocked out by Sporting Lisbon.

···→ Bolton goalscorer Ricardo Gardner tries to get past Bayern Munich duo Marcell Jansen and Andreas Ottl during the 2–2 UEFA Cup Group F draw between the two clubs at the Allianz Arena in October 2007.

Burnley

Burnley became the 43rd team to play in the Premier League in 2009/10. Their stay in the competition lasted just one season, though, as they suffered relegation at the end of the campaign. The Clarets have won the top-flight title twice in their history and the FA Cup once, and they will be hoping to bounce back to the big time before long.

SO CLOSE FOR CLARETS

The Clarets were two minutes away from reaching the Carling Cup final in 2009. It was the fourth time that Burnley had made it to the last four of the competition, and they had done it the hard way, knocking out London trio Fulham, Chelsea and Arsenal before losing 4–1 in the first leg of their semi-final at Tottenham. The Lancashire club, who were playing in the second tier at the time, managed to force extra time with a stunning 3–0 win at Turf Moor, but goals in the 118th and 120th minutes from Roman Pavlyuchenko and Jermain Defoe snatched victory for Spurs.

↑ Wade Elliott (11) turns away after scoring the only goal of the Championship Play-Off Final against Sheffield United at Wembley.

ELLIOTT WADES IN

Wade Elliott scored the goal that earned Burnley a place in the top tier in 2008/09. The Clarets finished fifth in the second tier to secure a play-off spot. A 3–0 aggregate win over Reading in the semi-finals set up a clash with Sheffield United at Wembley. Winger Elliott sent the Burnley fans wild with a stunning strike, finding the top corner with a superb first-time curling effort after he had created the chance with a jinking run from inside his own half.

⟵ Chris McCann scored Burnley's second goal in the Carling Cup semi-final second leg against Spurs, but the Londoners scored twice in extra time to win 6–4 on aggregate.

GOAL-CRAZY CLARETS

Burnley went goal crazy in the top-flight campaign of 1960/61, netting 102 times to set a club record. However, the feat did not bring the title to Turf Moor, with the Clarets finishing fourth in the table. In fact, their haul was bettered by both champions Tottenham, who scored 115, and third-place Wolves, who scored 103 times.

BEEL SETS HIS STALL OUT

George Beel is Burnley's record league goalscorer and has also netted the most goals in a single season for the club. Striker Beel played for the Clarets between 1923 and 1932, scoring 179 league goals in that time. His most prolific season came in 1927/28, as he scored 35 times in the top flight to help the club finish 19th in the table.

↑ *Tyrone Mears (14) congratulates team-mate Robbie Blake after a stunning goal in the 1–0 win over defending champions Manchester United at Turf Moor.*

BURNLEY'S 10-YEAR LEAGUE RECORD

2000/01	7th	(Second tier)
2001/02	7th	(Second tier)
2002/03	16th	(Second tier)
2003/04	19th	(Second tier)
2004/05	13th	(Second tier)
2005/06	17th	(Second tier)
2006/07	15th	(Second tier)
2007/08	13th	(Second tier)
2008/09	5th	(Second tier)
2009/10	18th	(Top flight)

FREEMAN FIRES WINNER

Burnley were FA Cup winners for the one and only time in their history in 1914. Bert Freeman scored the only goal of the game as the Clarets snatched a 1–0 victory against Liverpool at Crystal Palace. The club had enjoyed a 3–0 success against local rivals Bolton in the third round. Cliff Britton was in charge when the Clarets were beaten 1–0 by Charlton in 1947, while they were also losing finalists in 1962, 3–1 against Tottenham.

MAGIC MOMENTS

Burnley may have suffered relegation at the end of the 2009/10 campaign, but they enjoyed some memorable moments in their first-ever Barclays Premier League campaign. Robbie Blake scored the only goal of the game as Manchester United were beaten 1–0 in the Clarets' first home match in the top flight, and a 1–0 success against Everton followed, with Wade Elliott on target. Burnley were leading 2–0 at Manchester City in November, although it took a Steven Fletcher strike three minutes from time to earn them a point in a thrilling 3–3 draw.

POOR START AT POTTERS

A Ryan Shawcross header and a Stephen Jordan own goal ensured Burnley started life back in the top division with a 2–0 defeat at Stoke. Both goals came from set-pieces, with Shawcross rising highest to nod in a Liam Lawrence free-kick and Jordan glancing Rory Delap's long throw past goalkeeper Brian Jensen.

← *Martin Paterson (left) and Danny Higginbotham tussle for possession on a difficult opening day for Burnley at Stoke's Britannia Stadium.*

← *When Burnley defender Clarke Carlisle appeared on the TV words and numbers game show* Countdown, *he managed to avoid asking for a 'foul'!*

ROCK ON TOMMY

Tommy Lawton is the youngest player to have pulled on a Burnley shirt. The former England striker was 16 years and 174 days old when he made his debut against Doncaster on March 28 1936. Lawton played seven games in the 1935/36 campaign, scoring five goals. He made 18 more appearances the following term before leaving for Everton in a £6,500 deal. Lawton was also a hit at Goodison Park and went on to play for Chelsea, Notts County and Brentford before a swansong at Arsenal in the mid-1950s.

CARLISLE'S COUNTDOWN

Clarke Carlisle proved himself to be something of a brainbox when the Burnley centre-back beat 12 other players to scoop the title of Britain's Brainiest Footballer in 2002 and then featured on popular daytime TV game show *Countdown* in February 2010. Carlisle was a winner on two occasions before losing on his third *Countdown* appearance. Following his first victory, the defender admitted: 'I can't say it's better than winning a big football game – but it's up there!'

Burnley

DAWSON'S DECISION

Jerry Dawson, Burnley's record appearance maker, missed the 1914 FA Cup final at his own request. Goalkeeper Dawson told manager John Haworth the day before the game that he did not think he would be able to play the full 90 minutes due to a rib injury he had sustained the week before. There were no substitutes in those days, meaning that the Clarets could have been left without a keeper. Dawson, who played 522 league games for the club between 1907 and 1928, was given a special winners' medal in recognition of his selfless decision.

BAD YEAR FOR CLARETS

Burnley set a club record of 24 league games without a win in 1979. The sequence started on April 16 when the Clarets were held to a goalless draw by Wrexham, and eight more matches of that second-tier season followed in which they failed to find a win. The streak continued for 16 more games at the start of the following campaign – including a 7–0 defeat at QPR – before their wretched run finally came to an end in style with a 5–3 victory against Cambridge.

↓ Wade Elliott appeared in all 38 matches of Burnley's 2009/10 Barclays Premier League campaign, four times coming on as a substitute.

NO CASE FOR DEFENCE

The Clarets were beaten 10–0 on two occasions in the 1920s, with the defeats remaining unwanted club records. Both games were away from home, with the first coming at Aston Villa in August 1925 before Sheffield United inflicted the same scoreline on them four years later. Burnley suffered a number of heavy losses during that period in their history, with Bury claiming an 8–1 win in December 1925 and Liverpool hitting eight without reply on Boxing Day 1928.

BEST-EVER START

The club made an impressive start to the 1972/73 campaign, going 16 games without suffering defeat. A 2–2 draw at home to Carlisle on the opening day started the run, with a first win of the season coming two games later against Aston Villa (4–1). Burnley claimed seven wins and nine draws during that sequence. They won the second-tier title that season, collecting a haul of 66 points.

EVER-PRESENT ACES

Three players featured in all 38 games of Burnley's first campaign back in the top flight. Goalkeeper Brian Jensen was an ever-present, as was defender Tyrone Mears, while Wade Elliott started 34 games and came off the bench four times. Striker Steven Fletcher made 35 appearances and finished as the club's top scorer with eight goals.

↑ Brian Jensen was in goal for almost all of Burnley's 2009/10 season, although he was hurt early in the 3–1 home loss to Wigan and went off after 15 minutes.

GOALS GALORE

The Lancashire club have been involved in some high-scoring matches over the years. In October 2002, Grimsby claimed a 6–5 win at Blundell Park, having led 4–3 at half-time. Gareth Taylor and Robbie Blake both scored twice, but it was not enough. The Clarets lost another 11-goal thriller that same season, with Watford running out 7–4 winners at Turf Moor, despite Taylor netting a hat-trick. The highest-scoring game involving Burnley came in 1898 when they were 9–3 winners against Loughborough.

⟵ *Robbie Blake (left) scores Burnley's third goal against Grimsby at Blundell Park in 2002. Grimsby, who were leading 4–3 at half-time, went on to win the match 6–5.*

EUROPEAN RUN

The Clarets reached the quarter-finals of the European Cup in 1961. The club had won their first top-flight title in 39 years in 1959/60 to take their place alongside Europe's elite. Burnley battled to a hard-fought 4–3 aggregate win against French side Reims to earn a last-eight clash with Hamburg. Brian Pilkington scored twice and Jimmy Robson added a third in the first leg at Turf Moor before the Germans grabbed a crucial away goal. Uwe Seeler stole the show in the return, scoring a brace as Hamburg claimed a 4–1 win to progress 5–4 on aggregate.

GOLDEN GRAHAM

Graham Alexander became the oldest debutant in Barclays Premier League history in 2009/10. The Scottish international was approaching his 38th birthday when he started the opening-day defeat at Stoke. He was the fifth oldest player to turn out in the top flight that term and is the third oldest goalscorer in the competition's history. Penalty specialist Alexander, who was named Burnley's Player of the Year at the end of the season, netted seven times in total, with six of them coming from the spot.

↑ *Scotland international Graham Alexander has played in more than 120 league games for every one of his four clubs: Scunthorpe (159), Luton (152), Preston (354) and Burnley (122 and counting).*

AWAY DAZE

Burnley became the first team in Premier League history to lose 17 away games in a season in 2009/10. They managed just one win on their travels, although it came in emphatic fashion against Hull. The Clarets had fallen behind to an early Kevin Kilbane strike but recovered to claim a 4–1 victory. The Lancashire club suffered heavy defeats to Liverpool (4–0), Tottenham (5–0), West Ham (5–3) and Aston Villa (5–2) on the road.

⬇ *Despite losing 5–2 at Aston Villa in February 2010, Burnley players salute their fans after the final whistle.*

BURNLEY LEAGUE APPEARANCES

Jerry Dawson	522
John Angus	439
Jimmy McIlroy	439
Alan Stevenson	438
Tommy Cummings	434
Jimmy Adamson	426
Martin Dobson	410
Fred Barron	400
Brian Miller	379
George Waterfield	371

Chelsea

Chelsea have long been established as a top-flight club but it is only relatively recently that they have enjoyed a prolonged spell of success, having been transformed into a worldwide name by Russian owner Roman Abramovich. The Blues were crowned champions in 2009/10, their third title in the last six seasons.

SEVEN UP FOR BLUES

Chelsea scored seven goals on three different occasions during 2009/10. Sunderland were the first to suffer, losing 7–2 at Stamford Bridge in January. Nicolas Anelka and Frank Lampard both netted twice in that game, while the latter hit four past Aston Villa in a 7–1 victory in March – the second time Lampard had achieved the feat in the Premier League. The Blues then hit seven past Stoke without reply a month later. Salomon Kalou scored a hat-trick, with Lampard grabbing two. Carlo Ancelotti's men went one better on the final day of the season, beating Wigan 8–0 to claim the title in style.

THE SPECIAL ONE

Jose Mourinho brought Chelsea their first top-flight title in 50 years when he led the club to glory in his first season in charge in 2004/05. 'The Special One', as he was dubbed by the press, went on to make it back-to-back Barclays Premier League titles the following term and also guided the Blues to two Carling Cup triumphs – in 2005 and 2007 – and an FA Cup victory in 2007. They also reached the last four of the Champions League under the Portuguese boss. Mourinho left Stamford Bridge in September 2007 as the most successful manager in the club's history.

A 'Special' moment for Chelsea as (left to right) Frank Lampard, Jose Mourinho and John Terry celebrate the 2005 Barclays Premier League title.

Frank Lampard has just scored the first of his four goals in Chelsea's 7–1 drubbing of Aston Villa at Stamford Bridge in March 2010.

LAMPS SHINES BRIGHT

Frank Lampard moved up to third in the list of Chelsea's all-time goalscorers during the 2009/10 campaign. Four goals against Aston Villa in March took the England midfielder above Roy Bentley and Peter Osgood. Lampard still has some way to go to catch the top two, though, with second-place Kerry Dixon having scored 193 in total and Bobby Tambling setting the benchmark with 202 goals.

A SCORE DRAW

Chelsea drew their first game in the Premier League on August 15 1992. Striker Mick Harford, a summer signing from Luton, had opened the scoring for the Blues in the home clash with Oldham, only for Nick Henry to net an equaliser following a mistake by goalkeeper Dave Beasant. The Londoners finished 11th that season.

CHELSEA MANAGERS DURING ROMAN ABRAMOVICH ERA

Claudio Ranieri	2000–2004
Jose Mourinho	2004–2007
Avram Grant	2007–2008
Luiz Felipe Scolari	2008–2009
Guus Hiddink	2009
Carlo Ancelotti	2009–Present

⟶ *In 2009/10, Carlo Ancelotti emulated Jose Mourinho by winning the Barclays Premier League title in his first season as Chelsea manager.*

FORTRESS STAMFORD BRIDGE

A 2–1 victory against Fulham at Stamford Bridge on March 20 2004 was the starting point for an amazing run of 86 home games in the League without defeat for the Londoners – a sequence that spanned four years! The 86th game was a 2–0 success against Aston Villa on October 5 2008, but Liverpool brought an end to their incredible run later that month, with Xabi Alonso's deflected strike, which went down as a Jose Bosingwa own goal, enough for the Reds to scrape a 1–0 win.

HARRIS CHOPS DOWN MARK

Ron 'Chopper' Harris is the Blues' record appearance maker, having turned out almost 800 times for the club between 1962 and 1980. Harris, who earned his nickname due to his uncompromising style, played 795 games for Chelsea in all competitions, 66 more than goalkeeper Peter Bonetti, who is second in the list. The tough-tackling centre-back captained the Londoners to FA Cup glory against Leeds in 1970 and was also skipper for the Cup Winners' Cup victory over Real Madrid a year later.

BLUES BREAK BANK

Chelsea broke their transfer record to bring striker Andriy Shevchenko to the club from AC Milan in 2006. The Ukraine international had been prolific in Serie A, prompting the Blues to splash out a fee thought to be in the region of £30million to sign him. Unfortunately, Shevchenko struggled to make an impact, scoring 22 goals in all competitions before he was loaned back to Milan.

GOALS GALORE

The Blues were involved in some incredibly high-scoring games during the 1940s and 50s. They were beaten 7–4 by Liverpool in September 1946 and narrowly lost out 6–5 to Manchester United in their title-winning season of 1954/55, despite Seamus O'Connell netting a hat-trick on his debut. Chelsea also claimed a 7–4 win against Portsmouth in 1957, and the next season they beat Newcastle 6–5.

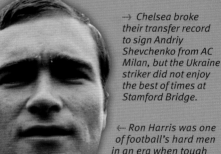

⟶ *Chelsea broke their transfer record to sign Andriy Shevchenko from AC Milan, but the Ukraine striker did not enjoy the best of times at Stamford Bridge.*

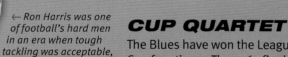

⟵ *Ron Harris was one of football's hard men in an era when tough tackling was acceptable, and he gave Chelsea fantastic service.*

CUP QUARTET

The Blues have won the League Cup four times. The 1965 final against Leicester was played over two legs, with a 3–2 win in the first clash at Stamford Bridge enough for the Blues to claim the trophy. It wasn't until 1998 that Chelsea next tasted glory in the competition, beating Middlesbrough 2–0, but they were winners again in 2005 with a 3–2 success over Liverpool after extra time. Didier Drogba scored both goals as Arsenal were beaten 2–1 at the Millennium Stadium two years later.

Chelsea

UEFA
Cup Winners' Cup

EURO GLORY

The Londoners may still be searching for an elusive first Champions League trophy, but they have tasted victory in the European Cup Winners' Cup on two occasions. Their first success came back in 1971 when they played Spanish giants Real Madrid in the final in Athens. They drew 1–1 in the first game before claiming a 2–1 win in the replay at the same venue two days later, with Peter Osgood scoring in both matches. A stunning volley from Gianfranco Zola was enough to earn them the trophy again when they beat German side Stuttgart in Stockholm in 1998.

⟵ Chelsea captain Dennis Wise lifts the European Cup Winners' Cup in Stockholm in 1998, as the Blues became England's last winners of the trophy before the competition was discontinued in 1999.

THE CREST OF TIMES

The Blues have had five different club badges throughout their history, with the current crest introduced in November 2004. It is based on the design from the 1950s and shows a blue lion holding a staff. The club's first badge featured a Chelsea pensioner, but it was never worn on a shirt, while the second had the Londoners' initials housed inside a shield. The club adopted their fourth badge in 1986. That depicted a lion draped over the letters 'CFC'. It was used for almost 19 years until the current emblem was unveiled.

CHELSEA PLAYER OF THE YEAR SINCE 2000

2000	Dennis Wise
2001	John Terry
2002	Carlo Cudicini
2003	Gianfranco Zola
2004	Frank Lampard
2005	John Terry
2006	John Terry
2007	Michael Essien
2008	Joe Cole
2009	Frank Lampard
2010	Didier Drogba

↓ Didier Drogba (scoring against Arsenal in November 2009) claimed the 2009/10 Barclays Premier League Golden Boot with a hat-trick on the final matchday

LEADING BLUES GOALSCORERS

Bobby Tambling	202
Kerry Dixon	193
Frank Lampard	157
Roy Bentley	150
Peter Osgood	150
Jimmy Greaves	132
Didier Drogba	130
George Mills	125
George Hilsdon	108
Barry Bridges	93

GOAL-DEN DROGBA

Didier Drogba has won the Barclays Premier League's Golden Boot award twice. He finished the 2009/10 campaign as top scorer with 29 goals. The Ivory Coast international won the prize for the first time in 2006/07 after scoring 20 goals. Drogba, who is also the reigning Chelsea Player of the Year, was the Blues' seventh highest all-time goalscorer going into the 2010/11 season, having netted 130 times in all competitions since arriving at the club from Marseille in July 2004.

← *A stunned Old Trafford crowd looks on as Joe Cole (second left) is congratulated by (left to right) Frank Lampard, Paulo Ferreira and Nicolas Anelka.*

BIG FOUR BEATEN

Chelsea's emergence in recent years as one of the most dominant forces in English football was underlined in 2009/10 by the fact that they took a maximum 18 points off the rest of the perceived 'Big Four'. Manchester United were beaten 1–0 at Stamford Bridge and 2–1 at Old Trafford, with Joe Cole scoring an audacious backheel in the latter game. Didier Drogba proved the scourge of Arsenal by scoring twice in both wins against the Gunners – 2–0 at home and 3–0 at the Emirates Stadium. And Liverpool could not stop the rampant Blues, who won 2–0 at home and 2–0 at Anfield – a result that all-but sealed the title. Manchester City, who finished fifth, did manage to beat the Londoners both home and away.

ZOLA'S THE BEST

Gianfranco Zola was voted as Chelsea's greatest player in an official poll held in 2003. The diminutive Italian spent seven seasons at Stamford Bridge between 1996 and 2003, scoring 80 goals in 312 games. Perhaps his most memorable strike came in an FA Cup replay against Norwich in January 2002 when he scored with a spectacular mid-air backheel.

↑ *Former Italy international Gianfranco Zola may be the finest player not to claim a Premier League winners' medal.*

NEW BLUES BENCHMARKS

Chelsea set new Premier League records for the most goals scored in a single season and the biggest goal difference on their way to winning the title in 2009/10. The Blues netted 103 times as they secured a fourth top-flight crown, with big wins over Blackburn (5–0), Sunderland (7–2), Portsmouth (5–0), Aston Villa (7–1), Stoke (7–0) and Wigan (8–0) among the highlights. They kept it tight at the other end of the pitch too, conceding just 32 goals in their 38 league matches to end the campaign with an impressive goal difference of +71.

FIRING BLANKS

Goals may have been a theme of the Blues' season in 2009/10, but it was a totally different story in 1923/24 when Chelsea managed just 31 goals as they were relegated from the top flight. That remains a club-record low. The Londoners were one of two teams relegated that term, along with Middlesbrough. Nottingham Forest stayed up, despite having collected the same number of points as the Blues. Both teams had a goal difference of -22, but Chelsea went down due to their inferior number of goals scored.

↓ *John Terry, Didier Drogba, Joe Cole and Florent Malouda celebrate yet another goal. Chelsea ran riot on six occasions against top-flight opponents during 2009/10.*

HIT FOR SIX

The FA Cup final victory against Portsmouth in 2010 was the sixth time the club have won the competition. The Blues lifted the trophy for the second successive year following their 2–1 win against Everton 12 months previously. They first tasted victory in the competition in 1970 when they beat Leeds 2–1 in a replay, but it was another 27 years before they won it again. Roberto Di Matteo scored after 42 seconds of the 1997 final to set Chelsea on their way to a 2–0 win against Middlesbrough. The Italian also netted the only goal as Aston Villa were beaten in 2000, and Didier Drogba was the hero in a 1–0 win against Manchester United in 2007.

Everton

Everton

Everton have won the top-flight title on nine occasions, with their last success coming in 1986/87. The 1980s were a hugely successful decade for the club, both domestically and in Europe. The last major trophy the Toffees won came in 1995 when they lifted the FA Cup, but they have made steady progress in recent years under boss David Moyes.

BEACON SHINES ON SHIRT

The motto 'Nil Satis, Nisi Optimum', which can be found underneath the Everton crest, means 'Nothing but the best is good enough'. The tower that features on the club badge is known as The Beacon and is located on Netherfield Road in the Everton area of Liverpool, while the laurels used either side were associated with winners in classical times. The shield design with the Latin text was not used on Everton's shirts until 1980.

EVERTON APPEARANCES

Neville Southall	750
Brian Labone	534
Dave Watson	528
Ted Sagar	497
Kevin Ratcliffe	493

⇢ Neville Southall was a binman, a waiter and a hod carrier before he turned professional. He rose to become one of the world's best goalkeepers in the 1980s.

⇢ Gary Lineker's 1985/86 season at Everton was very successful on a personal level, but the Toffees were pipped to the league title and FA Cup by neighbours Liverpool. His goals in the 1986 World Cup then earned him a move to Barcelona.

ONE-SEASON WONDER

Gary Lineker may have only spent one season at Goodison Park, but he still managed to score 40 goals in all competitions and finished the 1985/86 campaign as the top flight's leading scorer. Unfortunately, Everton finished as runners-up to Liverpool in both the league and the FA Cup that year. Lineker won the Golden Boot at the 1986 World Cup after scoring six times for England. He moved to Barcelona that summer.

CHAMPIONS LEAGUE WOE

Everton finished the 2004/05 season in fourth place in the Barclays Premier League and qualified for the Champions League for the first time. Sadly for the Toffees, they missed out on the group stages after they were beaten 4–2 over two legs by Spanish side Villarreal in the third qualifying round. They dropped into the UEFA Cup, as it was then known, but lost at the first hurdle to Romanian side Dinamo Bucharest.

LAST-DAY DRAMA

The Toffees have escaped relegation on the last day of the season twice since the Premier League began. They did it the hard way in season 1993/94, falling 2–0 behind against Wimbledon at Goodison Park before a screamer from Barry Horne and two goals from Graham Stuart snatched a 3–2 victory to keep them up. Gareth Farrelly was the unlikely hero four years later, scoring early as Everton held on to draw 1–1 with Coventry and claim the point they needed to survive on goal difference.

EVERTON'S LEADING GOALSCORERS

Dixie Dean	383
Graeme Sharp	159
Bob Latchford	138
Alex Young	125
Joe Royle	119

---> *William Ralph Dean did not like being called Dixie and how he got the nickname is lost in time. His goalscoring feats, however, are the stuff of legend and record.*

---> *Few players have ever made as big an impact at such a young age as Wayne Rooney. After his stunning goal to beat Arsenal in 2002, veteran striker Kevin Campbell gave him a piggy-back ride.*

REMEMBER THE NAME!

Wayne Rooney announced his arrival on the big stage with a stunning goal to earn Everton a 2–1 win against Arsenal in October 2002. Debutant Rooney was just 16 when, in the dying seconds of the Goodison Park clash, he expertly controlled a high ball, turned and curled a superb shot into the top corner past the despairing dive of David Seaman. The wonder strike also ended the Gunners' 30-match unbeaten run. Rooney moved to Manchester United for a club-record fee – reported to be £27million – in August 2004.

DIXIE IS GOODISON GREAT

William Ralph Dean, or Dixie Dean as he was more popularly known, was a goalscoring hero for Everton between 1925 and 1937. The hot-shot striker still holds the Football League record for the most goals in a single season, having netted an incredible 60 times in the club's top-flight campaign of 1927/28. He is also the Merseysiders' all-time top goalscorer with 383 in all competitions – 224 more than Graeme Sharp. There is a statue of him standing outside Goodison Park.

TOTTENHAM TORN APART

One of the most memorable matches in Everton's recent history came against Tottenham in the semi-final of the FA Cup in 1995. Spurs started as strong favourites, but they were blown away by a stunning Toffees display. The game is best remembered for striker Daniel Amokachi bringing himself on as a substitute while Paul Rideout was receiving treatment. Manager Joe Royle was apparently furious, but the Nigerian went on to secure a 4–1 victory with two goals. Everton shocked Manchester United in the final – the last time they lifted the trophy.

EVERTON ON TOP

Everton were a dominant force in the 1980s, tasting success both at home and in Europe. With a team featuring club legends such as Kevin Ratcliffe, Peter Reid and Graeme Sharp, the Toffees scooped a host of major trophies. They won the top-flight title in 1984/85 and again in 1986/87, finishing as runners-up in between. They edged past Watford to win the FA Cup in 1984 but were beaten finalists in 1985, 1986 and 1989. They also reached the final of the League Cup in 1984, before enjoying their finest hour a year later when they won the European Cup Winners' Cup.

<-- *Andy Gray runs away after scoring in the 1984 FA Cup final against Watford. It was the first of many trophies Everton won during Howard Kendall's first spell in charge during the 1980s.*

Everton

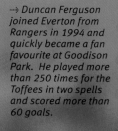
Everton

A SWEET TRADITION

The club's nickname, the Toffees, is thought to have been adopted after a sweet shop called Mother Noblett's, situated in the Everton area of Liverpool, started selling Everton Mints. The Merseysiders have a tradition at Goodison Park where a Toffee Lady walks around the side of the pitch on a matchdays throwing Everton Mints into the crowd.

TOFFEES COME UNSTUCK

Barry Horne scored on his debut as Everton drew 1–1 with Sheffield Wednesday in their first Premier League game on August 15 1992. The Toffees fell behind to a goal from Nigel Pearson after quarter of an hour before Horne equalised just short of half-time. Midfielder Horne failed to find the target again until February 3 1996 when he scored against his former club Southampton in a 2–2 draw at The Dell.

⟶ *Duncan Ferguson joined Everton from Rangers in 1994 and quickly became a fan favourite at Goodison Park. He played more than 250 times for the Toffees in two spells and scored more than 60 goals.*

RED AND WHITE DELIGHT

Everton have been 7–1 winners in the Premier League on two occasions – their biggest victories since the competition began. Gary Speed scored a hat-trick and Andrei Kanchelskis bagged a brace as the Toffees beat Southampton at Goodison Park in November 1996. They managed the same scoreline in November 2007 against another team playing in red and white stripes, this time securing victory against Sunderland. Ayegbeni Yakubu and Tim Cahill both netted two goals each, with Steven Pienaar, Andrew Johnson and Leon Osman also on target.

↑ *Welsh midfielder Gary Speed was Everton's unlikely hat-trick hero when they beat Southampton 7–1 at Goodison Park in 1996.*

EVERTON'S BIGGEST LEAGUE WINS

9–1	v	Manchester City	(September 3 1906)
8–0	v	Stoke	(November 2 1889)
8–0	v	Southampton	(November 20 1971)
9–2	v	Leicester	(November 28 1931)
8–1	v	Darwen	(October 21 1893)

BIG DUNC

Duncan Ferguson became a cult hero at Goodison Park during two spells at the club between 1994 and 2006. The fiery Scottish striker arrived on an initial three-month loan deal from Rangers and, after scoring a towering header against Liverpool to set up a famous 2–0 derby victory, he made a permanent £4million switch. 'Big Dunc', who has an Everton-related number nine tattoo on his arm, left for Newcastle in November 1998 but returned to Merseyside in 2000 to spend another six years with the Toffees before retiring.

FREE-SCORING EVERTON

The club scored in a record 47 consecutive home league matches between April 1984 and September 1986. A 2–0 win against Wolves started the sequence before QPR finally ended the run by holding the Merseysiders to a goalless draw more than two years later.

RECORD TOTAL

The Merseyside giants claimed their biggest points total under two points for a win in season 1969/70. Everton finished their title-winning top-flight campaign on 66 points, nine ahead of nearest challengers Leeds. Joe Royle was their top scorer that term with 23 goals, with Alan Whittle adding 11 and Alan Ball netting 10. The Toffees were league winners again in 1984/85 with a 90-point haul, which is a club record since three points for a win was introduced.

REDS GIVEN THE BLUES

The Toffees have not beaten Merseyside rivals Liverpool in the league since September 2006. However, that 3–0 home victory – when two goals from Andrew Johnson added to Tim Cahill's opener – was Everton's biggest derby success since 1964. The Blues knocked Liverpool out of the FA Cup on their way to the final in 2009, with youngster Dan Gosling scoring the only goal in extra time of a Goodison Park replay.

A START TO FORGET

The club suffered their worst start to a season in 1994/95 when they went 12 games without a win under manager Mike Walker. A 1–0 victory at home to West Ham in November ended the sequence, but the run cost Walker his job, with Joe Royle coming in to replace him. Everton's Premier League safety was assured at the end of April that term, while they went on to win the FA Cup, with Paul Rideout scoring the only goal of the final against Manchester United.

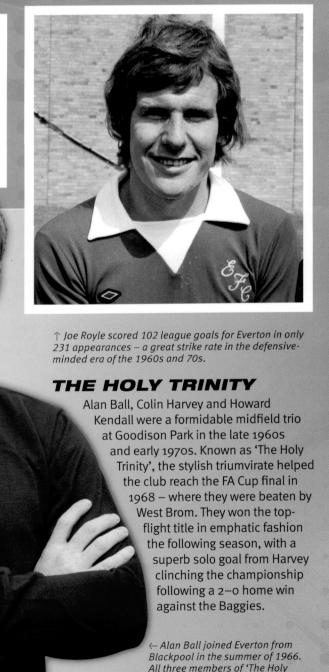

↑ *Joe Royle scored 102 league goals for Everton in only 231 appearances – a great strike rate in the defensive-minded era of the 1960s and 70s.*

THE HOLY TRINITY

Alan Ball, Colin Harvey and Howard Kendall were a formidable midfield trio at Goodison Park in the late 1960s and early 1970s. Known as 'The Holy Trinity', the stylish triumvirate helped the club reach the FA Cup final in 1968 – where they were beaten by West Brom. They won the top-flight title in emphatic fashion the following season, with a superb solo goal from Harvey clinching the championship following a 2–0 home win against the Baggies.

↑ *Colin Harvey was nicknamed 'The White Pele', but he wasn't given a real chance to shine on the international stage, making just one appearance for England.*

← *Alan Ball joined Everton from Blackpool in the summer of 1966. All three members of 'The Holy Trinity' became managers, but only Ball didn't manage Everton.*

Fulham

Fulham are relative newcomers to the Barclays Premier League, having gained their place among the elite in time for the start of the 2001/02 campaign. The London club enjoyed their highest league finish in 2008/09, and the following term was one of the most memorable in their history as they reached the Europa League final.

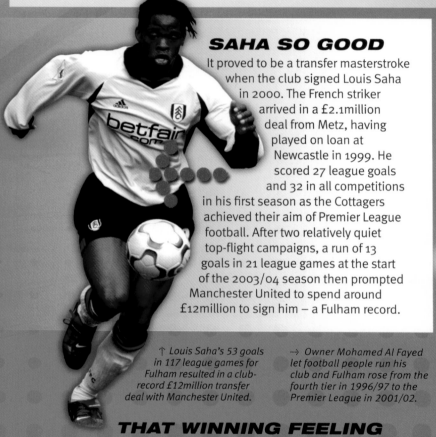

SAHA SO GOOD

It proved to be a transfer masterstroke when the club signed Louis Saha in 2000. The French striker arrived in a £2.1million deal from Metz, having played on loan at Newcastle in 1999. He scored 27 league goals and 32 in all competitions in his first season as the Cottagers achieved their aim of Premier League football. After two relatively quiet top-flight campaigns, a run of 13 goals in 21 league games at the start of the 2003/04 season then prompted Manchester United to spend around £12million to sign him – a Fulham record.

↑ Louis Saha's 53 goals in 117 league games for Fulham resulted in a club-record £12million transfer deal with Manchester United.

⇢ Owner Mohamed Al Fayed let football people run his club and Fulham rose from the fourth tier in 1996/97 to the Premier League in 2001/02.

THAT WINNING FEELING

The west Londoners managed a club-record run of 12 straight league victories in 2000. The last game of the 1999/2000 season started the sequence, with Fulham claiming a 3–0 win at home to Huddersfield. A 2–0 success against Crewe on the opening day of the following campaign continued the streak, and big wins followed against Stockport and Barnsley. The Cottagers were held to a goalless draw by Wolves on October 2 – that stalemate starting a three-game winless run.

CUP OF PLENTY

The Cottagers were one of three Intertoto Cup winners in 2002, earning a place in the UEFA Cup. Now defunct, the summer knockout competition was made up of a series of two-legged matches involving the highest-ranked applicants from Europe's many leagues. Fulham beat Finnish side FC Haka, Greek club Egaleo and Sochaux of France to set up a final clash with Italians Bologna. Junichi Inamoto scored a hat-trick in a 3–1 home win to secure a 5–3 aggregate victory. They lost to Hertha Berlin in the third round of the UEFA Cup.

AL FAYED FULFILS PREMIER LEAGUE DREAM

Mohamed Al Fayed, the former owner of London department store Harrods, transformed the club when he took over in 1997. The ambitious Egyptian brought in Kevin Keegan and Ray Wilkins to replace Micky Adams, who had achieved promotion to the third tier in season 1996/97. The Cottagers reached the play-offs in 1997/98 before Wilkins left and Keegan oversaw an incredible title-winning campaign the following term. He also departed soon after to concentrate on the England job, paving the way for Jean Tigana to help realise Al Fayed's Premier League dream in 2000/01.

HERO HAYNES

Johnny Haynes is the player to have made the most appearances for the club, having pulled on the Fulham shirt 657 times during an 18-year stay at Craven Cottage. Inside-forward Haynes, who was the first player in Britain to earn £100 a week, captained England in 22 of the 56 games he played for his country, securing him another record as Fulham's most capped player. Having made his debut for the club in 1952, he left for South Africa in 1970 at the age of 35, joining Durban City.

→ *Johnny Haynes (with ball) was Fulham captain for almost a decade and, but for a knee injury that ended his international career in 1962, might have been the England skipper when they won the 1966 World Cup.*

A LEG UP

Graham Leggat scored one of the fastest hat-tricks in history – three in three minutes – when Fulham recorded their biggest league victory, against Ipswich on Boxing Day 1963. Former Scotland international Leggat scored four times and Bobby Howfield, who went on to play American football in the NFL as a kicker for the Denver Broncos and New York Jets, hit a treble in a 10–1 win.

POINTS MEAN PRIZES

A number of club records were broken on the way to achieving a place in the top flight, with Kevin Keegan's 1998/99 side setting a new points record of 101 to claim the third-tier title. However, Frenchman Jean Tigana equalled that feat in 2000/01 when the Cottagers gained promotion to the Premier League in emphatic style.

SEVENTH HEAVEN

Fulham secured their best-ever Barclays Premier League finish in 2008/09, ending the campaign in seventh spot and qualifying for the Europa League. Roy Hodgson's men, who had escaped relegation on goal difference the season before, finished above two of the top flight's big spenders in Tottenham and Manchester City. Notable results that term included a 1–0 win against Arsenal and a 2–0 victory at home to Manchester United.

A FINAL TOO FAR

Fulham were beaten FA Cup finalists in 1975 – the closest they have come to winning the competition. A side including club legends such as Bobby Moore and skipper Alan Mullery lost 2–0 to London rivals West Ham, with Alan Taylor scoring both goals. Fulham had endured some epic battles on the way to Wembley, playing Hull three times and Nottingham Forest four times before winning through.

→ *Alan Mullery began and ended his league career with Fulham. He led out the team at Wembley in 1975, with World Cup-winning skipper Bobby Moore behind him.*

↑ *Roy Hodgson performed miracles in transforming Fulham from relegation favourites in 2007 to one of the most respected teams in the top flight and 2010 UEFA Europa League finalists. He moved to Liverpool for the start of the 2010/11 season.*

FULHAM'S RECENT MANAGERS

Ray Wilkins	1997–1998
Kevin Keegan	1998–1999
Paul Bracewell	1999–2000
Jean Tigana	2000–2003
Chris Coleman	2003–2007
Lawrie Sanchez	2007
Roy Hodgson	2007–2010

Fulham

UNITED REELING

Fulham have beaten Manchester United at Craven Cottage in the last two seasons. A Danny Murphy penalty and a late strike from Zoltan Gera secured a 2–0 win in the 2008/09 campaign. The Cottagers went one better in 2009/10 when they claimed a 3–0 victory, with former Liverpool midfielder Murphy again opening the scoring. Bobby Zamora made it two shortly after half-time, with Damien Duff clinching the points. Fulham's only other Premier League win against United came at Old Trafford in October 2003.

↓ Danny Murphy (front) has scored five goals against Manchester United, three for Liverpool and two for Fulham – and all were opening goals in wins.

RECORD CLIPS CANARIES' WINGS

Fulham's record Premier League victory came against Norwich on the final day of the 2004/05 campaign – a result that relegated the Canaries. Brian McBride opened the scoring in the 10th minute, with Papa Bouba Diop doubling their advantage before the break. Zat Knight made it three and Steed Malbranque added a fourth, with McBride's second and a late Andrew Cole strike completing a 6–0 victory. Fulham also hit West Brom for six in February 2006, although the Baggies scored a late consolation.

↑ Fulham's hopes of escaping relegation in 2007/08 stayed alive when Diomansy Kamara (right) scored a stoppage-time match-winner against Manchester City at Eastlands. Clint Dempsey is also pictured.

A GREAT ESCAPE

Former manager Roy Hodgson masterminded a great escape in season 2007/08, with Fulham winning four of their last five games to stay up. The amazing run began with an away victory at Reading, although they were then beaten 2–0 by Liverpool. The Cottagers looked to be heading for relegation when they fell 2–0 behind at Manchester City in their next game, but Diomansy Kamara snatched an injury-time winner as they hit back to win 3–2. The Londoners then won a tense relegation clash against Birmingham, and safety was secured with a 1–0 win against Portsmouth on the final day.

SWANS SUNK

The Cottagers' record cup victory came in November 1995 when they scored seven without reply against Swansea. Mike Conroy bagged a hat-trick in the FA Cup first-round tie at Craven Cottage, with Paul Brooker, Nick Cusak, Duncan Jupp and Martin Thomas also getting in on the act. Fulham were in the fourth tier at the time, with the Swans in the division above.

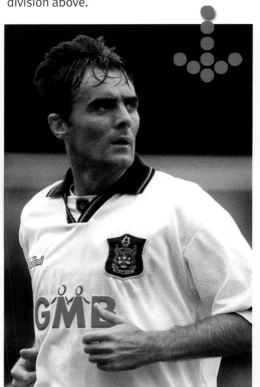

←·· Mike Conroy scored only three FA Cup goals in his three seasons with Fulham and all came in the record 7–0 victory over Swansea on November 11 1995.

BY GEORGE

World Cup winner George Cohen is regarded as one of Fulham's greatest players, having spent his entire 13-year career at Craven Cottage. Full-back Cohen made 459 appearances for the club and helped them into the top flight in 1958/59. He was a regular for his country, with the pinnacle of his career coming in 1966 when he was in the England team that beat West Germany to lift the World Cup. Cohen was described by Sir Alf Ramsey as 'England's greatest right-back'.

··→ George Cohen's career was cut short by injury in 1969. His nephew, Ben Cohen, was also a World Cup winner with England, at rugby in 2003.

FLASH GORDON

Gordon Davies scored 178 goals for Fulham in two spells between 1978 and 1991, making him the club's all-time top goalscorer. The Welsh striker, who bagged two goals in 18 appearances for his country, left Craven Cottage for Chelsea in October 1984 but returned two years later via Manchester City to carry on scoring and move to the top of the Cottagers' goal charts.

BEST OF TIMES

George Best played 42 games for Fulham in the late 1970s. The legendary winger, who made his name at Manchester United, scored eight goals for the Cottagers – one of those coming 71 seconds into his debut. Northern Irishman Best had lost some of his pace by the time he moved to Craven Cottage, but he still wowed the crowds alongside the likes of Rodney Marsh and Bobby Moore.

BINGO FOR BONZO

Frank Newton holds the club record for the most league goals scored in a single season. Newton, affectionately known as 'Bonzo', netted 43 times in 39 games during the 1931/32 campaign to help the Cottagers secure the first promotion in their history by winning the third tier title. He scored his 50th goal for the club in only his 42nd game and ended his first spell at Craven Cottage with 72 in 74 matches.

FREE-SCORING ZAMORA

Bobby Zamora scored almost five times more goals in the 2009/10 season than he had during the previous campaign. He struck 19 in all competitions, having only netted four in 2008/09. Zamora grabbed eight goals during the Cottagers' run to the Europa League final and eight in the Barclays Premier League, with the remaining three coming in the FA Cup. It was the striker's best haul since scoring 32 for Brighton in 2001/02.

←·· The criticism of Bobby Zamora at the highest level was that he didn't score enough goals. He put that right with 19 in 2009/10, his best return in the top flight – and his most for eight seasons.

FULHAM'S LEADING GOALSCORERS

Gordon Davies	178
Johnny Haynes	158
Bedford Jezzard	154
Jim Hammond	150
Graham Leggat	134
Arthur Stevens	124
Steve Earle	108

HULL CITY A.F.C.

'THE TIGERS'

Hull City

Prior to 2008, Hull was the biggest city in Europe never to have had a top-flight football team, but that all changed when they were promoted via the play-offs for their first Barclays Premier League campaign. The Tigers avoided relegation in 2008/09, but they could not repeat the feat a year on and they slipped back down to the second tier.

⇡ *Martin Carruthers models one of the most memorable kits in English football history. These Tigers didn't scare too many teams as they tried vainly to climb out of the third tier.*

EYE-SORE OF THE TIGERS

Several clubs have sported some 'questionable' kits over the years, but Hull fans have had to endure a few of their own. From 1992 until the end of the 1994/95 season the Tigers made the most of their nickname, taking their famous amber and black stripes one step further by wearing tiger-print shirts!

HULL'S 10-YEAR LEAGUE RECORD

2000/01	6th	(Fourth tier)
2001/02	11th	(Fourth tier)
2002/03	13th	(Fourth tier)
2003/04	2nd	(Fourth tier)
2004/05	2nd	(Third tier)
2005/06	18th	(Second tier)
2006/07	21st	(Second tier)
2007/08	3rd	(Second tier)
2008/09	17th	(Top flight)
2009/10	18th	(Top flight)

VOLLEY GOOD SHOW

Dean Windass cemented his popularity with Hull fans by scoring the goal that earned the club a place in the top flight. Windass, who scored 77 goals in 236 league appearances for City over two spells, volleyed home the only goal of the game in the 2008 Championship Play-Off Final against Bristol City to complete a remarkable campaign.

⋯⋯> *Dean Windass celebrates the final whistle after his goal had given Hull City their first-ever place in England's top tier. His goals had already made him a legend on Humberside.*

MUTRIE'S THE MAN

Les Mutrie set a club record when he scored 14 goals in nine consecutive games in season 1981/82. The sequence started on February 13 1982 with a brace in a 2–2 draw at Tranmere, and the prolific striker followed that up with four goals in a 5–2 success against Hartlepool. The last game of his remarkable scoring run came on March 20, with Mutrie netting in a 3–1 win at home to Port Vale. Keith Edwards came close to equalling the record in 1989 when he managed 13 goals in eight consecutive matches.

A SEASON OF FIRSTS

Hull's first game in the Barclays Premier League in 2008 ended with a victory thanks to a late goal from substitute Caleb Folan which secured a 2–1 win against Fulham. Seol Ki-Hyeon had opened the scoring early on for the visitors, but summer signing Geovanni equalised with a superb 20-yard drive before striker Folan sent the home fans wild with an 81st-minute winner, coolly side-footing home a pass from Craig Fagan.

GRABBING THE BULL BY THE HORNS

Jimmy Bullard became Hull's record signing when he joined the club from Fulham for a reported £5million fee in January 2009. The midfielder suffered a serious knee injury on his debut and didn't play again that season. Bullard scored four goals for the Tigers in 2009/10 – all from the penalty spot.

┈▶ *Hull's hopes of staying in the top flight were dealt a severe blow following the knee injuries suffered by record signing Jimmy Bullard.*

◀┈ *Caleb Folan celebrates after scoring Hull's match-winning goal in their top-tier debut against Fulham at the KC Stadium in August 2008.*

DUANE AT THE DOUBLE

Duane Darby scored a double hat-trick for Hull in an extraordinary FA Cup tie against Whitby Town in November 1996. The non-league side had forced a replay at Boothferry Park after holding City to a goalless draw. However, the two teams more than made up for a lack of goals in the first match, with the Tigers going on to claim an amazing 8–4 victory! Striker Darby scored four goals in normal time – the fourth coming in the 89th minute to send the game into extra time – and he went on to net two more as Hull finally secured their progress.

CITY SLICKERS

The Tigers made it to the semi-final of the FA Cup in 1930 – their best run in the competition. City, who were playing in the second tier at the time, knocked out top-flight duo Newcastle and Manchester City on their way to the last four. They were beaten 1–0 by Arsenal in a replay at Villa Park on March 26 after the initial Elland Road tie had ended 2–2. Hull suffered relegation to the third tier that term.

TIGERS ROAR AT KC

City played their first competitive game at the KC Stadium on Boxing Day 2002. Hartlepool were their opponents in a fourth-tier clash, with Dean Keates and Stuart Green scoring in a 2–0 victory. The stadium, which can hold 25,404 spectators, replaced Boothferry Park, where Hull had played their home games since 1946. City share the ground with rugby league side Hull FC.

STU BETTER BELIEVE IT

Stuart Elliott is revered by Hull fans for his goalscoring exploits during the promotion-winning season of 2004/05. He scored 27 league goals to finish as the joint top scorer in the third tier alongside City legend Dean Windass, who was playing for Bradford at the time. Winger Elliott's feat was made even more impressive due to the fact that he spent six weeks on the sidelines that season with an injury.

┈▶ *Northern Ireland international Stuart Elliott was Hull's leading scorer in the league three times in four seasons between 2002 and 2006. He averaged almost a goal every three games in more than 200 appearances.*

Hull City

'THE TIGERS'

SIMPLY THE CREST

City's tiger-head crest was first introduced in 1947. There have been a number of different variations over the years, while the badge was also dropped for a time, with the club opting to put their initials on their shirts between 1975 and 1979. The current crest features the tiger's head in an amber shield with Hull City A.F.C written at the top and the club's nickname along the bottom.

---> Ken Wagstaff was a prolific marksman for Hull with his 173 league goals bettered only by his 1965/66 team-mate and strike partner Chris Chilton.

<-- Chris Chilton averaged 20 goals a season for 11 years at Hull City.

MAKING A POINT

The title-winning campaign of 1965/66 saw Hull record their biggest points haul under two points for a win, while they also scored a club-record amount of goals that term. They earned 69 points to finish at the summit, although Millwall were only four behind in second. Cliff Britton's side netted 109 goals, 14 more than third-place QPR, with Chris Chilton, Ken Wagstaff, Ian Butler and Ken Houghton contributing 77 between them.

HULL'S LEADING GOALSCORERS

Chris Chilton	222
Ken Wagstaff	197
Sammy Stevens	116
Paddy Mills	110
John Smith	102

THE GREAT ESCAPE

Hull were bottom of The Football League in November 1998 and they looked likely to slip into the Conference when Warren Joyce replaced Mark Hateley in the managerial hot-seat. It was not until the turn of the year that results finally began to pick up, but City lost just four times in their last 22 games to pull clear of danger, confirming their fourth-tier status with just a few games to spare.

---> As player-manager, Warren Joyce oversaw Hull's escape from relegation to the Conference in 1998/99.

CHILTON IS HOT-SHOT

Chris Chilton is the club's all-time top goalscorer, having netted 222 times in all competitions between 1960 and 1971. He left for a brief spell at Coventry but returned to Boothferry Park as youth-team manager, nurturing talents such as Steve McClaren, who was England coach between 2006 and 2007, and Brian Marwood. He also spent a spell as assistant manager under Colin Appleton and then Brian Horton.

LATICS LOVING LIFE

The club equalled their record home league defeat in August 2008 when they were beaten 5–0 by Wigan at the KC Stadium. An early own goal from Sam Ricketts put the Latics ahead, with Antonio Valencia doubling their lead in the 13th minute. Amr Zaki scored the third and fifth goals, with England striker Emile Heskey adding a fourth in between. It was the Tigers' heaviest home defeat since they lost to Lincoln by the same scoreline 49 years previously.

TIGERS ARE TAMED

The Tigers were the only team who failed to win away from home in the top division in 2009/10. They came agonisingly close at Fratton Park in March when Caleb Folan's brace put them 2–1 up against Portsmouth. However, two crazy final minutes saw Jamie O'Hara equalise and then Nwankwo Kanu snatch a 3–2 win for the home side with virtually the last kick of the game. Steve Gohouri scored a last-minute leveller for Wigan in Hull's last away game of the campaign.

FLYING HIGH

Phil Brown oversaw an amazing turnaround in fortunes as the club recovered from a poor start to reach the Championship Play-Off Final in 2008. They were struggling at the turn of the year, but lost just four times in 19 games between January 29 and May 4 to finish third. The Tigers took their good form into their first Barclays Premier League campaign, with a 3–0 win at West Brom at the end of October sending them up to third place in the table. Unfortunately, that run didn't last and they eventually avoided relegation by just a single point.

⤊ *Hull manager Phil Brown directs his players from the touchline during a match against West Ham at Upton Park.*

A FALSE START

City suffered their worst start to a season in 1989/90 when they went 16 games without a league win. They started the campaign with a 1–1 draw against Leicester but were not able to celebrate a first victory until they were 3–2 winners at Bradford on November 11. They drew 10 of those 16 matches and went on to finish 14th in the second tier that term.

TEEN MAKES HIS MARK

Mark Cullen was the youngest Barclays Premier League goalscorer of the 2009/10 season. The striker was 18 years and nine days old when he was handed his first start in the clash at Wigan on May 3. He repaid his manager's faith with a goal, heading in a cross from George Boateng to put his side 2–1 ahead.

⤑ *Mark Cullen's first goal for Hull was not enough to bring them victory over Wigan at the Latics' DW Stadium because the Tigers conceded a goal from Steve Gohouri deep in stoppage time to draw 2–2.*

Liverpool

The Reds are England's most successful club. They have won more trophies than any of their rivals, claiming 18 top-flight titles, seven FA Cups, seven League Cups, three UEFA Cups and five European Cups. However, they have yet to win the Premier League, with their last championship success coming back in 1989/90.

LIVERPOOL'S LEADING GOALSCORERS

Ian Rush	346
Roger Hunt	286
Gordon Hodgson	241
Billy Liddell	228
Robbie Fowler	176
Kenny Dalglish	172
Michael Owen	158
Harry Chambers	151
Jack Parkinson	130
Sam Raybould	128

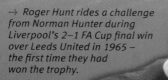

⟶ Roger Hunt rides a challenge from Norman Hunter during Liverpool's 2–1 FA Cup final win over Leeds United in 1965 – the first time they had won the trophy.

GOAL RUSH

Ian Rush is Liverpool's record goalscorer in all competitions, having netted 346 times in two spells between December 1980 and May 1996. The Welsh striker scored 39 FA Cup and 48 League Cup goals, which are both club records. Season 1983/84 was the most productive for Rush – he bagged 47 goals as the Reds claimed the top-flight title, the League Cup and the European Cup. Rush scored five in one game against Luton during that campaign – a feat managed by three other Liverpool players, including Robbie Fowler.

⟵ Ian Rush runs away in celebration after giving Liverpool the lead in the 1986 FA Cup final against Everton.

IN THE HUNT

Roger Hunt is one of the few men to have rivalled Ian Rush in terms of goalscoring for the Reds. Hunt, who played for Liverpool for 10 years between 1959 and 1969, netted on his debut against Scunthorpe and went on to score 245 league goals for the club – a Reds record. Striker Hunt, who grabbed three goals for England during the tournament as they won the World Cup in 1966, also holds the record for the most league goals in a single season for the club, scoring 41 times – including five hat-tricks – as Liverpool claimed the second-tier title in 1961/62.

PFA PRIDE

Five Liverpool players have been awarded the PFA Player of the Year trophy. Steven Gerrard was the last Reds recipient, claiming the prize in 2006. Terry McDermott was the first in 1980, with the club's dominance of English football during that decade also resulting in Kenny Dalglish (1983), Ian Rush (1984) and John Barnes (1988) winning the accolade.

TORRES TOPS GOAL POLL

Fernando Torres scooped Liverpool's Goal of the Season award in 2009/10 for a stunning strike in a 3–0 win against Sunderland at Anfield. Goalkeeper Pepe Reina picked him out wide on the left touchline and Torres dribbled inside Michael Turner and curled a shot over Craig Gordon and perfectly into the top corner. Torres also took second place for his goal against Manchester United, with Ryan Babel's long-range thunderbolt against Lyon completing the top three.

BRUCE ALMIGHTY FOR REDS

The Reds' European Cup success of 1983/84 is best remembered for the antics of goalkeeper Bruce Grobbelaar. They had played out a 1–1 draw with Italian side Roma after extra time, meaning the game went to a penalty shootout. Grobbelaar was all smiles as he prepared for Bruno Conti to take his kick, biting the back of the net in front of a mass of photographers. Conti blazed his effort high and wide. The Liverpool goalkeeper then tried to distract Francesco Graziani by wobbling his legs on the goal-line. He succeeded and Graziani also missed, with the Merseysiders claiming a 4–2 shootout win.

REINA IS RESOLUTE

Goalkeeper Pepe Reina and a stubborn Liverpool defence set a club record of 11 games without conceding a goal between October and December 2005. The run started with a 2–0 win at home to West Ham on October 29, with Xabi Alonso and Boudewijn Zenden scoring. After seven Barclays Premier League matches and three Champions League games without being beaten, Reina kept an 11th shut-out in the FIFA Club World Championship clash with Saprissa on December 15.

⬆ Bruce Grobbelaar looks behind him as Francesco Graziani's penalty flies high over the crossbar to give Liverpool their fourth European Cup victory in 1984.

GUNNERS TAKE AIM

The club's record League Cup defeat came in January 2007 when Arsenal claimed a thrilling 6–3 victory at Anfield. A young Gunners side were 5–1 up at one stage, with Brazilian forward Julio Baptista scoring four of the Londoners' goals. Robbie Fowler, Steven Gerrard and Sami Hyypia were the Reds' goalscorers.

⬇ Phil Neal was the first signing made by Bob Paisley after he had replaced Bill Shankly as Liverpool boss. The full-back won almost every honour available.

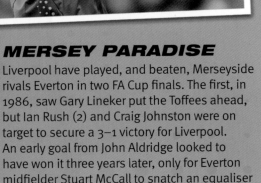

⬅ Pepe Reina isn't celebrating another clean sheet. He's actually got an assist after setting up a goal for Albert Riera against Aston Villa at Anfield in 2009.

RELIABLE RED

Phil Neal made an incredible 365 consecutive league appearances for Liverpool between December 1974 and September 1983. The dependable right-back held down a first-team spot for almost a decade before he was sidelined through injury and Steve Nicol stepped in. Neal claimed a club-record 20 medals during those nine ever-present seasons and played in five European Cup finals. He was a winner on four occasions.

MERSEY PARADISE

Liverpool have played, and beaten, Merseyside rivals Everton in two FA Cup finals. The first, in 1986, saw Gary Lineker put the Toffees ahead, but Ian Rush (2) and Craig Johnston were on target to secure a 3–1 victory for Liverpool. An early goal from John Aldridge looked to have won it three years later, only for Everton midfielder Stuart McCall to snatch an equaliser in the 89th minute to send the game to extra time. Rush restored the Reds' advantage and, after McCall had levelled again, the Welsh striker grabbed the winner.

Liverpool

CALLAGHAN A TRUE RED

No one has played for Liverpool more times than Ian Callaghan. The legendary midfielder featured 857 times in an 18-year spell with the club between 1960 and 1978. He made his debut against Bristol Rovers in April 1960 aged 17 and played his part in the club's progression from a second-tier side to the champions of Europe. Callaghan was named the Football Writers' Player of the Year in 1974 and was awarded an MBE for his services to football before leaving for Swansea in 1978.

···▷ *Ian Callaghan gave Liverpool great service over 18 years and enjoyed many glorious moments at Anfield. He was also in the England 1966 World Cup squad.*

JACK THE LAD

Jack Robinson became the youngest player to have pulled on a Liverpool shirt when he was brought on as a substitute at Hull on the final day of the 2009/10 season. Robinson, who had not even played for the reserves at the time, was 16 years and 250 days old when he entered the action in the 88th minute of the 0–0 draw. The defender smashed Max Thompson's record of 17 years and 129 days set in 1974. After the game, Robinson said: "Sitting on the bench would have been good enough but it became even better to get on."

MOLBY IS SPOT ON

Midfielder Jan Molby scored a club-record 42 penalties during his Liverpool career. The former Denmark international, who spent 11 years at Anfield between 1984 and 1995, was prolific from the spot. Molby only missed three penalties, two coming in 1985/86 against Sheffield Wednesday and QPR and the other against Chelsea in 1989/90. He scored a hat-trick of spot-kicks in a League Cup replay against Coventry in 1986.

REINA'S GOLDEN GLOVES

Pepe Reina has won the Barclays Golden Glove award for the best goalkeeper in three of the last five seasons. The Spanish shot-stopper, who was an ever-present in the top flight for the third consecutive season in 2009/10, narrowly missed out on the most recent honour to Chelsea's Petr Cech, despite keeping 17 clean sheets.

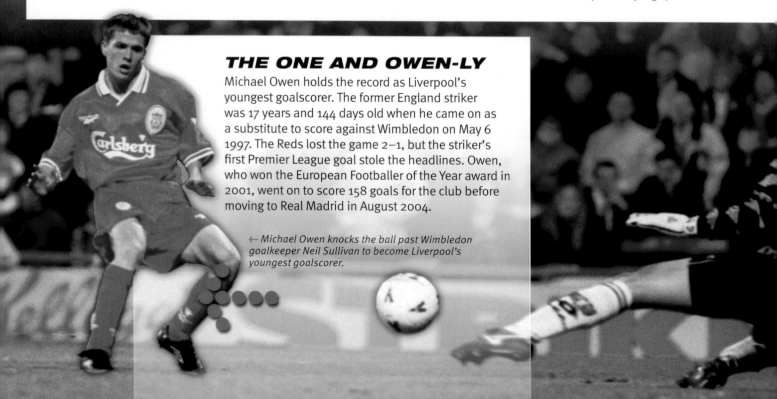

THE ONE AND OWEN-LY

Michael Owen holds the record as Liverpool's youngest goalscorer. The former England striker was 17 years and 144 days old when he came on as a substitute to score against Wimbledon on May 6 1997. The Reds lost the game 2–1, but the striker's first Premier League goal stole the headlines. Owen, who won the European Footballer of the Year award in 2001, went on to score 158 goals for the club before moving to Real Madrid in August 2004.

◀─ *Michael Owen knocks the ball past Wimbledon goalkeeper Neil Sullivan to become Liverpool's youngest goalscorer.*

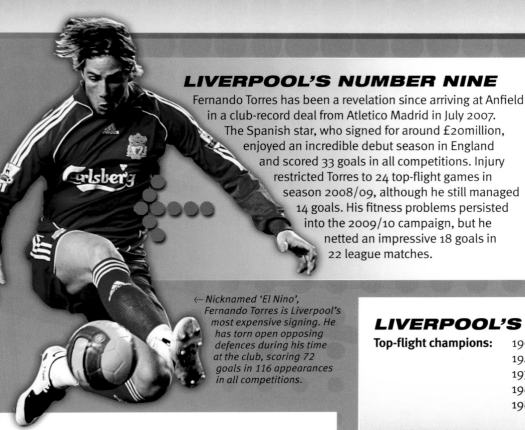

LIVERPOOL'S NUMBER NINE

Fernando Torres has been a revelation since arriving at Anfield in a club-record deal from Atletico Madrid in July 2007. The Spanish star, who signed for around £20million, enjoyed an incredible debut season in England and scored 33 goals in all competitions. Injury restricted Torres to 24 top-flight games in season 2008/09, although he still managed 14 goals. His fitness problems persisted into the 2009/10 campaign, but he netted an impressive 18 goals in 22 league matches.

←·· Nicknamed 'El Nino', Fernando Torres is Liverpool's most expensive signing. He has torn open opposing defences during his time at the club, scoring 72 goals in 116 appearances in all competitions.

EURO AGONY

Liverpool's seventh-place finish in 2009/10 was their lowest in the top flight for 11 years. The Reds missed out on Champions League qualification, instead having to settle for a place in the Europa League. The Merseysiders suffered 19 defeats in all competitions – the most they have lost since the first Premier League season back in 1992/93.

LIVERPOOL'S HONOURS TABLE

Top-flight champions:	1900/01, 1905/06, 1921/22, 1922/23, 1946/47, 1963/64, 1965/66, 1972/73, 1975/76, 1976/77, 1978/79, 1979/80, 1981/82, 1982/83, 1983/84, 1985/86, 1987/88, 1989/90
Second-tier champions:	1893/94, 1895/96, 1904/05, 1961/62
European Cup winners:	1976/77, 1977/78, 1980/81, 1983/84, 2004/05
FA Cup winners:	1964/65, 1973/74, 1985/86, 1988/89, 1991/92, 2000/01, 2005/06
League Cup winners:	1980/81, 1981/82, 1982/83, 1983/84, 1994/95, 2000/01, 2002/03
UEFA Cup winners:	1972/73, 1975/76, 2000/01

NO GREEK TRAGEDY

Liverpool memorably won the European Cup for the fifth time in their history in 2004/05, but they were actually seconds away from exiting the Champions League that season at the group stage. Having fallen behind to Greek side Olympiacos at Anfield, the Reds needed three second-half goals to ensure their progress. They were leading 2–1 heading towards injury-time when captain Steven Gerrard lashed an unstoppable first-time shot into the bottom corner to send the Anfield fans wild with delight.

↓ The glorious night in Turkey in May 2005 wouldn't have happened if Steven Gerrard hadn't scored a last-gasp third goal against Olympiacos to book Liverpool's place in the last 16 of the Champions League.

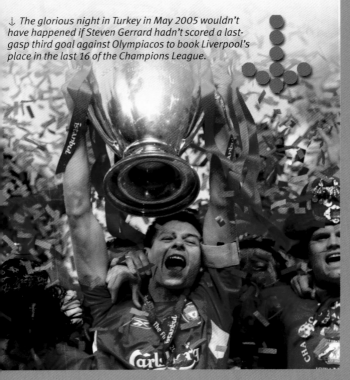

PAISLEY IS TROPHY KING

Bob Paisley is the club's most successful manager. He won six top-flight titles, the League Cup on three occasions, the UEFA Cup once and the Charity Shield five times. However, the biggest achievements of his nine-year stay at Anfield were the three European Cup victories of 1977, 1978 and 1981. Other hugely successful Reds bosses include Bill Shankly and Kenny Dalglish, who both won three top-flight titles and two FA Cup finals. Joe Fagan (1984) and Rafael Benitez (2005) have both led the club to European Cup glory.

··→ Bob Paisley with the European Cup in 1977, after the Reds had won the trophy for the first time.

Manchester City

City have not won a major trophy since they lifted the League Cup in 1976. They suffered relegation twice in three years during the 1990s but have now established themselves in the Barclays Premier League and have high hopes that silverware is on its way back to the City of Manchester Stadium.

PRIDE IN BATTLE

A new club badge was unveiled in 1997. The crest is based on the coat of arms of the city of Manchester. The shield standing in front of a golden eagle features a ship in the upper half, which represents the Manchester Ship Canal, and three diagonal stripes in the lower half, which symbolise the city's three rivers. Club motto 'Superbia in Proelio' translates from Latin as 'Pride in Battle'.

MAINE MOVE

City left Maine Road, their home of 80 years, to move into the City of Manchester Stadium, or Eastlands as it is also commonly known, in 2003. Built for the Commonwealth Games of 2002, it was later converted into a football stadium which can hold 47,405 spectators. Barcelona were the Blues' opponents for the first football match to be played at the ground, with Nicolas Anelka scoring the opening goal as City claimed a 2–1 win.

CITY'S GROUNDS

1880	Clowes Street
1881	Kirkmanshulme Cricket Ground
1882	Queens Road
1884	Pink Bank Lane
1887	Hyde Road
1923	Maine Road
2003	City of Manchester Stadium

→ The 1999 third-tier play-off trophy is in safe hands as Manchester City goalkeeper Nicky Weaver celebrates his team's dramatic victory over Gillingham.

← Paul Stewart was one of the three hat-trick heroes in Manchester City's 10–1 destruction of Huddersfield Town in 1987.

HAT-TRICK HEROES

The Blues' record league victory came against Huddersfield in the second tier in November 1987. Three players scored hat-tricks that day as City raced to a 10–1 win at Maine Road. David White, Tony Adcock and Paul Stewart netted nine of the goals between them, with Neil McNab the other goalscorer. Bobby Marshall scored five goals when City recorded their biggest cup victory – also 10–1 – against Swindon in 1930.

BACK TO THE PREMIER LEAGUE

Back-to-back promotions in 1998/99 and 1999/00 secured City a return to the Premier League. Goalkeeper Nicky Weaver was the hero against Gillingham in the third-tier Play-Off Final, saving two penalties in a shootout to send City up. The following term, Joe Royle led the club back to the top flight via a runners-up finish in the second tier behind Charlton. Unfortunately, the Blues' stay in the Premier League was shortlived. They finished third from bottom and were relegated back down 12 months later.

UNITED RED-FACED

Manchester City recorded the biggest home derby victory in their history in 1989 when Manchester United were beaten 5–1 at Maine Road. Mel Machin's side had started the season with one win in six league games, but they ran riot against their fierce rivals. They were 3–0 up at half-time, with David Oldfield, Trevor Morley and Ian Bishop on target. Mark Hughes, who later managed City, pulled a goal back for United with a stunning scissor-kick, but Oldfield's second and a superb header from Andy Hinchcliffe wrapped up the victory.

⟵ Sven-Goran Eriksson made Eastlands a fortress in 2007/08 as Manchester City won their first nine home Barclays Premier League games.

CUP DOUBLE

City won the European Cup Winners' Cup in 1970, beating Polish side Gornik Zabrze in the final in Vienna. Goals from Neil Young and Francis Lee earned them a 2–1 victory and completed a cup double, following their League Cup success of a few weeks earlier. Joe Mercer was in charge as City knocked out Athletic Bilbao, Belgian club Lierse, Academica Coimbra of Portugal and Schalke on the way to the final.

CITY GO UP IN STYLE

City's title-winning campaign of 2001/02 in the second tier saw the club finish with a record-breaking total of 99 points. They also equalled a 75-year-old club goalscoring record, as Kevin Keegan's men netted 108 times on their way to the title. Notable results that season came against Crewe (5–2), Sheffield Wednesday (6–2), Burnley (5–1) and Barnsley (5–1). Hot-shot striker Shaun Goater scored 28 league goals and Darren Huckerby added 20 more, with Ali Benarbia pulling the strings in midfield.

↓ Kevin Keegan's attacking tactics brought Manchester City great success in the 2001/02 promotion season. He managed the club until 2005.

ON THE RUN

Manchester City created a club record when they won the first nine home games of the 2007/08 campaign under Sven-Goran Eriksson. Michael Johnson set the ball rolling by scoring the only goal of the game against Derby, and Manchester United were beaten 1–0 four days later when Brazilian Geovanni snatched the winner. The last victory of the sequence came against Bolton on December 15, with the Blues coming back from 2–1 down to win 4–2. City were held to a 2–2 draw by Blackburn on December 27.

⟶ Carlos Tevez celebrates one of his two goals in the Carling Cup semi-final first leg against Manchester United at Eastlands. He also scored the goal that levelled the match 3–3 on aggregate at Old Trafford, though United went on to win 4–3.

TEVEZ ON TARGET

Carlos Tevez was the club's top scorer in 2009/10. The Argentina international finished his first City campaign with 29 goals in all competitions – 23 in the Barclays Premier League and six in the Carling Cup. The powerful forward scored two hat-tricks, with the first coming in a 4–1 win against Blackburn and the second a 3–0 success at home to Wigan. Tevez's haul put him fourth in the overall Premier League goalscoring charts.

Manchester City

DRAW SPECIALISTS

The club drew more away games than any other top-flight side in 2009/10 and also suffered the least defeats on their travels. Nine of their 19 away matches ended all-square, while they only lost on four occasions. Yossi Benayoun's equaliser a minute after Stephen Ireland had put City 2–1 ahead denied them victory at Liverpool in November, while they needed a last-gasp wonder goal from Adam Johnson to snatch a point in a 1–1 draw at Sunderland. The Blues were beaten by Manchester United, Tottenham, Everton and Hull.

↓ Alan Oakes won a second League Cup winners' medal in his final season with Manchester City – a 2–1 defeat of Newcastle in 1976.

FA CUP SUCCESS

City have won the FA Cup on four occasions, with their last success coming in 1969. The Blues beat Bolton 1–0 in the 1904 final, claimed a 2–1 win against Portsmouth 30 years later and enjoyed a 3–1 success against Birmingham in 1956. The 1969 final saw City come up against Leicester, with a single goal from Neil Young enough to secure the trophy. The last time they reached the Wembley showpiece was in 1981, when they lost 3–2 to Tottenham in a replay following a 1–1 draw.

← Tony Book, the Manchester City captain and co-winner of that season's Footballer of the Year award, shows off the FA Cup in 1969.

SIMPLY THE BEST

City enjoyed their highest Barclays Premier League finish in season 2009/10. Roberto Mancini's side narrowly missed out on a Champions League spot, but fifth was still three places better than their previous high, achieved in 2004/05. The Manchester club were three points behind fourth-place Tottenham and a further five adrift of Arsenal in third.

FAMILY TIES

Alan Oakes made a club-record 565 league appearances for Manchester City in a 17-year spell between 1959 and 1976. He made his debut in a 1–1 draw with Chelsea in November 1959, with his last game coming as a substitute against derby rivals Manchester United in May 1976. Oakes' cousin, Glyn Pardoe, is the Blues' youngest-ever player. He was just 15 years and 314 days old when he made his debut in April 1962.

CITY'S LEADING LEAGUE GOALSCORERS

Eric Brook	158
Tommy Johnson	158
Billy Meredith	145
Joe Hayes	142
Billy Gillespie	126
Tommy Browell	122
Colin Bell	117
Frank Roberts	116
Francis Lee	112
Fred Tilson	110

JOHNSON'S JOY

Tommy Johnson shares the record for scoring the most league goals for the club, having netted 158 times between 1919 and 1930. The forward scored 38 goals in 39 games in the top-flight campaign of 1928/29 – still the most by any Blues player in a single season. Johnson is also one of four players to have scored five times in a game for the club. He stole the show in a 6–2 win against Everton at Goodison Park on September 15 1928. Eric Brook also bagged 158 league goals and 178 in total – 12 more than Johnson.

FIRST-ROUND EXIT

Manchester City were briefly involved in the European Cup in season 1968/69. Joe Mercer's men secured their place in the competition by winning the top-flight title in 1968, but they failed to get past the first round. City played out a goalless draw in the first leg of their clash with Turkish side Fenerbahce at Maine Road, but they lost the away leg 2–1.

WRIGHT MOVE FOR SHAUN

Chelsea paid Manchester City a reported £21million to sign Shaun Wright-Phillips in July 2005 – a record for the biggest transfer fee received by the club. But Wright-Phillips found himself back at the City of Manchester Stadium three years later, with Mark Hughes paying less than half of that figure to re-sign the diminutive winger. In total, the England star has made over 200 league appearances for City.

⟵ Shaun Wright-Phillips, Manchester City's most expensive transfer sale in 2005, completed 200 league appearances for City in 2010, two years after returning from Chelsea.

⟶ Roberto Mancini couldn't bring Champions League football to Eastlands as Manchester City ended three points behind fourth-place Tottenham in 2009/10.

BERT PUTS HIS NECK ON THE LINE

Legendary Manchester City goalkeeper Bert Trautmann played the last 15 minutes of the 1956 FA Cup final with a broken neck! The German was knocked out when he collided with Birmingham's Peter Murphy. Trautmann was in obvious discomfort when he came round, but there were no substitutes in those days, so he stayed on. He made a string of fine saves to preserve City's 3–1 lead. An X-ray three days after the game revealed he had dislocated five vertebrae in his neck, one of which was cracked in two!

MANCINI TAKES CHARGE

Roberto Mancini was appointed manager of Manchester City on December 19 2009 following the departure of Mark Hughes. The Italian won his first game in charge against Stoke, and that was followed by a first away victory in two months at Wolves. He masterminded a 4–2 success at Chelsea and oversaw big wins against Burnley (6–1) and Birmingham (5–1). In 21 Barclays Premier League games at the helm in 2009/10, Mancini secured 11 victories, five draws and suffered five defeats.

↑ Bert Trautmann is helped from the field by team-mates Dave Ewing (left) and Bill Leivers after Manchester City's 3–1 victory over Birmingham City in the 1956 FA Cup final. Trautmann had played on despite suffering a broken neck.

Manchester United

United rank as one of the biggest and most widely-supported clubs in world football. They have won 18 top-flight titles, a record 11 FA Cups, four League Cups and three European Cups, among a host of other trophies. Manager Sir Alex Ferguson is the most successful boss in their history, while record appearance holder Ryan Giggs is still turning out for the club.

THE BUSBY BABES

The 'Busby Babes' were a group of young and talented players who progressed through Manchester United's youth system to win the top-flight title under the management of Sir Matt Busby in 1955/56 and 1956/57. Tragically, in February 1958, eight members of the squad – including Duncan Edwards and Tommy Taylor – were killed when the passenger plane they were travelling on crashed on the runway at Munich Airport. The team had been returning from a European Cup match in Belgrade.

↑ *As Manchester United boss, Sir Matt Busby created three outstanding teams: the 1948 FA Cup-winning side, the 'Busby Babes' of the 1950s and finally the 1968 European champions.*

NEWTON HEATH

Manchester United were formed as Newton Heath in 1878. The club were elected to The Football League in 1892 and were renamed in 1902 by a group of businessmen who had saved them from bankruptcy. United released a green and yellow third shirt in 1992 to celebrate 100 years since Newton Heath's election.

UNITED'S LEADING LEAGUE GOALSCORERS

Bobby Charlton	199
Jack Rowley	182
Denis Law	171
Dennis Viollet	159
Joe Spence	158
George Best	137
Stan Pearson	128
Mark Hughes	120
David Herd	114
Tommy Taylor	112

⋯→ *Arguably England's greatest ever player, Bobby Charlton is both Manchester United's and his country's all-time leading goalscorer.*

WEMBLEY WONDERS

The Red Devils became the first English club to win the European Cup in 1968 when they claimed a 4–1 win against Portuguese side Benfica at Wembley. United took the lead through a Bobby Charlton header, but Benfica equalised to take the game into extra time. George Best went around the goalkeeper and slotted home to make it 2–1, before Brian Kidd and another Charlton strike secured a famous victory.

CHARLTON'S DOUBLE LANDMARK

Bobby Charlton is Manchester United and England's record goalscorer. Charlton netted 249 times in all competitions for the Red Devils – 199 in the league – and hit 49 for England. Gary Lineker was one goal away from equalling his international record when he retired. Charlton survived the Munich air disaster of 1958, and having already played a part in the title-winning season of 1956/57, he went on to win the FA Cup, two more top-flight titles, the World Cup and the European Cup in a glittering career for both club and country.

GREY DAY FOR UNITED

United famously changed their grey away shirts at half-time during a 3–1 defeat at Southampton in April 1996. Sir Alex Ferguson claimed that his players were struggling to pick each other out due to the colour of the kit, with United 3–0 down at the time. They appeared for the second half sporting a blue-and-white-striped shirt and managed to pull a goal back. The Red Devils lost four and drew one of the five games they played in the grey shirt. It was retired from use two days after the Dell defeat.

THE BABY-FACED ASSASSIN

Ole Gunnar Solskjaer wrote his name into United's history books when he scored the winning goal in the dying seconds of the 1999 European Cup final. The 'Baby-Faced Assassin', as he was affectionately known due to his boyish looks and finishing ability, stabbed the ball home in injury time to snatch United a 2–1 win against Bayern Munich. United had been 1–0 down going into time added on. The Norwegian striker scored 91 league goals in 235 appearances for United. Four of those came as a substitute in the last 10 minutes of an 8–1 win at Nottingham Forest in February 1999.

⟶ *Ole Gunnar Solskjaer scores Manchester United's dramatic winner in the 1999 UEFA Champions League final.*

POST-WAR UNITED MANAGERS

Matt Busby	1945–1969
Wilf McGuinness	1969–1970
Matt Busby	1970–1971
Frank O'Farrell	1971–1972
Tommy Docherty	1972–1977
Dave Sexton	1977–1981
Ron Atkinson	1981–1986
Alex Ferguson	1986–Present

A FAMOUS FIRST

Manchester United were the inaugural winners of the Premier League in 1992/93 – their first top-flight title for 26 years. They finished the season 10 points ahead of Aston Villa in second, but things had not started well when they lost their first game of the newly-formed competition at Sheffield United. Brian Deane scored twice for the Blades – the opener creating history as the first-ever Premier League goal – before Mark Hughes pulled one back just after the hour.

⬆ *Brian Kidd had celebrated his 19th birthday by winning the European Cup in 1968. As assistant manager, Kidd (left) helped 'Fergie's Fledglings' to the 1996 Premier League title.*

FERGIE'S FLEDGLINGS

'Fergie's Fledglings' were the modern-day equivalent of the 'Busby Babes', with Sir Alex Ferguson nurturing talents such as David Beckham, Ryan Giggs, Gary Neville and Nicky Butt. When a new-look Manchester United side lost 3–1 at Aston Villa on the opening day of the 1995/96 season, TV pundit Alan Hansen famously said: 'You'll never win anything with kids.' How wrong he was. The youngsters clawed back Newcastle's 14-point lead at the top of the Premier League to claim the title by four points. They also won the FA Cup that year to secure the double.

⟵ *Steve Bruce (left) and Bryan Robson with the Premiership trophy at the end of the first season of the new competition, Manchester United's first top-tier title for 26 years.*

Manchester United

EDWIN THE UNBEATABLE

Goalkeeper Edwin van der Sar and the Manchester United defence went a record-breaking 1,311 minutes without conceding a league goal in the 2008/09 season. They beat a Premier League benchmark set by Chelsea's Petr Cech in the 2004/05 campaign and then surpassed Steve Death's English league record of 1,103 minutes without conceding four days later. The British top-flight record fell against West Ham on February 8 2009 and the world record was broken on February 18. The Dutchman was finally beaten by Newcastle forward Peter Lovenkrands on March 4.

ROAD TO SUCCESS

The Red Devils won more games on their travels than any other top-flight team during the most recent campaign. United won 11 away matches – one more than champions Chelsea – with notable results including a 5–0 victory at Wigan, 3–1 wins at Tottenham and Arsenal and a 1–0 derby success at Manchester City.

LUCKY NUMBER SEVEN

The number seven shirt has become iconic at Manchester United. Some of the club's greatest players have worn it, with George Best starting the tradition in the 1960s. 'Captain Marvel' Bryan Robson also had the honour, before Eric Cantona took over. David Beckham was next to be handed the shirt, with Cristiano Ronaldo taking it on when the England talisman left for Real Madrid. Michael Owen currently has the squad number, having been handed it following his arrival at the club in July 2009.

⇢ George Best was the first superstar footballer. With Denis Law and Bobby Charlton, he was part of the most entertaining and lethal strike force in England in the 1960s.

OOH AAH CANTONA!

Eric Cantona was voted as the greatest Manchester United player of all time in an official poll in 2001. He helped Sir Alex Ferguson's men to two Premier League titles and an FA Cup in his first two seasons at Old Trafford. Arguably his finest hour came in the 1995/96 season, as he returned from a nine-month suspension to almost single-handedly win the club another double and scored eight goals in United's last 11 games, including a late winner against Liverpool in the FA Cup final. 'King Eric' retired the following year after another title success.

⇠ Eric Cantona celebrates a derby goal for Manchester United against City in 1993, in his first season with the Reds.

UNITED'S GREATEST PLAYERS*

1   Eric Cantona
2   George Best
3   Ryan Giggs
4   Bobby Charlton
5   Peter Schmeichel
6   Bryan Robson
7   Roy Keane
8   David Beckham
9   Duncan Edwards
10 Denis Law

* As voted by the club's fans in 2001

EURO DOMINATION

The Manchester giants hold the record for the longest unbeaten run in the Champions League – a staggering 25 matches without defeat. That sequence started with a 1–0 win at Sporting Lisbon in their opening group game of the 2007/08 campaign, with a 3–1 success at Arsenal in the semi-finals of the 2008/09 competition completing the run. Their streak came to an end when they were beaten 2–0 by Barcelona in the final. Dutch outfit Ajax had previously held the record with a run of 20 unbeaten matches.

OWN GOAL RECORD

Manchester United benefited from a record 11 own goals in 2009/10. Arsenal put through their own net in both fixtures against the Red Devils, with Abou Diaby helping United to a 2–1 win at Old Trafford in August and goalkeeper Manuel Almunia scooping a cross from Nani into his own net as the Gunners were beaten 3–1 at the Emirates Stadium in January. Portsmouth scored two own goals in a single game in February to help United to a 5–0 win.

Michael Owen (7) gets past Shaun Wright-Phillips to score the dramatic winner in the 2009/10 derby match at Old Trafford. United won 4–3.

DERBY DOUBLE

The Red Devils took maximum points off local rivals Manchester City for the third time in four seasons in 2009/10. Their Old Trafford clash in September was one of the most memorable of recent years, with City equalising three times – their last goal coming in the 90th minute through Craig Bellamy – only for Michael Owen to snatch a 4–3 win for the home side in injury time. Paul Scholes also left it late to head home the only goal of the game in the return at the City of Manchester Stadium in April.

BECKS IS BACK

David Beckham was given a hero's welcome when he returned to Old Trafford for the first time with AC Milan in March 2010. The England midfielder made his name at United during a 10-year spell between 1993 and 2003. A stunning lob from the halfway line against Wimbledon at the start of the 1996/97 season shot him to stardom, and he went on to win six Premier League titles, two FA Cups and a European Cup with the club. Beckham left to join Real Madrid in July 2003. He then moved to MLS side LA Galaxy, who loaned him out to AC Milan for part of 2008/09 and 2009/10.

David Beckham, wearing a United scarf, leaves the pitch after playing for AC Milan against Manchester United at Old Trafford in 2010.

CRISTIANO IS THE RON

Cristiano Ronaldo is the only player in Manchester United's history to have won the FIFA World Player of the Year award. The Portuguese forward claimed the prize in 2008 following a memorable campaign. He scored 42 goals in all competitions as United won the Barclays Premier League title and also lifted the European Cup. Ronaldo headed the opener against Chelsea in the Champions League final, with Sir Alex Ferguson's men going on to win the trophy on penalties. The Portuguese also claimed the Ballon d'Or, the European Golden Shoe and the UEFA Footballer of the Year trophies that season.

Cristiano Ronaldo was the catalyst for Manchester United's championship runs of 2007–09. In the 2007/08 season he scored 42 goals in all competitions, mainly from midfield.

Portsmouth

Portsmouth's seven-year stay in the Premier League came to an end in 2009/10 after a difficult season both on and off the field ended in relegation, but the club still managed to reach the FA Cup final for the second time in three years and they are now rebuilding for another crack at the big time.

↑ In 2008, Harry Redknapp became the first English manager to win the FA Cup since 1995.

HAPPY AS HARRY

Harry Redknapp became the first English manager to lift the FA Cup since 1995 when Portsmouth beat Cardiff 1–0 at Wembley in 2008. A single goal from Nigerian striker Nwankwo Kanu was enough for victory as the south-coast club won the trophy for the second time in their history. Cliff Parker was the hero in the 1939 final, scoring twice to help Pompey to a 4–1 win against Wolves.

BACK-TO-BACK TITLES

Only five teams have won back-to-back top-flight titles since World War II – and Portsmouth are one of them. Bob Jackson led the club to glory in 1948/49 and again in 1949/50, with a team featuring club legends such as Jimmy Dickinson, Jack Froggatt, Duggie Reid and Peter Harris. Harris finished the first championship-winning season as top scorer with 22 goals, while Ike Clarke led the way with 20 the following term.

DERBY DELIGHT

The 4–1 FA Cup win against Southampton in February 2010 was the first time Pompey have ever beaten their fierce rivals in a major cup competition. In four previous FA Cup clashes and one League Cup game, Saints had always come out on top. To the end of the 2009/10 campaign, there had been 36 derby games between the two sides in total, with Southampton winning 19, Pompey claiming victory nine times and eight games ending all-square.

WHAT A GUY!

Guy Whittingham scored a club-record 42 league goals in season 1992/93, but Pompey missed out on promotion to the top flight on goal difference. They finished third in the second tier, with Newcastle and West Ham going up automatically before Portsmouth were beaten by Leicester at the semi-final stage of the play-offs. Prolific striker Whittingham scored over half of the club's total goals that term and left for Aston Villa in the summer of 1993 having scored 88 times in 160 league matches.

← It was ironic that despite 42 goals in the league from striker Guy Whittingham, Portsmouth missed out on promotion into the Premier League on goal difference.

CROUCH IS NO SLOUCH

Peter Crouch has been Portsmouth's record signing twice. The striker – famous for his robotic dance celebration while playing for England – first arrived at Fratton Park in July 2001 in a £1.5million deal from QPR. He moved to Aston Villa for £5million three years later but was then brought back to the south coast in the summer of 2008, leaving Liverpool for a fee reported to be £11million. The England forward played 38 league games and scored 11 goals in 2008/09 before joining Harry Redknapp at Tottenham.

RECORDS TOPPLE

The club's title-winning season of 2002/03 saw them break two significant records. They claimed a best-ever points haul of 98 and also scored the most goals they have managed in a single league season with 97. Paul Merson pulled the strings in midfield, netting 12 times, while Bulgarian striker Svetoslav Todorov finished the campaign as the second tier's leading marksman with 26.

← Peter Crouch (left) is congratulated by Jermain Defoe after scoring Portsmouth's equaliser against West Brom in November 2008. The duo are now team-mates at both Tottenham and England.

PRETTY IN PINK

Portsmouth have not always played in a blue and white kit. Between 1898 and 1909 they wore salmon pink shirts with white shorts and maroon socks! The club then changed to a white shirt with navy shorts and socks for two years before the current royal blue top was introduced. The only change since then came in 1947 when red socks were worn for the first time.

POMPEY'S BEST XI*

GK	David James
DEF	Glen Johnson
DEF	John Beresford
DEF	Sol Campbell
DEF	Jimmy Dickinson
MID	Paul Merson
MID	Peter Harris
MID	Robert Prosinecki
ATT	Duggie Reid
ATT	Guy Whittingham
ATT	Jack Froggatt

* As voted by the club's fans

GENTLEMAN JIM

Jimmy Dickinson holds the record for the most appearances in a Portsmouth shirt and is also the club's most capped player. Dickinson, who earned the nickname 'Gentleman Jim' due to the fact that he was never booked or sent off, featured 845 times in all competitions for Pompey between 1946 and 1965. His 764 league appearances for one club is bettered only by John Trollope, who played 770 games for Swindon. Dickinson was capped 48 times by England and went to both the 1950 and 1954 World Cups.

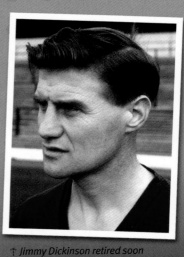

↑ Jimmy Dickinson retired soon after his 40th birthday, having helped to save Portsmouth from relegation to the third tier.

MILAN MEMORIES

Portsmouth's one and only taste of European football brought with it a memorable clash against AC Milan. The club played in the UEFA Cup in 2008/09, qualifying for the group stages by beating Portuguese side Vitoria de Guimaraes in the first round. A tough draw threw up trips to Braga and Wolfsburg and Fratton Park clashes with Milan and Heerenveen. Pompey were 2–0 up against the Italian giants, with Younes Kaboul and Nwankwo Kanu scoring, but a trademark free-kick from Ronaldinho and late Filippo Inzaghi strike snatched a 2–2 draw.

← Richard Hughes (right) tangles with Gennaro Gattuso of AC Milan during Portsmouth's UEFA Cup Group E tie at Fratton Park in 2008. Pompey missed out on a place in the last 32, finishing fourth in the group.

Portsmouth

WINLESS RUN PROVES COSTLY

Portsmouth went on a club-record run of 25 league games without a win between November 1958 and August 1959. The sequence started with a 2–1 defeat at Bolton in the top flight and continued until the second game of the 1959/60 season, with the winless streak having seen the club relegated to the second tier. Pompey suffered heavy defeats to West Ham (6–0), Wolves (5–3 and 7–0), Newcastle (5–1), Manchester United (6–1) and Arsenal (5–2) along the way as they were sent down.

OPENING-DAY SUCCESS

The south-coast club marked their first Premier League outing with a victory in August 2003, beating Aston Villa 2–1 at Fratton Park. Teddy Sheringham opened the scoring from close range three minutes before the break, with fellow summer signing Patrik Berger making it two with a superb strike midway through the second half. Gareth Barry pulled a goal back from the penalty spot late on for Villa, but Pompey held on.

↓ Benjani (25) is congratulated by Niko Kranjcar after scoring Portsmouth's first goal in the 11-goal thriller against Reading in 2007.

↑ The honour of scoring the first Premier League goal in Portsmouth's history belongs to Teddy Sheringham (10).

A COMMON SCORELINE

The amazing 7–4 win against Reading in September 2007 was nothing new – it was actually the fourth time the club have been involved in games with that scoreline. The first came against Newcastle in November 1930, with the club winning on Tyneside. It was raining goals again on Christmas Day 1957, but there was no festive cheer for Portsmouth, who lost out to Chelsea. Charlton were 7–4 victors in October 1960, before the most recent battle against the Royals. Striker Benjani Mwaruwari scored a hat-trick for Pompey in that game.

POMPEY'S LEADING GOALSCORERS

Peter Harris	211
Jack Weddle	181
Ron Saunders	162
Duggie Reid	135
Billy Haines	128
Ray Hiron	119
Johnny Gordon	116
Guy Whittingham	115
Jimmy Easson	106
Albert McCann	98

HARRIS HITS THE HEIGHTS

Peter Harris is Pompey's all-time top goalscorer. He netted 211 times in total for the club – 194 in the league – between 1946 and 1960. Harris is one of two Portsmouth players to have scored five times in a game, achieving that feat against Aston Villa in September 1958. He also bagged a hat-trick in the south-coast club's record cup victory, helping his side to a 7–0 success against Stockport in January 1949.

FUN ON THE ROAD

Portsmouth's longest winning streak away from home in the Premier League is six consecutive games, achieved in 2007/08. That run began on September 23 2007 when Nwankwo Kanu scored the only goal of the game at Blackburn. Wins against Fulham, Wigan, Newcastle, Birmingham and Aston Villa followed. Liverpool claimed a 4–1 victory at Anfield on December 22 to bring the sequence to an end.

UNITED NATIONS

Pompey used 33 different players during the 2009/10 season – more than any other top-flight club. Players from 18 different countries took to the field in the famous blue shirt, including two Nigerians (John Utaka and Nwankwo Kanu), two Algerians (Nadir Belhadj and Hassan Yebda) and two Ghanaians (Kevin-Prince Boateng and Quincy Owusu-Abeyie). There were also 11 English players involved, with boss Avram Grant introducing youngsters Joel Ward and Matt Ritchie to his squad towards the end of the campaign.

Nigeria international Nwankwo Kanu has played in England since 1999, joining Portsmouth in 2006. To the end of 2009/10, exactly half of his 122 appearances in all competitions had been as a substitute.

Harry Redknapp took Portsmouth to eighth in the Barclays Premier League in 2008 – their best finish since 1954/55 – and they also won the FA Cup for the first time in 69 years.

CHELSEA GIVE POMPEY THE BLUES

Chelsea's 5–0 win at Fratton Park in March 2010 equalled Portsmouth's record home defeat in the league. Didier Drogba and Florent Malouda both scored twice, with Frank Lampard wrapping up the win late on. Pompey had previously been beaten by the same scoreline against Birmingham in October 1955.

ON A HIGH

Pompey enjoyed their best Barclays Premier League campaign in season 2007/08, finishing in eighth place. Harry Redknapp was in charge as the club ended the term above the likes of Manchester City and Tottenham, while they were only three points off sixth-place Aston Villa. They were impressive 4–1 winners at Newcastle and enjoyed a 3–1 success at Villa Park during the course of that campaign, while they also held Manchester United and Chelsea to 1–1 draws at Fratton Park.

GOAL MILESTONES

The club had the honour of scoring both the 500th and the 1,000th Barclays Premier League goals of the 2009/10 campaign. Nadir Belhadj netted the 500th when he put Pompey ahead against Liverpool at Fratton Park on December 19. That tally was chalked up in record time, with the Algerian's strike coming in just the 168th fixture of the season – 17 games quicker than the previous fastest mark, set in 1994/95. John Utaka scored the 1,000th goal with Portsmouth's second in a 3–1 home win against Wolves on May 1.

Nadir Belhadj's goal against Liverpool on December 19 2009 was the 500th of the season and it gave them a 2–0 victory.

Stoke City

Stoke, who were founded in 1863, are the oldest club in the top division and are thought to be the second oldest professional club in the world after Notts County. The Potters regained their top-flight status in 2008 and have finished in a creditable mid-table position in their two seasons back there so far.

BRITANNIA RULES

Stoke's first season at the Britannia Stadium ended in disappointment when they were relegated to the third tier. The Potters finished second from bottom in the second tier in season 1997/98, with Reading at the foot and Manchester City also going down. The club had played their home games at the Victoria Ground since 1878, but moved to their new 27,500-capacity ground in 1997. Graham Kavanagh scored the first goal at the stadium in a League Cup clash against Rochdale.

⇡ *Terry Conroy (arm raised) scored after four minutes of the 1972 League Cup final. It was only the second domestic honour won by Stoke keeper Gordon Banks.*

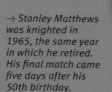

⇢ *Stanley Matthews was knighted in 1965, the same year in which he retired. His final match came five days after his 50th birthday.*

A FIRST POT

The Potters scooped their first major trophy in 1972 when they beat Chelsea to win the League Cup. Stoke, who had finished 17th in the top flight that season, were underdogs going into the game at Wembley, but goals from Terry Conroy and veteran forward George Eastham earned them a 2–1 victory. Tony Waddington was in charge as City also reached the semi-final of the FA Cup that year, losing out to Arsenal in a replay.

MATTHEWS HONOURED

Sir Stanley Matthews' ashes are buried under the centre circle of the Britannia Stadium pitch. There are also three nine-foot statues showing the forward at different stages of his career standing outside the ground. Matthews is a Potters legend, having scored 51 league goals in 259 appearances for the club.

WHITEHEAD WALKS

He may be known for his tough tackling, but Dean Whitehead's red card in Stoke's 2–1 defeat to Tottenham in March 2010 was his first for nine years! Whitehead walked for two bookings in the Britannia Stadium clash, both for late challenges on Spurs playmaker Luka Modric. The midfielder's previous dismissal came during his time at Oxford. He was sent off in the first half of a 2–0 defeat to Swindon.

AZTEX LINK-UP

Stoke forged links with American side Austin Aztex at the start of 2008. The Texas-based club, who play in the United Soccer Leagues, benefit from the partnership by getting the pick of City's young players for a short spell, while the Potters are keen to unearth talented American players to bring to the Barclays Premier League. Stoke great Adrian Heath is the Aztex head coach, while former forward Gifton Noel-Williams turned out for the club in 2009. They play in similar red and white stripes to their English allies.

STEIN MAKES MARK

Stoke have won the Football League Trophy on two occasions. The first came in season 1991/92 when Mark Stein scored the only goal to see off Stockport at Wembley. County gained revenge in the play-offs, though, beating the Potters over two legs at the semi-final stage. Diminutive forward Stein netted five goals in the Trophy that season and 17 in the third tier. City were winners of the competition for the second time in 2000 when Graham Kavanagh and Peter Thorne were on target in a 2–1 victory against Bristol City.

···→ *Matthew Etherington was voted Stoke's Player of the Year in 2009/10. He appeared in 34 Barclays Premier League matches, scoring five goals.*

SUPER SUB SOULEYMANE

Souleymane Oulare may have only played 80 minutes in two substitute appearances for Stoke, but he is fondly remembered for his part in the club's promotion to the second tier in 2002. Following his debut against Northampton in January 2002, Oulare was diagnosed as having a blood clot on his lung and was told he would not play again that season. However, the striker came off the bench against Cardiff in the semi-final of the play-offs to score the winning goal via his backside in extra time!

THORNE IN THE SIDE

Peter Thorne scored 20 goals in the last 17 games of the 1999/00 season as Stoke narrowly missed out on promotion but won the Football League Trophy. Having started the campaign with three goals in his first three matches, the striker had only netted 10 when Chesterfield arrived at the Britannia Stadium on March 4 2000. However, Thorne scored four times in a 5–1 win to spark an incredible run of form. He bagged a hat-trick against Bristol Rovers and the winner against Bristol City in the Football League Trophy final.

···→ *Peter Thorne stretches to knock the ball into an unguarded goal to give Stoke a 2–1 victory over Bristol City in the 2000 Football League Trophy final at Wembley.*

STOKE'S PLAYER OF THE YEAR SINCE 2000

2000/01	Brynjar Gunnarsson
2001/02	Wayne Thomas
2002/03	Sergei Shtaniuk
2003/04	Ade Akinbiyi
2004/05	Clint Hill
2005/06	Carl Hoefkens
2006/07	Danny Higginbotham
2007/08	Liam Lawrence
2008/09	Abdoulaye Faye
2009/10	Matthew Etherington

↓ *Tony Pulis masterminded Stoke's return to English football's top flight in 2008 and defied the odds by keeping the club in the Barclays Premier League.*

PULIS IS PREMIER CLASS

Tony Pulis led Stoke to the Barclays Premier League in season 2007/08. The Potters finished second in the Championship – two points behind West Brom – to gain automatic promotion. Ricardo Fuller finished as the club's top scorer with 15 league goals, while midfielder Liam Lawrence netted 14 – his best goalscoring season since 2003/04.

Stoke City

VALE RIVALRY

Port Vale are Stoke's traditional rivals, but the clubs have not faced each other in competitive action since the third-tier campaign of 2001/02. The Valiants, who are currently in The Football League's bottom division, were 1–0 winners at the Britannia Stadium the last time the two sides met, with Michael Cummins scoring the only goal of the game. The two Potteries teams have played each other 44 times in the league, with Stoke edging the number of wins 16 to 13, while 15 games have been drawn.

SHERON'S SEVEN

Mike Sheron scored in a club-record seven consecutive matches for Stoke in 1995/96. Striker Sheron joined the club from Norwich in November 1995 and netted 15 goals in 28 appearances as the club reached the play-offs the following year. His impressive goalscoring run started in City's 2–1 defeat at Charlton on March 23 1996 and ended against the same opposition at the Victoria Ground on April 17. Sheron scored a total of 34 league goals in 69 matches for the club before leaving for QPR.

⇢ *Mike Sheron (left), trying to get the better of Wolves' Eric Young, was a prolific goalscorer throughout his career, averaging a goal every three starts. His best strike rate came at Stoke.*

⬆ *Ricardo Fuller's goal against Bolton was the first of 11 he scored in 34 appearances in the league for Stoke in 2008/09.*

FULLER IS FIRST UP

Jamaican striker Ricardo Fuller scored the club's first goal in the Barclays Premier League, but it was only a consolation strike as Stoke went down 3–1 at Bolton. Goals from Gretar Steinsson, Kevin Davies and Johan Elmander had put Wanderers firmly in control of the game in August 2008, with Fuller's injury-time header proving too little, too late.

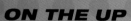

ON THE UP

City's 11th-place finish in 2009/10 saw them go one spot better than in their debut Barclays Premier League season. They recorded three less home wins, dropping to seven from the previous campaign's 10, but their away record improved, as they doubled their number of wins from two to four. They also lost just seven games away from the Britannia Stadium – a marked improvement on 2008/09, when they suffered 13 defeats.

POTTERS SINK GREENS

Stoke scored nine goals without reply against Plymouth in December 1960 – the biggest winning margin in the club's history. Johnny King grabbed a hat-trick that day, while Bill Asprey and Don Ratcliffe both got their name on the scoresheet twice. A Dennis Wilshaw strike and an own goal from Gordon Fincham completed the scoring as City ran riot. The Potters finished 18th in the second tier that season.

CITY KEEP IT CLEAN

The Potters set a club record when they went seven games without conceding a goal during the 2006/07 campaign. A 1–0 win against Coventry at the Britannia Stadium on November 6 kicked off the run, with their seventh clean sheet coming just over a month later in a 1–0 victory against QPR. Goalkeeper Steve Simonsen went a total of 658 minutes without being beaten during that streak.

⇢ *Steve Simonsen made only eight Barclays Premier League appearances for Stoke in their first two seasons in the top flight, but he did play in nine cup ties.*

STOKE'S LEADING GOALSCORERS

Tommy Sale	282
Freddie Steele	240
Frank Bowyer	205
John Ritchie	171
Charlie Wilson	118
Johnny King	113
Harry Oscroft	108
Harry Davies	101
Jimmy Greenhoff	97
Bobby Liddle	96

HENRY IS SUPER SUB

Karl Henry has made the most substitute appearances for Stoke, having come off the bench 60 times in his five years at the club between 2001 and 2006. Midfielder Henry went on to join Wolves for an initial £100,000 fee and has since captained the midlands side on numerous occasions. Jon Parkin holds the record for the most sub appearances in a single season for the Potters. The striker was brought on 26 times in 2007/08.

† *As well as his 61 substitute appearances for Stoke, Karl Henry started 75 times, though he scored just one goal. At Wolves, however, he has come off the bench only four times and been in the starting line-up in 163 matches.*

AWAY-DAY BLUES

Stoke matched Portsmouth's unwanted feat by scoring the least Barclays Premier League goals away from home in 2009/10. The Potters found the back of the net just 10 times on their travels, winning four and drawing eight of their 19 matches. Three of those were 1–0 victories, with the highlight coming at White Hart Lane in October when Glenn Whelan's late strike snatched maximum points against high-flying Tottenham.

DEBUT DELIGHT FOR SHAWCROSS

Ryan Shawcross was the last player to score on his Stoke debut, netting the only goal of the game at Cardiff on the opening day of the 2007/08 season. It took the defender just 27 minutes of his first professional start in English football to get his name on the scoresheet. Shawcross was on loan from Manchester United at the time and signed a permanent deal with City in January 2008.

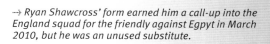

⇢ *Ryan Shawcross' form earned him a call-up into the England squad for the friendly against Egypt in March 2010, but he was an unused substitute.*

Sunderland

Sunderland were the only team from the north-east in the Barclays Premier League in 2009/10, following Newcastle and Middlesbrough's relegation. The Black Cats have won the top-flight title on six occasions, although the last time was in 1936. They have also won the FA Cup twice, in 1937 and 1973.

A NEW LOW...TWICE!

Sunderland have held the record for the lowest points total in a Premier League season twice – but they no longer have that unfortunate mark against their name. The Black Cats won just four games as they were relegated with 19 points in season 2002/03, but they broke their own record in the 2005/06 campaign, winning three times as they posted a total of 15 points. Derby's 11-point season of 2007/08 is the current low.

NEIGHBOURHOOD WATCH

Sunderland's record league victory came against derby rivals Newcastle at St James' Park in December 1908. Billy Hogg and George Holley scored hat-tricks and Arthur Bridgett netted twice as the visitors romped to a 9–1 win. Gary Rowell was the hero when the Black Cats got the better of their near-neighbours in another memorable Tyne-Wear battle in February 1979, scoring a hat-trick in a superb 4–1 away win.

BOB STOKES CUP FIRE

Bob Stokoe led the club to FA Cup glory in 1973 – the second time Sunderland had won the competition. Ian Porterfield's first-half strike was enough to snatch a shock 1–0 victory for the then second-tier side against Leeds, although goalkeeper Jimmy Montgomery played a starring role, pulling off a string of superb saves. The club's first FA Cup success had come in 1937 with a 3–1 win against Preston.

⇢ John Byrne's 1992 FA Cup run ended when Sunderland faced Liverpool in the final. For the first time in that season's competition, Byrne didn't score.

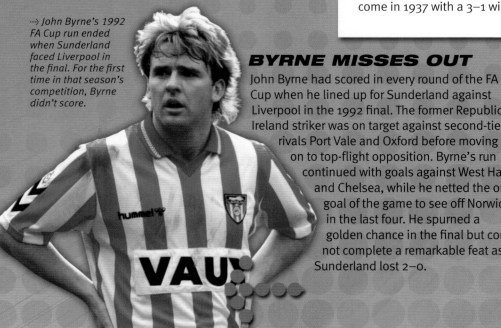

BYRNE MISSES OUT

John Byrne had scored in every round of the FA Cup when he lined up for Sunderland against Liverpool in the 1992 final. The former Republic of Ireland striker was on target against second-tier rivals Port Vale and Oxford before moving on to top-flight opposition. Byrne's run continued with goals against West Ham and Chelsea, while he netted the only goal of the game to see off Norwich in the last four. He spurned a golden chance in the final but could not complete a remarkable feat as Sunderland lost 2–0.

↑ Sunderland's Bobby Kerr sits on the shoulders of Dennis Tueart after captaining the team to their shock victory in the 1973 FA Cup final.

SUNDERLAND'S PREMIER LEAGUE RECORD

1996/97	19th	40 points
1999/00	7th	58 points
2000/01	7th	57 points
2001/02	17th	40 points
2002/03	20th	19 points
2005/06	20th	15 points
2007/08	15th	39 points
2008/09	16th	36 points
2009/10	13th	44 points

FANS VOTE FOR NEW NAME

Sunderland changed their nickname to the Black Cats after leaving Roker Park, with supporters having the final say. There have been a number of historical links between the club and black cats, with one appearing on a team photograph and another turning up at the old ground to be fed and watered. A kitten owned by young fan Billy Morris was said to have brought the Wearsiders luck when it sat in his pocket during the 1937 FA Cup final.

MONTY IS THE DON

Legendary goalkeeper Jimmy Montgomery is Sunderland's record appearance holder, having featured in 537 league games for the club between 1962 and 1977. He is best remembered for a stunning double save in the 1973 FA Cup final against Leeds when he kept out Trevor Cherry and then Peter Lorimer. Montgomery moved to Birmingham in 1977 after 15 years on Wearside.

⤏ Jimmy Montgomery's first and last games for Sunderland were in the League Cup, 15 years and two days apart, against Walsall and Manchester United respectively.

↑ The North Stand at Sunderland's Stadium of Light is behind the goal where the home fans sit. The slogan is common to fans of most clubs in the north-east.

SUNDERLAND LEAGUE APPEARANCES

Jimmy Montgomery	537
Ned Doig	418
Len Ashurst	409
Stan Anderson	402
Charlie Buchan	379
Gary Bennett	369

⤏ Kevin Phillips averaged 22 goals per year in all competitions in his six seasons with Sunderland. His eight England caps came while he was on Wearside.

GOLDEN BOY PHILLIPS

Kevin Phillips won the Premier League Golden Boot in 1999/00. The Black Cats enjoyed an impressive seventh-place finish that term, with Phillips and strike partner Niall Quinn scoring 44 of the club's 57 goals. Phillips finished the campaign with 30 in the league, seven more than nearest rival Alan Shearer. He scored a hat-trick in a 5–0 win at Derby and two in a stunning 4–1 victory against Chelsea.

ENTER THE LIGHT

Sunderland moved to the Stadium of Light in 1997. The club were relegated from the Premier League in their final season at Roker Park, meaning the first campaign at their new home was in the second tier. The Black Cats missed out on promotion that term after losing the Play-Off Final to Charlton, but they went up in style the following year. The capacity of the stadium was expanded to around 49,000 in 2002, making it the fifth largest of any English football ground.

Sunderland

ROY KEEN TO IMPRESS

Roy Keane led Sunderland to the Championship title in 2006/07 after the club had got off to the worst possible start. The Black Cats lost their first four matches, with Keane in the stands to watch them secure a first win against West Brom on August 28 2006. He started work the next day and a run of 17 games unbeaten – 14 of them wins – put the club firmly in the promotion hunt. A 5–0 victory at Luton on May 6 2007 clinched the title and with it a place in the top flight.

SUNDERLAND'S RED CARD RECORD

Kieran Richardson	v Manchester United	2–2
Kenwyne Jones	v West Ham	2–2
Lorik Cana	v Aston Villa	0–2
Michael Turner	v Manchester City	3–4
Lee Cattermole	v Portsmouth	1–1
David Meyler	v Portsmouth	1–1
Alan Hutton	v Hull	1–0
Jack Colback	v Wolves	1–2
Michael Turner	v Wolves	1–2

† Roy Keane turned around Sunderland's fortunes in 2006/07, working for former international team-mate Niall Quinn, who had recently taken over as club chairman.

⇢ Darren Bent scored three times in Sunderland's 4–0 defeat of Bolton in March 2010. Unusually, all his goals came in the final 26 minutes of the match.

DARREN HELL-BENT ON SCORING

Darren Bent justified his club-record price-tag by scoring 25 goals in all competitions in 2009/10. The striker, who joined the club from Tottenham in a reported £10million deal in August 2009, netted the only goal on his debut at Bolton and carried on scoring for the rest of the campaign. The longest he went without finding the back of the net was three matches. Bent scored 10 of his 24 top-flight goals in the opening 15 minutes of games.

⇢ Michael Turner (4) is aghast after being shown a straight red card at Eastlands at the end of Sunderland's 4–3 defeat to Manchester City.

BLACK CATS SEE RED

Sunderland set a new record in 2009/10 when they became the first side to have nine players sent off in a single Premier League season. Michael Turner saw red on two occasions, with the first coming in the dying seconds of a 4–3 defeat at Manchester City in December and the second in the latter stages of a 2–1 loss at Wolves on the final day. A double dismissal proved costly at Portsmouth in February, with Aruna Dindane snatching a last-gasp equaliser three minutes after substitute David Meyler had joined Lee Cattermole in being sent off.

← *Michael Bridges' career was blighted by injuries following his record move to Leeds in 1999. He made his Sunderland debut as a 17-year-old, but 51 of the 92 appearances in his three seasons on Wearside were as a substitute.*

GOAL-MAD GURNEY

Bobby Gurney is the club's all-time record goalscorer, having netted 228 times in 390 games in all competitions. The prolific striker was the club's top scorer for six successive seasons during the 1930s and grabbed the Black Cats' first-ever goal at Wembley in the FA Cup final victory of 1937. Gurney earned one England cap against Scotland in 1935. Charlie Buchan holds the record for the most league goals for the Wearsiders, with 209 between 1911 and 1925.

SUNDERLAND'S TOP LEAGUE GOALSCORERS SINCE 2000

Season	Player	Goals
2000/01	Kevin Phillips	14
2001/02	Kevin Phillips	11
2002/03	Kevin Phillips	6
2003/04	Marcus Stewart	14
2004/05	Marcus Stewart	16
2005/06	Liam Lawrence	3
	Anthony Le Tallec	
	Tommy Miller	
2006/07	David Connolly	13
2007/08	Kenwyne Jones	7
2008/09	Djibril Cisse	10
	Kenwyne Jones	
2009/10	Darren Bent	24

NO TROUBLE FOR BRIDGES

The £5million Leeds paid to Sunderland to sign Michael Bridges remains the biggest transfer fee ever received by the Wearsiders. The forward had scored 16 goals in 79 league appearances for the Black Cats when Leeds, then a high-flying Premier League club, moved to sign him in July 1999. Bridges netted 19 top-flight goals in his first season at Elland Road as the Whites finished third and reached the semi-finals of the UEFA Cup.

GOALLESS STALEMATE

Sunderland made an uninspiring start to life in the Premier League in August 1996, as their first game in the competition ended goalless. The Black Cats took on Leicester, who had also been promoted the season before, at Roker Park, but neither of the top-flight new-boys could find a breakthrough.

EUROPEAN TOUR

The Black Cats made it into the second round of the European Cup Winners' Cup in 1973/74, having qualified via their FA Cup success. They played Vasas SC of Hungary in the first round, winning 2–0 at home and 1–0 in the away leg, to land a tricky test against Sporting Lisbon. The Portuguese side proved too strong and they claimed a 3–2 aggregate win, despite Sunderland securing a 2–1 success at Roker Park. It remains the Wearsiders' only taste of European competition.

← Republic of Ireland international defender Charlie Hurley holds a number of Sunderland records and was named as Player of the Century by fans during the club's centenary celebrations in 1979.

HURLEY IS THE KING

Charlie Hurley is widely regarded as the best player ever to turn out for the club. The classy defender recovered from a 7–0 defeat to Blackpool on his debut to spend 12 seasons on Wearside, making 401 appearances in all competitions and scoring 26 goals. Hurley missed out on the Footballer of the Year award to Bobby Moore in 1964. He is Sunderland's most capped player, with 38 of his 40 caps for the Republic of Ireland having come during his time at Roker Park.

Tottenham Hotspur

Spurs have an illustrious history. They were the first club in the 20th Century to achieve a league and cup double and were also the first English club to taste success in Europe when they lifted the Cup Winners' Cup in 1963. They have won the UEFA Cup twice, the League Cup four times and the FA Cup on eight occasions.

ROUGH DIAMONDS

Tottenham legends Glenn Hoddle and Chris Waddle released a single called 'Diamond Lights' in April 1987. The song reached number 12 in the charts, with the pair performing the track on *Top of the Pops*. Hoddle left White Hart Lane for Monaco at the end of the 1986/87 season, although it's not thought that the embarrassment of his short music career had anything to do with him leaving the country!

←-- Glenn Hoddle was probably ranked higher than 12 in the England football charts when 'Diamond Lights' peaked.

EURO FIRST FOR SPURS

Spurs became the first English side to lift a European trophy when they crushed Atletico Madrid 5–1 in the European Cup Winners' Cup final of 1963. Jimmy Greaves and Terry Dyson both scored twice against the Spaniards, with John White completing the victory. The win went some way to erasing the memory of the previous season's European Cup campaign, which had ended in semi-final disappointment.

DOUBLE DELIGHT

The Londoners were the first double winners of the 20th Century in 1961. Tottenham scored 115 goals on their way to the top-flight title, finishing eight points ahead of Sheffield Wednesday. They then claimed a 2–0 win against Leicester in the FA Cup final at Wembley to complete a memorable campaign. Captain Danny Blanchflower landed the Player of the Year award for the second time. Spurs then repeated their FA Cup win by triumphing again in 1962.

SPURS' MAJOR HONOURS

Top flight
Winners   1950/51, 1960/61
Runners-up 1921/22, 1951/52, 1956/57, 1962/63

Second tier
Winners   1919/20, 1949/50
Runners-up 1908/09, 1932/33

FA Cup
Winners   1900/01, 1920/21, 1960/61, 1961/62, 1966/67, 1980/81, 1981/82, 1990/91

League Cup
Winners   1970/71, 1972/73, 1998/99, 2007/08

European Cup Winners' Cup
Winners   1962/63

UEFA Cup
Winners   1971/72, 1983/84

←-- Bobby Smith (left) and Maurice Norman chair captain Danny Blanchflower after Tottenham had beaten Burnley in the 1962 FA Cup final.

GREAVES IS THE GREATEST

Jimmy Greaves is widely regarded as one of the greatest goalscorers of all time, with an incredible 220 league goals in 321 appearances from a nine-year stay at Tottenham between 1961 and 1970. He also holds the distinction of having scored the most league goals in a single season for Spurs – 37 as the club lifted the title in 1962/63. His record in cup competitions was also amazing, with the striker netting 32 goals in 36 FA Cup games, five in eight League Cup matches and nine goals in 14 games on the European stage.

KLINSMANN DIVES IN

Jurgen Klinsmann made a huge impact in his one full season at White Hart Lane in 1994/95. The German striker scored 20 Premier League goals and 29 overall as Spurs finished seventh and reached the semi-finals of the FA Cup. Klinsmann returned to the club in December 1997 to aid their successful battle against relegation and scored nine times before the end of the campaign, including four goals in a 6–2 win at Wimbledon.

⇢ *Jurgen Klinsmann's first goal for Spurs, at Sheffield Wednesday in 1994, was followed by a dive on the Hillsborough turf. It has become one of the most copied goal celebrations.*

SPURS' LEADING GOALSCORERS

Jimmy Greaves	266
Bobby Smith	208
Martin Chivers	174
Cliff Jones	159
George Hunt	138

ARGIE BARGY

Tottenham pulled off a transfer coup in 1978 when they signed two of Argentina's World Cup-winning squad. Ossie Ardiles and Ricky Villa arrived at White Hart Lane fresh from starring at the finals in their home country. Villa scored 25 goals in 179 appearances but is best remembered for a stunning solo effort against Manchester City in the replay of the 1981 FA Cup final. He left in 1983, but Ardiles stayed on to add a UEFA Cup winners' medal to his collection a year later. He also netted 25 goals but played 311 games.

⌐ *Manager Keith Burkinshaw is flanked by Ricky Villa (left) and Ossie Ardiles, who had just starred in Argentina's 1978 World Cup win.*

TOP OF THE BILL

Bill Nicholson both played for and managed Tottenham during their golden era. Having made over 300 appearances for the club, winning two titles, he became manager in October 1958 and enjoyed a hugely successful 16-year spell in charge. Nicholson led Spurs to the double in 1961 and won the FA Cup again in 1962. The Londoners claimed the European Cup Winners' Cup in 1963, the FA Cup again in 1967, the League Cup in 1971 and 1973 and the UEFA Cup in 1972. Nicholson scored after just 19 seconds of his only England appearance.

⌐ *Bill Nicholson (second left) with (left–right) Frank Saul, Joe Kinnear, Terry Venables and Pat Jennings before the 1967 FA Cup final.*

UP FOUR THE CUP

Spurs won the League Cup for the fourth time in 2008, beating London rivals Chelsea 2–1 after extra-time. Didier Drogba had put the Blues ahead in the first half, but a Dimitar Berbatov penalty made it 1–1 and a 94th-minute header from Jonathan Woodgate snatched victory. Tottenham were also winners of the competition in 1971, 1973 and 1999, while they finished runners-up in 1982, 2002 and most recently 2009, when they lost on penalties to Manchester United.

Tottenham Hotspur

GUNNERS SHOT DOWN

Mark Falco and Chris Hughton both scored twice when Tottenham equalled their biggest victory against arch-rivals Arsenal in April 1983. Spurs first claimed a 5–0 win on Christmas Day 1911, and 72 years later they matched that success. More recently, there were five different goalscorers when a young Gunners side were beaten 5–1 in the Carling Cup at White Hart Lane in January 2008.

ARSENAL BEATEN... AT LAST!

Spurs got the better of north London rivals Arsenal in the Premier League for the first time in 11 years in 2009/10. Youngster Danny Rose scored a spectacular 30-yard volley early on and Gareth Bale added a second just after half-time to help Harry Redknapp's side claim a 2–1 victory. Steffen Iversen and Tim Sherwood were the last players to earn Tottenham victory over the Gunners in November 1999 when they both scored in another 2–1 win.

A UEFA FIRST

The north London club were the first winners of the UEFA Cup in 1972. That year saw an all-English final, with Spurs claiming a 3–2 aggregate victory over Wolves. The first leg at Molineux finished 2–1 to the visitors, with Martin Chivers scoring a stunning late winner. A 1–1 draw in the second leg at White Hart Lane was enough to secure the trophy. Tottenham won the same competition for the second time in 1984, beating Anderlecht of Belgium 4–3 on penalties after both legs had finished 1–1.

← Danny Rose (right) scored a spectacular volley in the 2–1 victory over Arsenal that was voted Goal of the Season in a poll in May 2010.

↑ Happy captain Alan Mullery waves to Tottenham fans after the team had beaten Wolves 3–2 on aggregate to win the UEFA Cup in 1972.

BILL'S FLYING START

October 11 1958 was an unforgettable afternoon for Spurs as it marked both the start of legendary manager Bill Nicholson's reign and Tottenham's highest-scoring league match. Nicholson's spell as manager could not have begun better – his new side claiming an incredible 10–4 win against Everton at White Hart Lane. The Londoners were leading 6–1 at the break, with Bobby Smith going on to score four goals and Alfie Stokes helping himself to a brace. Nicholson led the club from 1958 to 1974 and is widely regarded as Spurs' greatest boss.

↑ *Paul Gascoigne's 1991 FA Cup final – the last game of his Tottenham career – was over after less than 20 minutes. Spurs went on to beat Nottingham Forest 2–1.*

THE GREAT EIGHT

The club have won the FA Cup on eight occasions, with their most recent success coming back in 1991. That final is best remembered for Paul Gascoigne's reckless challenge on Gary Charles that saw the Tottenham playmaker come off worst. Gascoigne left the field with a serious knee injury. In his absence, Gary Lineker had a penalty saved by Mark Crossley with Forest 1–0 up, but Paul Stewart equalised to force extra time. An own goal from Des Walker eventually handed Tottenham the cup. The Londoners were a non-league club when they won the trophy for the first time in 1901, while their other wins came in 1921, 1961, 1962, 1967, 1981 and 1982.

DEFOE'S TON TARGET

Jermain Defoe ended the 2009/10 season just eight goals short of a century for the club in all competitions. The England striker, who scored 18 top-flight goals that term, reached that total in 230 games over two spells. Defoe first arrived at White Hart Lane from West Ham in a £7million switch in February 2004, but he was sold to Portsmouth four years later. He returned in a £15million deal in January 2009, following Harry Redknapp back to Spurs from Pompey.

ON CLOUD NINE

Tottenham's biggest margin of victory came in a second-tier clash with Bristol Rovers in 1977 when they claimed a 9–0 win at White Hart Lane. Colin Lee scored four goals on his debut, having signed from Torquay for £60,000, with Ian Moores netting a hat-trick. Glenn Hoddle and Peter Taylor completed the rout. Spurs went close to matching that feat when they beat Wigan 9–1 in 2009/10.

A RECORD RUN

Steve Perryman is Spurs' record appearance holder, having featured in 854 games for the club between 1969 and 1986. Defender Perryman also holds the distinction of having won more medals than any other Tottenham player. He lifted two League Cups, two FA Cups and two UEFA Cups in his 17-year stay at White Hart Lane and also scooped the Football Writers' Player of the Year award in 1982.

↑ *Steve Perryman made his Spurs debut at the age of 17 and, as a 20-year-old, became the youngest player in modern times to be appointed club captain.*

SPURS APPEARANCES

Steve Perryman	854
Gary Mabbutt	611
Pat Jennings	590
Cyril Knowles	506
Glenn Hoddle	490
Ted Ditchburn	452
Alan Gilzean	439
Jimmy Dimmock	438
Phil Beal	420
Maurice Norman	411

WHITES EARN EURO SPURS

Tottenham secured their highest Premier League finish in 2009/10 and with it qualified for the Champions League for the first time. England striker Peter Crouch scored the most important goal in the club's recent history in the 1–0 win against Manchester City at Eastlands in May to ensure that Spurs could not be caught in the race for fourth place.

←··· *Peter Crouch heads home the goal that gave Spurs a Barclays Premier League fourth-place finish and a spot in the qualifying rounds of the UEFA Champions League for 2010/11.*

West Ham United

West Ham have been members of the Premier League for all but three seasons since the competition began in 1992. They have never won the top-flight title, but they have lifted the FA Cup on three occasions. The Hammers also claimed the now defunct European Cup Winners' Cup back in 1965.

ALAN SEALS CUP WIN

Alan Sealey scored twice as the east Londoners beat 1860 Munich to lift the European Cup Winners' Cup in 1965. The Hammers beat Belgian side Gent, Sparta Prague of the Czech Republic, Swiss team Lausanne and Spanish club Real Zaragoza to reach the final at Wembley. They were runners-up in the same competition in 1976, losing 4–2 to Anderlecht in Belgium after Pat Holland had put John Lyall's men in front.

⤑ *Alan Sealey (left) and Bobby Moore, with happy West Ham team-mates, run around Wembley with the European Cup Winners' Cup in 1965. Bobby Moore was a cup-winning captain at Wembley three years in a row – 1964 (FA Cup), 1965 and 1966 (World Cup).*

HAMMERS ARE HIT

Manchester United and Blackburn have both inflicted 7–1 defeats on West Ham during the Premier League years – the club's heaviest losses. Midfielder Paul Scholes scored a hat-trick for United as they cruised to victory at Old Trafford in April 2000 on their way to the title. But there were seven different scorers when Rovers achieved the same feat in October 2001, with Grant McCann putting through his own net. Michael Carrick was the Hammers' goalscorer.

WORLD CUP WONDERS

West Ham had three players in England's World Cup-winning squad of 1966 – and the trio played a major part in claiming the trophy. Defensive rock Bobby Moore captained the side and midfielder Martin Peters was on target in the final, but it was striker Geoff Hurst who stole the headlines. Having scored the only goal against Argentina in the quarter-final, Hurst netted a hat-trick in the final as England beat West Germany 4–2 after extra time.

HAMMER TIME FOR ENGLAND

There were seven players with an affiliation to West Ham on the pitch at the same time during the second half of England's friendly clash with Holland in August 2009. Current goalkeeper Robert Green and former Hammers trio Rio Ferdinand, Glen Johnson and Frank Lampard all played the full 90 minutes, while Michael Carrick, Jermain Defoe and Joe Cole came on as substitutes. Six of those players had come through the Hammers' Academy set-up, although Defoe arrived from Charlton at the age of 14.

↓ *West Ham fans like to say that their team won the World Cup in 1966.(Left to right) Bobby Moore captained England to glory in the final, Martin Peters scored the second goal and Geoff Hurst got the other three.*

TEVEZ TIMES HIS RUN

Carlos Tevez wrote his name into West Ham folklore in season 2006/07 when his goals helped the club to survive relegation. The Argentina international opened his Hammers account in a 4–3 defeat at home to Tottenham on March 4 2007, starting a spree of seven goals in 10 games. Tevez was on target against Manchester United at Old Trafford on the final day of the campaign to secure a shock 1–0 win that guaranteed the club's top-flight status.

ZAMORA THE SCORER

Bobby Zamora scored the only goal of the 2005 Play-Off Final as West Ham claimed a 1–0 win against Preston at Cardiff's Millennium Stadium to book a return to the Premier League. There had been heartbreak for the Hammers on the same stage a year earlier when London rivals Crystal Palace edged a close contest 1–0, with Neil Shipperley on target. West Ham beat Ipswich in the semi-finals on both occasions.

RECORD-BREAKING RIO

Rio Ferdinand created a British transfer record when he left West Ham for Leeds in an £18million switch in November 2000. The England skipper came through the ranks at Upton Park, making his debut as a substitute on the last day of the 1995/96 season. The central defender played 127 league games for the Hammers and scored two goals. Ferdinand, who now plays for Manchester United, no longer holds the British transfer record, although the fee remains the biggest ever received by the east Londoners.

↑ *Rio Ferdinand mde his West Ham debut aged 17. He was only 22 when Leeds broke the British transfer record to sign him.*

HOW DID THEY MANAGE THAT?

Avram Grant is the 13th manager in West Ham's history. Syd King, the club's first and longest-serving boss, was in charge for over 30 years, while Charlie Paynter spent 18 years at the helm and John Lyall 15. Ted Fenton and Ron Greenwood were also in the Upton Park hot-seat for long spells. Scot Lou Macari became the Hammers' first non-English manager in 1989, while Italian Gianfranco Zola, who departed at the end of 2009/10, was the club's first overseas manager.

WEST HAM MANAGERS

Syd King	1901–1932
Charlie Paynter	1932–1950
Ted Fenton	1950–1961
Ron Greenwood	1961–1974
John Lyall	1974–1989
Lou Macari	1989–1990
Billy Bonds	1990–1994
Harry Redknapp	1994–2001
Glenn Roeder	2001–2003
Alan Pardew	2003–2006
Alan Curbishley	2006–2008
Gianfranco Zola	2008–2010
Avram Grant	2010–Present

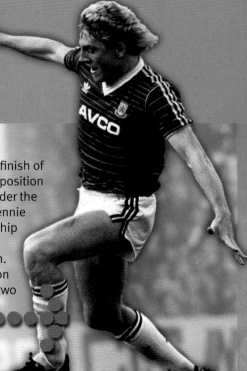

←--- *Tony Cottee scored almost 150 goals in his two spells at West Ham in the 1980s and 1990s, including 116 in 280 league matches. He also played seven times for England and was the PFA Young Player of the Year in 1986.*

ON THE UP

The club achieved their highest Premier League finish of fifth in 1998/99, but their best overall top-flight position came in the 1985/86 campaign. West Ham – under the management of John Lyall and with Frank McAvennie and Tony Cottee forging a superb strike partnership – finished third, but they were in with a chance of the title going into the last week of the season. Liverpool were the eventual winners, with Everton two points behind and the Londoners a further two adrift on 84.

····➤ *Frank McAvennie enjoyed his most productive season in 1985/86, helping West Ham to within four points of what would have been a first top-flight title.*

West Ham United

BILLY MAKES BONDS

Billy Bonds is West Ham's record appearance holder, having played for the club almost 800 times in all competitions between 1967 and 1988. He featured in 663 league games during his 21-year stay at Upton Park, captaining the side to two FA Cup final victories. Bonds, who started his career at right-back then switched to midfield before ending up in the centre of defence, enjoyed two promotions in four seasons as manager of the Hammers in the early 1990s.

←·· Billy Bonds had played more than 100 times for Charlton before he joined West Ham as a 20-year-old and then appeared in almost 800 matches for the Hammers over the next 21 years.

WEST HAM APPEARANCES*

Billy Bonds	793
Frank Lampard Snr	674
Bobby Moore	646
Trevor Brooking	635
Alvin Martin	600
Jimmy Ruffell	548
Steve Potts	505
Vic Watson	505
Geoff Hurst	502
Jim Barrett	467

* Excludes war-time matches

THE BOLEYN GROUND

The Hammers' home is commonly known as Upton Park, but that is only the area of east London where their stadium is situated. West Ham actually play their home games at the Boleyn Ground, and have done since 1904. When they were known as Thames Ironworks, the club played at Hermit Road in Canning Town. They briefly played at Browning Road in East Ham before moving to the Memorial Grounds in Plaistow in 1897. They moved to the Boleyn Ground four years after they had become West Ham United.

TON UP

The 1957/58 promotion-winning campaign saw West Ham break the 100-goal barrier, setting a club record for the most scored in a single season. Ted Fenton was in charge as the Hammers found the net 101 times to finish the season at the top of the second tier with 57 points, one ahead of second-place Blackburn. The Londoners recorded an 8–0 victory against Rotherham that term, with John Dick scoring four times.

CULT HERO DI CANIO

Paolo Di Canio was a fans' favourite during his time at the club. The Italian joined West Ham from Sheffield Wednesday for £1.7million in January 1999, scoring 46 goals in 118 league appearances, one of which is considered to be among the best goals in Premier League history – a stunning volley from a tight angle against Wimbledon. Di Canio also won the FIFA Fair Play Award in 2001 for an act of sportsmanship at Everton. He was presented with a clear sight of goal when goalkeeper Paul Gerrard was lying injured on the ground having twisted his knee attempting to clear, but Di Canio caught the ball instead and stopped play to allow the shot-stopper to get treatment.

←·· Paolo Di Canio celebrates a match-winner against Fulham at Craven Cottage in 2002. The Italian arrived at Upton Park with a passionate reputation and he stayed at West Ham for four years.

THE TWO FRANKIES

Two generations of the Lampard family have played for the London club, with Frank Snr turning out between 1967 and 1985 and his son, Frank Jnr, making his name at Upton Park from 1995 until 2001. Frank Snr won two FA Cups with the club, in 1975 and 1980, and was also part of the promotion-winning team of 1981. He is second only to Billy Bonds in the list of record appearance makers. Frank Jnr, who now plays for Chelsea, helped West Ham to their highest Premier League finish in 1998/99.

⬅---➡ Between them, the two Frank Lampards made more than 850 appearances for West Ham. Frank Senior (left) is second on the all-time list with nearly 700, while Frank Junior played more than 170 times before joining Chelsea in 2001.

ILAN'S LATE SHOW

West Ham narrowly avoided equalling the club record of seven successive defeats in 2009/10. It took an 87th-minute diving header from substitute Ilan to rescue a point in a 2–2 draw at Everton in April, which means the sequence set in 1967 still stands. The run had started with a 3–0 defeat at Manchester United, with the sixth straight loss coming at home to Stoke.

NO CAPITAL GAIN

West Ham failed to win a game against any of their London rivals in the Barclays Premier League in season 2009/10. They were beaten home and away by Tottenham and drew home games with Chelsea, Arsenal and Fulham but lost away on each occasion. An injury-time strike from Junior Stanislas rescued a point against the Cottagers in a 2–2 draw at Upton Park in October 2009, while it took two late goals from Carlton Cole and Alessandro Diamanti to snatch the same scoreline in the home clash with Arsenal.

WATSON BAGS A HATFUL

Vic Watson is West Ham's all-time top scorer. He netted 298 times in the league and 326 in total in a 15-year spell with the club between 1920 and 1935. Watson also scored 13 hat-tricks and once bagged six in one game in February 1929 against Leeds. Geoff Hurst equalled that feat in October 1968 against Sunderland in an 8–0 win.

---➡ Trevor Brooking acknowledges the crowd after his goal decided the 1980 FA Cup final. Two of West Ham's three FA Cup final wins have been in London derbies.

TRIPLE WHAMMY FOR HAMMERS

The club have won the FA Cup on three occasions, with their last success coming in 1980. The Hammers' first triumph in the competition came in 1964, when a last-gasp goal from Ron Boyce snatched a 3–2 win against Preston. Alan Taylor scored twice as Fulham were beaten 2–0 in the 1975 final, while Trevor Brooking was practically on the floor when he headed the only goal of the game against Arsenal in 1980.

Wigan Athletic

Wigan reached the top flight for the first time in 2005 and have now established themselves in the Barclays Premier League. They have won the Football League Trophy twice, but the nearest they have come to claiming a major domestic trophy was in 2006 when they were beaten finalists in the Carling Cup.

WIGAN'S HONOURS

Second tier
Runners-up   2004/05

Third tier
Champions   2002/03

Fourth tier
Champions   1996/97
Promoted (third) 1981/82

Football League Trophy
Winners   1984/85, 1998/99

League Cup
Runners-up   2005/06

A TOP FINISH

Wigan achieved their best top-flight finish in their debut season back in 2005/06. The Lancashire club's first Premier League game ended in a last-gasp 1–0 defeat at home to Chelsea but, after losing by the same scoreline at Charlton, the Latics embarked on an impressive run of nine games without defeat – eight of those victories – to climb to second in the table. Paul Jewell's side were unable to sustain that impressive form, but they still ended the season in 10th place.

LEAGUE CUP LATICS

Wigan made it to their first major domestic final in 2006 when they played Manchester United in the Carling Cup at the Millennium Stadium. Jason Roberts had scored with only a few seconds remaining in extra time of the semi-final second-leg clash against Arsenal at Highbury to secure a win on away goals. That earned the Latics their Cardiff date but, unfortunately for Paul Jewell's side, they were beaten 4–0 by a Wayne Rooney-inspired United.

⤑ Jason Roberts (right) scored in the opening minute of his Wigan debut, in a Lancashire derby against Preston, and quickly formed a dangerous partnership with Nathan Ellington (left).

DEADLY DUO

Nathan Ellington and Jason Roberts formed a superb strike partnership in the club's promotion-winning team of 2004/05. The Latics scored 79 league goals that term, with the pair contributing 45 of them. Ellington netted 24 times, with Roberts scoring 21 as the duo finished first and second in the scoring charts.

↑ Roberto Martinez (left) and Isidro Diaz (right), along with Jesus Seba, brought Spanish flair to Springfield Park in 1995. Two seasons later, they were celebrating promotion.

THE THREE AMIGOS

The 'Three Amigos' arrived at Wigan amid a wave of publicity in the summer of 1995. Spanish trio Roberto Martinez, Isidro Diaz and Jesus Seba were signed from Balaguer and Zaragoza by chairman Dave Whelan when the club were playing in the fourth tier. Playmaker Martinez made the biggest impact, completing 187 league appearances and scoring 17 goals for the Latics. He is now the manager of the club.

N'ZOGBIA SCOOPS AWARD

Charles N'Zogbia won the club's Player of the Year award at the end of his first full season at the DW Stadium. The winger became the Latics' record signing when he made a £6million switch from Newcastle in February 2009, with Ryan Taylor moving the other way. N'Zogbia, whose first goal for the club was a superb solo effort in a 2–1 win at Sunderland in March 2009, netted a stunning curling winner against Arsenal in April 2010 to complete an amazing comeback which effectively secured the club's top-tier status.

····> *Wigan's record signing, Charles N'Zogbia contributed five league goals from midfield to help Wigan retain their top-flight status in 2010.*

↓ *When Graeme Jones scored 31 goals for Wigan in 1996/97, he was playing in the bottom tier. Eight seasons later, the Latics were promoted to the Barclays Premier League.*

JEWELL IN THE CROWN

Paul Jewell masterminded a meteoric rise that saw Wigan move from the third tier to the Barclays Premier League within four seasons. They reached the second tier for the first time in emphatic fashion by winning the title with 100 points – their biggest-ever haul. The Latics narrowly missed out on the play-offs the following term, before they finished second to Sunderland in 2004/05 to secure automatic promotion and a place in the top flight for the first time in their history.

† *Paul Jewell makes a point during Wigan's December 2006 match against West Ham at Upton Park. The Latics just avoided relegation at the end of the season, after which Jewell resigned.*

KEEPING UP WITH THE JONESES

Assistant manager Graeme Jones was a goalscoring legend for the club between 1996 and 1999. Jones established the Latics record for the most goals in a single season when he netted 31 times in the promotion-winning campaign of 1996/97. He scored four hat-tricks during that term, including two in consecutive games against Leyton Orient and Darlington.

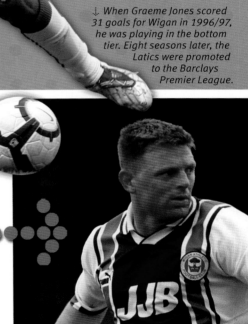

DOUBLE TROPHY JOY

The Latics have won the Football League Trophy on two occasions. Their first success came in 1985 when goals from Mike Newell, Tony Kelly and David Lowe secured a 3–1 win against Brentford, and they won it again in 1999 in dramatic fashion. Midfielder Paul Rogers scored the only goal of the final against Millwall in the dying seconds.

A LEAGUE OF THEIR OWN

The Lancashire outfit are the youngest club in the top division, having formed in 1932. The Latics were elected to the fourth tier of The Football League in 1978 thanks to a slice of good fortune. They had finished second to Boston United in the Northern Premier League, but the champions' ground did not meet the required criteria for a Football League club and so Wigan went up instead.

Wigan Athletic

THE DW STADIUM

The Lancashire club moved to the DW Stadium – or the JJB Stadium as it was first known – in time for the start of the 1999/2000 campaign. The Latics share the 25,133-capacity ground with the town's rugby league team, Wigan Warriors. Simon Haworth scored the first league goal at the stadium, going on to grab a brace in a 3–0 win against Scunthorpe. Prior to their move, Wigan had played their home games at Springfield Park for 67 years.

←·· Record goalscorer Andy Liddell (centre) is congratulated by Nicky Eaden (left) and Jimmy Bullard after scoring Wigan's second equaliser in a 2–2 home draw with Nottingham Forest.

LONG-SERVING LIDDELL

Andy Liddell scored a club-record 70 league goals for Wigan between 1998 and 2004. Liddell joined the Latics from Barnsley in a £350,000 switch in October 1998 and went on to score 10 goals in his first season. He was Wigan's top scorer in the 2001/02 campaign, netting two hat-tricks against Brighton and Cambridge on his way to an 18-goal haul. He was the club's longest-serving player when he left for Sheffield United in 2004.

↓· Kevin Langley scored 12 goals in his 317 appearances for Wigan in their early years in The Football League. He returned to the club as a coach in the Centre of Excellence.

WIGAN'S TOP SCORERS SINCE 2001

2001/02	Andy Liddell	18
2002/03	Andy Liddell	16
2003/04	Nathan Ellington	18
2004/05	Nathan Ellington	24
2005/06	Henri Camara	12
2006/07	Emile Heskey	8
2007/08	Marcus Bent	7
2008/09	Amr Zaki	10
2009/10	Hugo Rodallega	10

A LANG TIME COMING

Kevin Langley made 317 league appearances in two spells with Wigan – a club record. Midfielder Langley was 17 when he made his debut in September 1981, and he went on to feature 160 times before moving to Everton five years later. He returned to Springfield Park from Birmingham in 1990 for another four-year stay, adding another 157 appearances.

CAP FITS FOR HESKEY

Emile Heskey became the first full-time Wigan player to represent England when he started the European Championship qualifier against Israel on September 8 2007. The striker failed to get on the scoresheet, but England were 3–0 winners at Wembley. Goalkeeper Chris Kirkland had earned his first cap in a friendly against Greece while with the Latics in August 2006, but he was only on loan from Liverpool at the time.

LAST EIGHT FOR LATICS

Wigan's best run in the FA Cup saw them reach the sixth round in 1986/87. The Latics, who were playing in the third tier at the time, claimed a 3–1 win against Lincoln in the first round and then scored five without reply at Darlington. A 2–1 victory against Gillingham got them into the fourth round, where they knocked out Norwich, who finished fifth in the top flight that season. Second-tier Hull were brushed aside 3–0 to secure a quarter-final clash with Leeds, before the Latics were eventually beaten 2–0 at Springfield Park.

VALENCIA WINGS IT

Antonio Valencia cost Manchester United in the region of £16million when he left the DW Stadium in June 2009 – a record transfer fee received by the Latics. The Ecuador winger had been snapped up by Paul Jewell from Spanish side Villarreal in 2006, initially on loan, before penning a full-time deal in January 2008 when Steve Bruce was in charge. Valencia scored seven goals in 84 league games for Wigan before moving to Old Trafford.

⤑ *Antonio Valencia spent 18 months on loan at Wigan before a permanent deal was done. A year and a half later, he was sold for £16million.*

SPOT THE DIFFERENCE

Wigan are the only side in Premier League history to have conceded more than 74 goals in a season and still avoided relegation. The Latics' goal was breached a total of 79 times in 2009/10, with 24 of those coming at the DW Stadium, compared to 55 on their travels. Roberto Martinez's side ended the campaign with a goal difference of -42, which was the worst in the top flight. There wasn't much in it, though, with relegated duo Hull and Burnley ending the season on -41 and -40 respectively.

⤓ *A rare happy moment for Wigan in the capital as Hugo Rodallega (left) celebrates with Mohamed Diame after scoring the equaliser against West Ham in April 2010, but the Hammers went on to net a 77th-minute winner.*

⤒ *Roberto Martinez's reputation is for producing teams playing open football. Wigan set a new record in 2009/10 when they conceded the most goals by a team avoiding relegation.*

LOSING STREAK

A 1–0 home loss to Arsenal in 2006/07 led to the club's worst league run of eight straight defeats in a row. Having been beaten by the Gunners, the Latics also went down to Chelsea, twice (3–2 and 4–0), and they were also second best against Manchester United (3–1), Everton (0–2), Sheffield United (1–0), Blackburn (3–0) and Reading (3–2). They finally secured a long-overdue win on February 3 2007 when Lee McCulloch scored the only goal of the game against Portsmouth.

LONDON MAULING

Wigan's recent record playing against sides from London makes miserable reading, with the club having conceded 26 goals in five matches and failed to take a single point from their visits to the capital in 2009/10! Tottenham and Chelsea scored 17 between them, with Spurs winning 9–1 in November and the Blues 8–0 on the last day of the season. Defender Thomas Vermaelen bagged two for Arsenal as they claimed a 4–0 victory in September, with Fulham enjoying a 2–1 win and West Ham securing a 3–2 success in the closing weeks of the campaign.

Wolverhampton Wanderers

Wolves were one of the leading names in English football during the 1950s and early 1960s, making back-page headlines both domestically and in Europe. They have been top-flight champions three times, have won the FA Cup on four occasions and were League Cup winners in 1974 and 1980.

BADGE OF HONOUR

Wanderers have used their current club badge since 1979. The first crest worn on the famous gold and black shirts was Wolverhampton's coat of arms, which was then changed in the late 1960s to a single leaping wolf. The badge was redesigned again in the 1970s, this time to show three leaping wolves, until the current crest was introduced. The city's coat of arms made a brief return between 1993 and 1996.

A RUN TO REMEMBER

Wolves set a club record when they went 21 league matches unbeaten in 2005. The run started on January 15 with a 4–2 win at home to West Ham. Kenny Miller scored twice in that game, with Paul Ince and Carl Cort also on target. Wanderers didn't lose any of their remaining 18 games that term, and their streak continued into the 2005/06 campaign. They managed three more league matches before they were finally beaten 2–0 by Leeds at Elland Road on August 20.

WOLVES' MAJOR HONOURS

Top flight
Champions   1953/54, 1957/58, 1958/59

Second tier
Champions   1931/32, 1976/77, 2008/09

Third tier
Champions   1923/24 (North), 1988/89

Fourth tier
Champions   1987/88

FA Cup
Winners   1892/93, 1907/08, 1948/49, 1959/60

League Cup
Winners   1973/74, 1979/80

Football League Trophy
Winners   1987/88

SYLVAN HAS GOLDEN TOUCH

Sylvan Ebanks-Blake enjoyed a season to remember in 2008/09, claiming the second tier's Golden Boot for the second year running to help the club into the Barclays Premier League. The striker finished the campaign with 25 league goals – two better than the previous term – and he was named the Championship Player of the Year. He also scored his first professional hat-trick in a 3–3 draw against Norwich at Molineux.

↑ Sylvan Ebanks-Blake was released by Manchester United without playing a Premier League game for them, but he has found great success with Wolves.

STEVE IS UNBEATA-BULL

There was no shortage of goals at Wolves when Steve Bull was around. The prolific striker holds the record as the club's all-time top goalscorer, having netted 306 times in all competitions and scored 250 in the league between 1986 and 1999. Bull scored an incredible 52 times in season 1987/88 – a club record for the most goals in a single campaign – and he also grabbed 18 hat-tricks for Wanderers.

← Steve Bull, the last third-tier player to earn a full England cap, acknowledges the Wolves fans after his testimonial against Brazil's Santos in August 1997.

↑ Billy Wright receives the FA Cup from Princess Elizabeth after Wolves defeated Leicester City 3–1 in the 1949 final.

CAPTAIN BILLY

Billy Wright captained Wolves and England with distinction. The defender, who was never booked or sent off, won three top-flight titles with Wanderers in 1954, 1958 and 1959 and the FA Cup in 1949. He also skippered England in three World Cup finals on the way to making a total of 105 appearances for his country. He was the first player in the world to win a century of international caps. Wright captained England a record 90 times and played in 70 consecutive internationals. There is a bronze statue of him outside Wolves' Molineux ground and also a stand named in his honour.

WOLVES ARE SAVAGED

The club made the worst possible start to life in the Barclays Premier League when they were beaten 5–1 by Blackburn on the opening day of the 2003/04 campaign. Wanderers were already losing 3–0 when Steffen Iversen pulled a goal back, but two late strikes from Andrew Cole ensured that Rovers got their campaign off to a flying start. Dave Jones' side went on to suffer relegation that season.

GOAL DROUGHT

Wolves scored the fewest goals of any team in the Barclays Premier League in 2009/10. Mick McCarthy's side finished eight points above the relegation zone, but they managed to hit the net just 32 times. Wanderers scored more away from home, hitting 19 league goals on their travels compared to just 13 at Molineux. They recorded more than two goals in a game just once during the last campaign – a 3–1 win at West Ham in March. Their total was not a club record, though. They were relegated from the top flight having scored just 27 goals in the 1983/84 campaign.

HONVED HEROES

Newspaper headlines hailed Wolves as the best team in the world when they restored some national pride with a 3–2 win over Budapest Honved on December 13 1954. England had been thumped 6–3 by Hungary at Wembley in 1953 and 7–1 in Budapest a year later, and seven of those Hungarian players, including striker Ferenc Puskas, were in the Honved line-up. Wanderers found themselves 2–0 down in the early stages, with Sandor Kocsis and Ferenc Machos scoring for the visitors. But Wolves hit back in the second half, with Johnny Hancocks pulling a goal back from the penalty spot and Roy Swinbourne scoring twice in as many minutes to snatch a famous victory.

⟵ Mick McCarthy organised his Wolves side expertly in 2009/10. They may have scored only 32 Barclays Premier League goals, but they conceded few enough to avoid relegation.

⟵ Steffen Iversen was signed by Wolves in 2003 to get goals, but he played in only 16 Premier League matches and scored just four times.

WANDERERS COMPLETE THE SET

When Wolves were crowned fourth-tier champions in 1987/88 they became the first club to have won all four professional leagues in English football. Their first success came in the third tier in 1923/24, while they scooped the second-tier title for the first time in 1931/32. The top-flight championship followed in 1953/54, and they completed the set 34 years later by claiming the fourth-tier title. The feat has since been matched by Burnley in 1992 and Preston in 1996.

Wolverhampton Wanderers

DROUGHT AT MOLINEUX

Mick McCarthy's side managed just five home league wins during the 2009/10 season – the joint lowest total in the top flight. They secured a first Molineux victory since returning to the division at their third attempt – a 2–1 win against Fulham – but then had to wait until December for another home success, this time against Bolton. Relegated Portsmouth shared their unwanted record.

CUP OF PLENTY

Wolves have been FA Cup winners on four occasions, although they last lifted the trophy back in 1960. Captain Harry Allen scored the only goal of the game against Everton in 1893, while a second-tier Wanderers side stunned high-flying Newcastle 3–1 in 1908. Jesse Pye bagged a brace in a 3–1 success against Leicester in 1949 and a Norman Deeley double helped the midlands club to a 3–0 win against Blackburn 11 years later.

TONS OF GOALS

Wolves became the first team to score more than 100 goals in three consecutive league seasons in the late 1950s. They hit the net 103 times in the title-winning campaign of 1957/58 and managed 110 the following season as they again celebrated the championship, finishing six points ahead of Manchester United. Their impressive feat was confirmed in 1959/60 when they scored 106 goals – 21 more than Burnley – but they had to settle for runners-up spot.

↑ *Eddie Clamp (left) and captain Bill Slater run around Wembley with the FA Cup after Wolves had beaten Blackburn 3–0 in 1960.*

PARKIN FINE FOR WOLVES

Derek Parkin holds the club record for the most appearances, having featured 609 times in all competitions – 501 of those league games – between 1968 and 1982. Full-back Parkin, who joined the club from Huddersfield, claimed two League Cup winners' medals and a second-tier championship medal with the club before signing for Stoke in 1982.

←--- *Derek Parkin was almost an ever-present for Wolves throughout the 1970s. He was called into the full England squad once, in Malta in 1971, but didn't play.*

WOLVES' LEADING APPEARANCES

Derek Parkin	609
Kenny Hibbitt	574
Steve Bull	561
Jimmy Mullen	546
Billy Wright	541
Ron Flowers	515
John McAlle	508
Peter Broadbent	497
Geoff Palmer	495
John Richards	486

EUROPE'S BIGGEST STAGE

Wolves' back-to-back top-flight titles in the late 1950s brought with them the added bonus of European Cup football, with the club playing in the competition for two successive seasons. Wanderers received a bye in the first round of the 1958/59 competition and were then beaten 4–3 on aggregate by German side Schalke at the next stage. Their second attempt saw them get through the preliminaries before they beat Red Star Belgrade in the first round, with Bobby Mason scoring two late goals at Molineux to make it 4–1 on aggregate. Stan Cullis' side were beaten 9–2 by Barcelona over two legs in the last eight.

ALL HAIL THE DOUG

Derek Dougan netted 12 European goals during his career with Wolves to make him the club's leading scorer in continental competition. Nine of those came in the memorable run to the UEFA Cup final in 1971/72, as Dougan finished that season as the competition's top scorer. The popular striker grabbed four goals against Portuguese side Academica de Coimbra, two against Dutch outfit Den Haag and a brace in the home leg against Carl Ziess Jena. Dougan scored again when Wolves faced Italian giants Juventus in the last eight, but he failed to find the net in the semi-final success against Ferencvaros or the aggregate defeat to Tottenham in the final.

FINAL JOY

The midlands club have made it to the League Cup final on two occasions, winning both times. Kenny Hibbitt and John Richards scored the goals in 1974 as Wanderers claimed a 2–1 win against Manchester City at Wembley. European champions Nottingham Forest were beaten 1–0 in the final in 1980, with Andy Gray scoring the only goal of the game.

↑ *Andy Gray scored the only goal of the 1980 League Cup final as Wolves became the first team to beat Nottingham Forest in the competition since 1976/77.*

JODY'S ART ATTACK

Defender Jody Craddock may be best known as a vital part of Wolves' rearguard, but off the pitch he has also made quite a name for himself as an artist. The centre-back, who has made over 200 appearances for the club, has sold paintings at art shows across the country and shown his work in several top galleries. His recent work has included paintings of England stars Wayne Rooney and David Beckham, as well as Wolves club legend Steve Bull and several of his team-mates.

↑ *As well as being an accomplished painter, Jody Craddock has brushed up on the art of scoring goals (he got five in 2009/10) as well as helping to keep them out.*

PLAY-OFF JOY

Wolves reached the Premier League for the first time by beating Sheffield United 3–0 at Cardiff's Millennium Stadium in the 2003 Play-Off Final. Wanderers had finished fifth in the second tier that season and played Reading in a two-legged semi-final. Goals from Mark Kennedy, Nathan Blake and Kenny Miller cut down the Blades in the final to seal promotion.

⇢ *(Left to right) Wolves goalscorers Kenny Miller, Nathan Blake and Mark Kennedy celebrate with the second-tier play-off trophy after the 3–0 defeat of Sheffield United won them promotion in 2003.*

npower Championship Club Records

The Championship may be the second tier of English football but, according to recent statistics, it is the fourth most popular league in Europe, beating Italy's Serie A and Ligue 1 in France in terms of total attendance. The 2009/10 Championship line-up was probably the strongest ever, with Newcastle and Middlesbrough joining the likes of Nottingham Forest, Sheffield Wednesday and Derby – just five of nine teams who can attract attendances of over 30,000.

Sheffield United's Darius Henderson (left) tussles with Darren Purse of Sheffield Wednesday during the September 2009 Steel City derby at Bramall Lane.

Nottingham Forest fans in full voice at the City Ground early in the 2009/10 season.

Barnsley

Barnsley joined The Football League in 1898 and play their home games at Oakwell. The South Yorkshire club spent one season in the Premier League in the mid-1990s but have since flitted between the second and third tiers. The Tykes finished the 2009/10 season seven points and four places clear of the Championship relegation zone.

BIG GUNS BEATEN

Barnsley stole the headlines in 2008 when they stunned two of the Barclays Premier League's big guns on the way to the semi-finals of the FA Cup. Brian Howard scored the winner as they knocked Liverpool out in the fifth round with a stunning 2–1 victory at Anfield. A home tie against Chelsea followed in the quarter-finals, with a header from Kayode Odejayi enough to dump the Londoners out of the competition. Barnsley's dream died in the last four when Cardiff claimed a 1–0 win at Wembley.

BARNSLEY BOSSES SINCE DANNY WILSON

John Hendrie	1998–1999
Dave Bassett	1999–2000
Nigel Spackman	2001
Steve Parkin	2001–2002
Glyn Hodges	2002–2003
Gudjon Thordarson	2003–2004
Paul Hart	2004–2005
Andy Ritchie	2005–2006
Simon Davey	2006–2009
Mark Robins	2009–Present

⤑ *Danny Wilson failed to keep Barnsley in the Premier League in 1997/98, but his was a hard act to follow.*

ROVERS AND OUT FOR WARD

The £4.5million deal that saw Ashley Ward leave for Blackburn in December 1998 remains the record transfer fee received by Barnsley. Striker Ward had moved to Oakwell from Derby for £1.3million ahead of the club's Premier League campaign, and he ended that season with 10 goals. He scored 15 times for the Tykes in 1998/99 before making his big-money move to Ewood Park.

⤑ *Ashley Ward scored 10 goals for Barnsley in their 1997/98 Premier League season and had netted 15 in half a season before the Tykes received a record transfer fee for him.*

TOP-FLIGHT TYKES

The Tykes made it to the Premier League for the only time in their history when they were promoted at the end of 1996/97. Danny Wilson was in charge as they finished runners-up to Bolton in the second tier. Sadly, all three teams promoted that season went down the following term, with the Yorkshire club finishing 19th, ahead of Crystal Palace.

HINE HOLDS SCORING MARK

Ernie Hine is the club's record league goalscorer, having netted 123 times overall in two separate spells. Hine spent five years at Oakwell between 1921 and 1926 before leaving for Leicester, where he also became a crowd favourite. Hine rejoined the Tykes in 1934 having also played for Huddersfield and Manchester United. During his time at Leicester, he played six games for England and scored four goals.

Blackpool

The Seasiders have enjoyed an illustrious history, with some of English football's finest players having graced Bloomfield Road over the years. However, 2009/10, under the management of the charismatic Ian Holloway, was the club's best of recent times. It culminated with an appearance at Wembley and promotion to the top flight.

↑ *Blackpool's longest-serving player, Jimmy Armfield, is approaching 'National Treasure' status.*

ARMFIELD A BLACKPOOL LEGEND

Jimmy Armfield spent the whole of his 17-year career with Blackpool and holds the club record for the most appearances, making a total of 568 in the league. Armfield, who played 43 times for England, was part of the Blackpool team that finished the 1955/56 campaign as runners-up in the top flight. Now working in the media as a radio pundit, Armfield is widely regarded as one of the finest players English football has ever produced. He is held in such high esteem at Blackpool that he has a stand at Bloomfield Road named after him, with a statue to follow.

THE MATTHEWS FINAL

The 1953 FA Cup final is fondly remembered as 'The Matthews Final' thanks to wing-wizard Stanley Matthews' amazing display in helping Blackpool come from 3–1 down to lift the trophy. Another club legend, Stan Mortensen, scored a hat-trick as the Seasiders hit back to snatch a 4–3 win against Bolton at Wembley, but it was Matthews who really shone. Bill Perry scored the winning goal from a Matthews cross in injury time.

← *Charlie Adam left Rangers for Blackpool permanently in August 2009 and his goals helped the club reach the Championship Play-Off Final in 2010.*

TROPHY JOY FOR SEASIDERS

The club have won the Football League Trophy on two occasions. They eased to a 4–1 victory against Cambridge in March 2002, with John Murphy, Chris Clarke, John Hills and Scott Taylor on the scoresheet. Two years later, they made it back to Cardiff's Millennium Stadium, with striker Murphy on target again in a 2–0 win over Southend.

↑ *Blackpool had to wait for 49 years after 'The Matthews Final' before they won another major trophy, beating Cambridge United 4–1 in the 2002 Football League Trophy final in Cardiff.*

BRETT THE HITMAN

Brett Ormerod scored 27 goals in the 2000/01 season – including five in three play-off games – to help the Seasiders gain promotion to the third tier. He scored four times against Hartlepool in two semi-final matches and the last goal in a 4–2 victory against Leyton Orient in the final at the Millennium Stadium. Ormerod rejoined the club in January 2009 and scored the first goal of his second spell against Norwich in March that year.

ADAM ARRIVES IN RECORD DEAL

Blackpool broke their transfer record to sign Charlie Adam from Rangers in August 2009. The talented midfielder had impressed during a loan spell at Bloomfield Road towards the end of 2008/09, scoring twice in 13 games, with manager Ian Holloway subsequently signing him on a permanent basis for £500,000. Chris Malkin had previously established the record when Blackpool paid £275,000 to sign him from Millwall in October 1996.

Bristol City

Bristol City have played their home games at Ashton Gate since 1904, although the club are hoping to move to a new stadium within the next few years. The Robins have recently embarked on a new era following Gary Johnson's departure during the 2009/10 season after almost five years as manager. Steve Coppell was appointed for the 2010/11 campaign.

TIGERS TAME ROBINS

The Robins were on the verge of reaching the Barclays Premier League when they made it to the second-tier Play-Off Final in 2007/08, but they suffered heartbreak in the Wembley showpiece. They had only been promoted to the second tier that season but defied the pundits to move within sight of making it into the top flight at the first attempt. However, they lost out to a solitary strike from veteran Dean Windass, as he volleyed home to give Hull a 1–0 victory.

← *Dejected Bristol City players (left to right) Dele Adebola, Liam Fontaine, Louis Carey and Marvin Elliott after losing to Hull City at Wembley in 2008.*

ATYEO IS GOAL KING

John Atyeo is both Bristol City's record appearance holder and their all-time leading goalscorer. He played 645 times for the Robins in a 15-year spell with the club between 1951 and 1966, helping himself to 351 goals – better than a goal every other game! Goal-machine Atyeo, who was only ever a semi-professional footballer, won six England caps, scoring five times.

WALSH WALLOPS GILLS

Tommy 'Tot' Walsh was one of the most prolific marksmen to pull on a City shirt, and he enhanced that reputation when he scored six times in a single match. The striker achieved the amazing feat against Gillingham in a 9–4 win on January 15 1927. The Robins went goal crazy during the course of that season, scoring a club-record haul of 104.

ROBINS NICK STRIKER

City broke their transfer record to sign Nicky Maynard from Crewe for £2.25million in August 2008. Maynard had scored prolifically during two full seasons at Gresty Road, prompting then Robins boss Gary Johnson to pounce. The striker repaid his new manager's faith with 11 goals in 2008/09 and he netted 21 times last term. Maynard scooped The Football League's Goal of the Year award for 2009 following an acrobatic effort at QPR on Boxing Day.

↑ *Bristol City's most expensive signing was Nicky Maynard, who joined the Robins from Crewe in the summer of 2008.*

CITY'S LEADING GOALSCORERS

John Atyeo	351
Tom Ritchie	132
Arnold Rodgers	111
Jimmy Rogers	108
Alan Walsh	99

Cardiff City

Cardiff were formed as Riverside FC in 1899 and played their home matches at Ninian Park until 2009 when the 26,828 all-seater Cardiff City Stadium opened. The Bluebirds have not played top-flight football since 1962 but came close again in 2009/10 when they made the play-offs and appeared at Wembley for the second time in three years.

↑ *Alan Cork's reign as Cardiff manager saw the Bluebirds score goals at a record pace.*

BLUEBIRDS ARE FLYING

Cardiff established a new club mark for the most league goals scored in a single season in 2000/01. Under boss Alan Cork, they rattled in 95 on their way to a second-place finish and automatic promotion from the fourth tier. They finished 10 points behind champions Brighton but had scored 22 more goals. Notable victories included a 6–1 win at home to Exeter and 5–2 success at Macclesfield. Cardiff scored four or more goals on nine occasions in the league that season. More success came as they managed to go through the entire term unbeaten at home in the league, completing that run with a 3–1 victory over Shrewsbury on the penultimate weekend of the campaign.

WELSH WONDERS

The Bluebirds have the honour of being the only club from outside of England to have won the FA Cup. Their solitary success came in 1927 when they beat pre-match favourites Arsenal 1–0 at Wembley. Forward Hughie Ferguson scored the only goal of the game to give the Welshmen a memorable victory. Captain Fred Keenor received the trophy from King George V just seven years after Cardiff had entered The Football League.

CARDIFF'S MAJOR HONOURS

FA Cup	Winners	1927
FA Cup	Runners-up	1925, 2008
FA Charity Shield	Winners	1927
Top flight	Runners-up	1924
Second tier	Runners-up	1921, 1952, 1960
Third tier (South)	Champions	1947
Third tier	Champions	1993
Third tier	Runners-up	1976, 1983
Fourth tier	Runners-up	1988, 2001

┅➔ *Cardiff's winning goal in the 1927 FA Cup final came courtesy of an error by Arsenal's Welsh international goalkeeper Dan Lewis.*

DIAMOND DAVIES

Len Davies is the club's all-time leading goalscorer, having netted 128 times in the league between 1920 and 1931. Davies also holds the distinction of having scored City's first Football League hat-trick, in a 6–3 victory over Bradford in January 1922.

← *Goalscorer Rob Earnshaw celebrates another strike at Ninian Park in February 2003, one of his 31 for the Bluebirds that season.*

ROB NETS A HATFUL

Robert Earnshaw has scored the most league goals in a single season for Cardiff. The Wales international netted 31 times in 2002/03 as the Bluebirds gained promotion from the third tier via the play-offs. Earnshaw, who came through the Cardiff ranks and has also scored regularly for his country, netted two hat-tricks in the league that season and another treble in the League Cup. He left the club when he signed for West Brom in August 2004.

Coventry City

Coventry were in the top flight for 34 years between 1967 and 2001 but have since occupied the second tier. They have played their home games at the Ricoh Arena since 2005, with some notable players having pulled on the famous Sky Blue shirt both there and at their former Highfield Road ground.

HAPPY AS CLARRIE

A superb career at Coventry helped make Clarrie Bourton one of the most prolific strikers ever to have graced English football. He is the Sky Blues' all-time top marksman, with 171 league goals between 1931 and 1937. He also holds the club record for scoring the most league goals in a single season – 49 in 1931/32.

DUBLIN'S NET RETURN

Dion Dublin scored a record-equalling 23 goals in a top-flight season for the club in 1997/98. Dublin, who joined the Sky Blues for £2million from Manchester United in September 1994 and scored 61 goals in 145 league matches, could not surpass the record set by Ian Wallace in the 1977/78 campaign. Dublin left City for Aston Villa in 1998.

↑ Robbie Keane's year at Coventry saw his transfer value double, with the Sky Blues paying and receiving club-record fees for his services in 1999 and 2000.

ROBBIE THE BANK

Robbie Keane holds two transfer records for Coventry. His arrival for a reported £6.5million from Wolves in August 1999 is the most the Sky Blues have ever paid for a player, although that record is held jointly with Craig Bellamy, who cost the same amount from Norwich in August 2000. Keane was sold for £13million to Italian giants Inter Milan in July 2000 – the biggest transfer fee that City have received.

⇢ Dion Dublin celebrates yet another goal for Coventry during the 1997/98 season. His haul of 23 goals is a joint club record in the top flight.

OGGY, OGGY, OGGY!

Steve Ogrizovic holds a special place in Coventry folklore as the club's record appearance holder. He featured in 601 matches in all competitions during a 16-year spell with the Sky Blues between 1984 and 2000. Goalkeeper Ogrizovic is also the third oldest player to have appeared in a Premier League game, aged 42 years and 237 days.

SKY BLUES' CUP OF CHEER

Coventry won the FA Cup for the only time in their history in 1987. John Sillett and George Curtis were in charge as the Sky Blues beat Tottenham 3–2, with Keith Houchen scoring one of the great FA Cup final goals. The striker arrived in the box to power home a stunning diving header which sent the game into extra time. City went on to secure the trophy thanks to an own goal from luckless Tottenham defender Gary Mabbutt, with the Spurs centre-back inadvertently turning the ball into his own net when he failed to deal with a cross from Lloyd McGrath.

↑ Keith Houchen's flying header is probably the most famous goal in Coventry's history. It was the second equaliser in their 3–2 FA Cup final defeat of Tottenham at Wembley in 1987.

Crystal Palace

Crystal Palace were founder members of the Premier League in 1992/93 but were relegated at the end of that campaign. They have been promoted to the top flight three times since then but have struggled in recent seasons to match those highs. A 10-point deduction hampered the Eagles in 2009/10, but they avoided relegation on the final day of the season.

UNSTOPPABLE SIMPSON

Peter Simpson scored 19 hat-tricks for the Eagles between September 1929 and November 1933 on his way to becoming the club's all-time leading goalscorer. Simpson, who scored six times in one game against Exeter in October 1930, also holds the club landmark for the most goals in a single campaign – 46 in 1930/31. He grabbed 165 goals for the club in total.

⌄ Ian Wright is third on Crystal Palace's all-time scoring charts, but is the leader in post-war goals.

TOFFEES STUCK ON JOHNSON

Palace received a club-record £8.6million from Everton for Andrew Johnson in May 2006. The hot-shot striker had netted 17 goals for the Eagles in the 2005/06 season, prompting interest from the Toffees. The Barclays Premier League outfit were impressed enough to beat their previous biggest spend in order to sign the prolific frontman. Johnson, who made 160 appearances in total for Palace, got off the mark after 15 minutes of his Everton debut – a 2–1 win against Watford. He later left the Toffees to sign for Fulham in 2008.

⌄ Andrew Johnson's 84 goals for Crystal Palace came at a rate of better than one every other match for the Eagles.

PALACE'S LEADING GOALSCORERS

Peter Simpson	165
Ted Smith	124
Ian Wright	117
Clinton Morrison	113
Mark Bright	113
Dougie Freedman	108
George Clarke	106
Johnny Byrne	101
Albert Dawes	92
Andrew Johnson	84

BOSTOCK SOARS FOR EAGLES

John Bostock is the youngest player to have pulled on a Palace shirt. He was 15 years and 287 days old when he came on as a substitute with 20 minutes remaining in a 2–0 home defeat against Watford in October 2007. Bostock left Selhurst Park for the top flight at the age of 16, joining Tottenham. He spent part of 2009/10 season on loan at Brentford.

⌄ Alan Pardew (11) heads home the Crystal Palace winner in the 1990 FA Cup semi-final.

SEMI-FINAL STUNNER

The Eagles were involved in one of the greatest FA Cup semi-finals of all time when they enjoyed their best-ever run in the competition in 1990. They lost the final to Manchester United following a replay, but their 4–3 extra-time success against Liverpool to reach Wembley is fondly remembered. Andy Gray's header in the last minute of normal time made it 3–3, with Alan Pardew grabbing the winner.

Derby County

Derby were among the 12 founder members of The Football League in 1888. They were one of the dominant forces in the top flight during the 1970s and impressed in Europe during that time. Current boss Nigel Clough is the son of legendary Rams manager Brian, who was in charge during the club's glory years.

EURO DREAM DIES

The Rams were 180 minutes away from a place in the European Cup final in 1973. Under the late, great Brian Clough, they had already knocked Eusebio's Benfica out of the competition in an earlier round when they came up against Juventus in a two-legged semi-final. The Italian giants won the first tie 3–1, and that proved too much for Derby to overcome, as they had Roger Davies sent off and Alan Hinton missed a penalty in a goalless return.

TITLE TRIUMPH FOR RAMS

Derby were top-flight champions twice during the 1970s. Brian Clough guided the Rams to the first title in their history in 1971/72 as they beat Leeds, Liverpool and Manchester City by a point. Dave Mackay then took over the helm and ensured further glory in 1974/75 in his first full season as manager, edging out Liverpool and Ipswich by two points.

← Brian Clough (left, with assistant Peter Taylor) made Derby a top club in the 1970s, winning their first league title in 1972.

GOAL WOE FOR WARD

Ashley Ward scored Derby's last league goal at the Baseball Ground and the first at their new Pride Park Stadium – although the second has since been wiped from the history books. Arsenal ran out 3–1 winners in May 1997 after Ward had opened the scoring in the final game at the Rams' old ground. The striker was then the first name on the scoresheet in the clash with Wimbledon in August of that year as they began life at their new stadium, only for the floodlights to fail and the match to be abandoned shortly after half-time with Derby leading 2–1.

← Ashley Ward's first competitive goal at Pride Park was negated when Derby's match with Wimbledon was abandoned.

HECTOR SETS APPEARANCE MARK

Kevin Hector holds the record for the most appearances in a Derby shirt. Hector, who played in the successful Rams team of the 1970s, featured in 486 league games and 589 in total in two spells at the club, with a stint at Canadian side Vancouver Whitecaps sandwiched in between.

BLOOMING MARVELLOUS

Steve Bloomer holds a special place in the club's history following his extraordinary goalscoring exploits. He netted 292 league goals and 332 in total for the Rams in two spells from 1892–1905 and 1910–1913. He is Derby's record all-time goalscorer – a feat that is celebrated by a bust of Bloomer next to the home dugout at Pride Park.

↑ Kevin Hector (taking the ball past Everton's Henry Newton) scored 201 goals in all competitions for Derby in two spells, having netted 113 for Bradford Park Avenue before first joining the Rams. He earned two England caps in 1973, both as a substitute.

Doncaster Rovers

Doncaster Rovers only returned to The Football League in 2003 but have gone on to make it to the Championship in impressive fashion, gaining promotion from the third tier in 2007/08. They have also won the Johnstone's Paint Trophy since making their return. A 12th-place Championship finish in 2009/10 made it Rovers' best season for 59 years.

TROPHY GLORY FOR ROVERS

Doncaster won their first cup final in April 2007 when they took the Johnstone's Paint Trophy, beating Bristol Rovers 3–2. Two goals in the opening five minutes from Jonathan Forte and Paul Heffernan put Doncaster in command, but the Pirates fought back to take the game into extra time. Graeme Lee's header won it for Doncaster. A year later, Doncaster beat Leeds 1–0 in the League 1 Play-Off Final.

⇡ Thirteen months after winning their first major cup final, Doncaster Rovers were back at Wembley and they were celebrating again following a 1–0 defeat of Leeds United to win the League 1 Play-Off Final.

DONCASTER'S ASCENT TO THE CHAMPIONSHIP

2002/03	Conference National	3rd (Promotion)
2003/04	Fourth tier	1st (Promotion)
2004/05	Third tier	10th
2005/06	Third tier	8th
2006/07	Third tier	11th
2007/08	Third tier	3rd (Promotion)

GOODBYE TO BELLE VUE

Rovers played their first competitive game at the Keepmoat Stadium on New Year's Day 2007, having spent 84 years at their Belle Vue ground. Huddersfield were the first visitors, beaten 3–0. Mark McCammon had the distinction of scoring the first goal at the new stadium, while Town's Adnan Ahmed was shown the first red card, with Pawel Abbott and Doncaster's Gareth Roberts also dismissed that day.

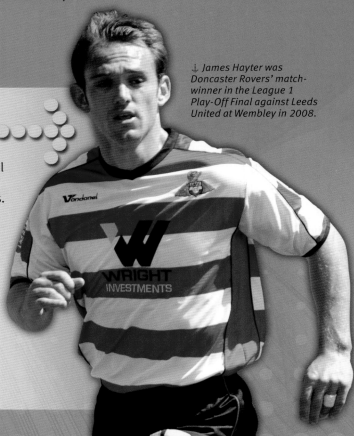

⇣ James Hayter was Doncaster Rovers' match-winner in the League 1 Play-Off Final against Leeds United at Wembley in 2008.

LUCKY BREAK FOR ALICK

Alick Jeffrey is the youngest player to have appeared for Doncaster in The Football League, aged 15 years and 229 days. Jeffrey made 262 appearances in two spells between 1954 and 1969, scoring 129 goals. Amazingly, Jeffrey actually retired from professional football in 1957 after failing to fully recover from a broken leg. But, after moving to Australia and taking up playing again, he returned to the club in 1963, going on to make another 191 appearances.

ROVERS MAKING PROGRESS

Doncaster have made a remarkable leap from playing Conference National football to becoming an established Championship club in just eight years. They made it back into The Football League in 2003 with a 3–2 play-off victory against Dagenham & Redbridge, before going on to claim the fourth-tier title the following season. A period of consolidation followed before a third-place finish in 2007/08 saw them book another Play-Off Final date, this time against Leeds. James Hayter scored the only goal of the game to send Rovers up.

Ipswich Town

Ipswich currently find themselves in the second tier, but they have a proud history which has seen them win the top-flight title and the UEFA Cup, among other trophies. The Tractor Boys have enjoyed two spells in the Premier League, from 1992–1995 and 2000–2002, and they hope that Roy Keane will lead them back to the promised land.

TOP BOSSES GET TOWN HONOUR

Ipswich have paid a special tribute to two of their greatest managers with statues which stand outside their Portman Road ground. Sir Alf Ramsey, who led the club to the top-flight title in 1961/62 before taking charge of England and guiding them to the 1966 World Cup, was first to be immortalised with a bronze sculpture in 2000, with a life-size statue of the late Sir Bobby Robson following two years later. Robson guided Town to FA Cup glory in 1978 and won the UEFA Cup with the club in 1981.

← A scarf adorns the statue of Sir Bobby Robson outside Portman Road in July 2009, placed there by a fan following the former manager's death.

JOHN WALKS OFF WITH AWARD

John Wark is the only Ipswich player to have won the PFA Player of the Year trophy. The Scot scooped the accolade following a string of impressive performances during the 1980/81 season which saw the Tractor Boys win the UEFA Cup. Wark scored 14 goals on the way to the final, netting 36 times in total over the course of the campaign. Another Town player has, however, won the PFA's Young Player of the Year award – Kevin Beattie claiming the inaugural prize in 1973/74.

KEEPERS IN THE SPOTLIGHT

Both the club's incoming and outgoing transfer records have involved goalkeepers. Manager George Burley splashed out a reported £5million on Matteo Sereni in August 2001, with the Italian making a total of 25 league appearances for the club before being loaned out to Brescia in his homeland. Richard Wright was sold to Arsenal in July 2001 for £6million. Wright was later re-signed by Ipswich from West Ham in July 2008.

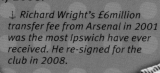

↓ Richard Wright's £6million transfer fee from Arsenal in 2001 was the most Ipswich have ever received. He re-signed for the club in 2008.

BADGE IS NO COMPETITION

Town's club badge actually came about as the result of a competition, run back in 1972. The winning entry, designed by John Gammage – a former treasurer of the Town supporters club – features the famous Suffolk Punch horse with a football at its feet. The current badge was given a facelift again in 2005, with a red border replacing the original yellow one.

IPSWICH HONOURS LIST

Top flight

Champions	1961/62
Runners-up	1980/81, 1981/82

Second tier

Champions	1960/61, 1967/68, 1991/92
Play-off winners	1999/00

Third tier (South)

Champions	1953/54, 1956/57

FA Cup

Winners	1977/78

UEFA Cup

Winners	1980/81

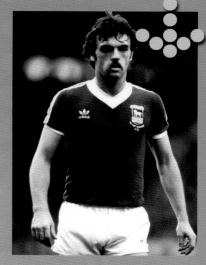

↑ John Wark's performances in 1980/81 earned him the PFA Player of the Year award. He also set a UEFA Cup record with 14 goals from midfield as Ipswich won their only European trophy.

Leicester City

Leicester bounced back from their recent relegation to the third tier in fine style, following up their promotion to the Championship in 2008/09 with another impressive showing in 2009/10. Arguably the Foxes' most impressive achievements of recent years have come in the League Cup, with two Wembley victories to their name.

TITLE CRUISE

The Foxes' haul of 96 points on the way to winning the League 1 title in 2008/09 is the most they have managed in a single season. Their relegation from the Championship the previous term was quickly banished from memory as manager Nigel Pearson led them to three wins from their first four games. They kept their good form going for the rest of the campaign and promotion was finally confirmed with a 2–0 win at Southend on April 18 2009.

↑ Graham Cross (white) is denied by Manchester United's David Gaskell and Maurice Setters in the 1963 FA Cup final.

MATT FINISHES FASTEST

Matt Fryatt broke the record for the fastest goal in Leicester's history when he scored after just nine seconds against Preston in 2006. Gareth Williams' chip over the defence released Fryatt, and he coolly slotted past Preston goalkeeper Carlo Nash. Unfortunately for Leicester, they went on to lose the game 2–1. Three other players – Tom Dryburgh, Derek Hines and Ian McNeil – had scored after 10 seconds for the Foxes in the 1950s. Fryatt also rewrote the record books in 2008/09 when he became the first Leicester player since Derek Dougan 42 years earlier to net 20 goals before Christmas.

← Matt Fryatt didn't only score early for Leicester, he also scored often, especially in the 2008/09 season, when he netted 32 times.

→ The £11million Leicester received from Liverpool for Emile Heskey in March 2000 was a club record.

LEICESTER'S LEADING APPEARANCES

Graham Cross	599
Adam Black	557
Hugh Adcock	460
Mark Wallington	460
Steve Walsh	449
Arthur Chandler	419
John Sjoberg	413
Mal Griffiths	409
Steve Whitworth	400
Sep Smith	373

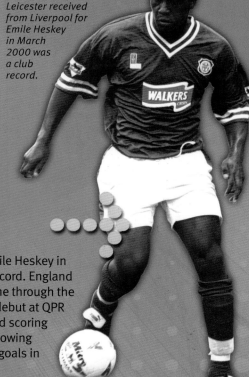

FOXES' SECOND HOME

City were regular visitors to Wembley between 1990 and 2000, featuring in seven finals. They reached the League Cup final three times during that period, drawing 1–1 with Middlesbrough then winning the replay 1–0 at Hillsborough in 1997, losing 1–0 to Tottenham in 1999 and beating Tranmere 2–1 in 2000. They also played in four play-off finals, losing against Blackburn (1992) and Swindon (1993) and beating Derby (1994) and then Crystal Palace (1996).

REDS RAID FOR HESKEY

Liverpool paid £11million to sign Emile Heskey in March 2000 – a Leicester transfer record. England international striker Heskey had come through the Foxes' ranks, making his first-team debut at QPR on March 8 1995 when he was 17 and scoring his first goal against Norwich the following season. Heskey scored a total of 46 goals in 197 appearances for Leicester.

Middlesbrough

Boro were one of the original members of the Premier League, but it hasn't always been an easy ride for the Teesside club. They were close to going out of business in 1986 but recovered with the help of chairman Steve Gibson, winning their first major trophy, the Carling Cup, in 2004. Middlesbrough suffered a third Premier League relegation in 2009.

BORO BREEZE PAST CITY

Middlesbrough recorded the biggest Premier League win since 1999 when they beat Manchester City 8–1 at the Riverside Stadium on the last day of the 2007/08 season. Afonso Alves scored a hat-trick, Stewart Downing grabbed two and Fabio Rochemback, Adam Johnson and Jeremie Aliadiere were also on the scoresheet as the Teessiders cruised to victory. Elano was on target for the visitors.

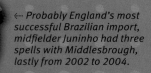

← Probably England's most successful Brazilian import, midfielder Juninho had three spells with Middlesbrough, lastly from 2002 to 2004.

BY GEORGE, THAT'S A RECORD!

George Camsell scored 59 league goals in a single season in the second tier in 1926/27 and netted 325 league goals in total for Middlesbrough between 1925 and 1939 – both club records. Camsell, who cost Middlesbrough just £600 from Durham City, scored 24 hat-tricks during his 14-year career on Teesside. He also made nine appearances for England, scoring 18 times.

↑ George Camsell's 59 goals in a season, in 1926/27, was a Football League record for only 12 months, but it remains the best ever in England's second tier.

MIDDLESBROUGH'S BIGGEST LEAGUE VICTORIES

9–0	v Brighton	(1958)
8–0	v Huddersfield	(1950)
8–0	v Sheffield Wednesday	(1974)
10–3	v Sheffield United	(1933)
9–2	v Blackpool	(1938)

SAMBA DUO DANCE IN... AND OUT

The club's record transfer cost them £12million, with the same figure also representing the biggest fee they have ever received for a player – and both deals involved Brazilians. Samba star Juninho moved to Teesside from Sao Paulo in October 1995, wowing the crowds for two years to make himself a fans' favourite before leaving for Atletico Madrid in a £12million move. He returned for two more spells with the club from 1999–2000 and 2002–2004.

Afonso Alves is Boro's record signing, costing £12million from Dutch side Heerenveen in January 2008. He made just 42 Barclays Premier League appearances and scored 10 goals before he left for Qatar in September 2009.

ARMSTRONG THE EVER-PRESENT

David Armstrong has made the most consecutive appearances for Boro. 'Spike', as he was affectionately known, played a remarkable 305 league games in a row for the club – 356 in all competitions – between March 1973 and August 1980. He was voted Middlesbrough's Player of the Year in 1980 and made his England debut in the same year against Australia. Ray Yeoman is second in the list of unbroken league appearances for Boro with 190.

Newcastle United

Newcastle fans have been on a real rollercoaster ride in recent seasons. The Magpies spent 16 years in the Premier League before they were relegated at the end of 2008/09. However, their stay in the second tier was shortlived and they claimed the Championship title in style in 2009/10, scoring 90 goals and amassing 102 points.

MAGPIES NUTTY OVER BRAZILIAN

Mirandinha became the first Brazilian to play in English football when he signed for Newcastle in 1987. The forward, who cost the Magpies £575,000 from Palmeiras, had hit the headlines with a goal for his country against England in the Rous Cup earlier that year. He failed to settle in the north-east and moved back to his former club in Brazil in 1989 having scored 33 goals – although he has since revealed that the Magpies tried to sign him again during Kevin Keegan's first spell as manager.

† *Andrew Cole scores one of his two goals against West Ham in Newcastle's 2–0 victory at St James' Park in September 1993.*

† *Mirandinha (right) was the first Brazilian to play in English football, but he only stayed with the Magpies for two seasons.*

SHEAR MAGIC

Alan Shearer scored 206 goals for Newcastle – 131 of those at St James' Park – in a 10-year spell with the club between 1996 and 2006, making him the Magpies' all-time leading goalscorer and a true club legend. Shearer scored 49 headers, 45 penalties, five free-kicks and four hat-tricks in the famous black and white shirt. In season 1996/97, the former England hot-shot netted in an amazing seven consecutive matches, including a memorable goal in Newcastle's stunning 5–0 win against Manchester United.

⟶ *Alan Shearer wheels away in celebration with his trademark raised arm after scoring against Southampton in September 1998 in a 4–0 win.*

RED-HOT COLE

Andrew Cole has the best strike rate of any post-war Newcastle player with 81 per cent. Cole scored an impressive 68 goals in 84 matches for the Magpies between 1993 and 1995, 41 of those coming in a single season (1993/94) – a club record that also earned him the PFA Young Player of the Year prize. Alan Shearer has a 51 per cent strike rate, having scored 206 goals in 404 matches, while Les Ferdinand netted 50 goals in 83 games – a strike rate of 60 per cent.

TEENAGE KICKS

Steve Watson is the youngest player to have featured in a league game for Newcastle at 16 years and 223 days old. The defender made his debut as a substitute in the Magpies' 2–1 defeat at Wolves in November 1990. He went on to make over 200 appearances for the club in an eight-year spell before being sold to Aston Villa for £4million in October 1998. Striker Andy Carroll became the club's youngest European debutant when he featured in the 1–0 UEFA Cup win in Palermo in November 2006.

NEWCASTLE'S LEADING ALL-TIME GOALSCORERS

Alan Shearer	206
Jackie Milburn	200
Len White	153
Hughie Gallacher	143
Malcolm MacDonald	121
Peter Beardsley	119
Bobby Mitchell	113
Tom McDonald	113
Neil Harris	101
Bryan Robson	97

Nottingham Forest

Nottingham Forest are one of the oldest football clubs in the world and one of the most successful in England. Among other things, they have won the top-flight title, the FA Cup, the League Cup and back-to-back European Cups, with their greatest spell of success coming in the late 1970s and early 1980s.

FOREST MANAGERS SINCE BRIAN CLOUGH

Frank Clark	1993–1996
Stuart Pearce	1996–1997
Dave Bassett	1997–1998
Ron Atkinson	1999
David Platt	1999–2001
Paul Hart	2001–2004
Joe Kinnear	2004
Gary Megson	2005–2006
Colin Calderwood	2006–2008
Billy Davies	2009–Present

CLOUGH REIGNS SUPREME

Brian Clough is the most successful manager in Nottingham Forest's history and is widely regarded as one of the greatest English football has ever seen. Clough also had spells in charge of Hartlepool, Derby, Brighton and Leeds during his long career, but his finest achievements came at the City Ground. Arguably his greatest feat was leading Forest to back-to-back European Cup triumphs in 1979 and 1980. Those successes came after the club had won the old Division One title in 1977/78 and claimed the runners-up spot the following season. Clough also took Forest to six League Cup finals during his 18 years in charge of the club from 1975–1993 – winning four and losing two. He also reached the FA Cup final in 1991.

⬆ *The charismatic Brian Clough (left) won two European Cups and one top-flight title at Forest.*

FOREST RECORD CHOPPED DOWN

After going through the entire 2003/04 Premier League season unbeaten, Arsenal broke a record that had been held by Nottingham Forest for 26 years. Prior to the Gunners' 49-game streak, the previous benchmark was 42, which the Reds had achieved under Brian Clough between November 26 1977 and November 25 1978. Forest's run spanned across two seasons, starting with a goalless draw at home to West Brom and ending almost a year later at Liverpool, where they lost 2–0.

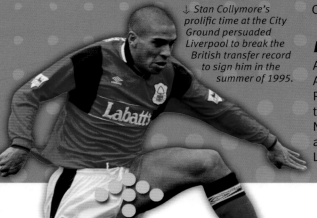

⬇ *Stan Collymore's prolific time at the City Ground persuaded Liverpool to break the British transfer record to sign him in the summer of 1995.*

STAN THE MAN

Both Nottingham Forest's incoming and outgoing transfer records involve strikers. The club paid Celtic £3.5million for Pierre van Hooijdonk in March 1997. The Dutchman is best remembered for the 34 goals he scored to help the Reds gain promotion back to the top flight at the first attempt in 1997/98. Stan Collymore joined the club in July 1993 from Southend and, after scoring 41 goals in 65 league appearances, he left the City Ground for Liverpool in a then British record £8.5million switch in June 1995.

FRANCIS IS ONE IN A MILLION

Nottingham Forest were the first British club to pay £1million for a player when they signed Trevor Francis from Birmingham in February 1979. Francis scored the winning goal in the European Cup final against Malmo in May of that year but missed out against Hamburg the following season due to injury.

⬅ *Trevor Francis repaid Brian Clough's faith in him by scoring the winner in the 1979 European Cup final.*

Peterborough United

Peterborough are relative newcomers to The Football League, having been admitted in 1960. The London Road club took little time to make their mark among English football's elite and they have since gone from strength to strength, spending 2009/10 in the second tier, although that term did end with relegation back to the third tier.

POSH SPICE UP THE LEAGUE

Peterborough scored a remarkable 134 league goals on the way to the fourth-tier title in 1960/1961. Incredibly, striker Terry Bly scored 52 of those as Posh also recorded a club-record 28 wins. Peterborough had only been elected to The Football League that season on the back of five successive title wins in the Midland League.

⬅ Terry Bly (back row, one from right) provided the firepower for Peterborough in their 1960/61 fourth-tier title run.

ETHERINGTON WINGS IN

Matthew Etherington is the youngest player to have represented Peterborough, appearing for 87 minutes of a 1–0 win at Brentford in May 1997 aged 15 years and 262 days. Etherington made almost 60 appearances for Posh before being sold to Tottenham in December 1999. Spurs snapped up Simon Davies at the same time, with Peterborough receiving a then club-record £700,000 for the Welsh winger.

BENNETT BREAKS RECORD

The club broke their transfer record to sign highly-rated defender Ryan Bennett from Grimsby in 2009/10. He penned a long-term deal after a successful loan spell. Although the exact fee was undisclosed, it did supersede the £400,000 paid to Norwich for goalkeeper Joe Lewis in January 2008.

LIKE FATHER, LIKE SON

Posh enjoyed back-to-back promotions in 2008 and 2009. Darren Ferguson secured runners-up spot in the fourth tier in his first full season as manager and then guided the club to another second-place finish the following year, taking them into the second tier. Ferguson, the son of Manchester United manager Sir Alex, left Peterborough by mutual consent in November 2009.

DUO STRIKE OUT

Hot-shot strike duo Aaron Mclean and Craig Mackail-Smith scored 41 of Peterborough's 78 goals in their promotion-winning season of 2008/09. Mclean, who had finished the previous campaign as the league's leading goalscorer, netted 18 times, while fellow forward Mackail-Smith bagged 23 in total, including a hat-trick in a 5–4 victory against Bristol Rovers. Winger George Boyd – who like the other two was signed by Posh from non-league football – contributed a further nine goals to the cause.

⤍ Ever since Barry Fry took over at Peterborough, Posh have been recognised as one of the most astute harvesters of non-league talent. Strikers Craig Mackail-Smith (left) and Aaron Mclean both thrived after leaving the Conference.

Plymouth Argyle

Plymouth is the largest city in England never to have hosted top-flight football, but the Pilgrims made steady enough progress at the start of the decade, moving up from the fourth tier to the Championship, where they were playing until their relegation at the end of the 2009/10 campaign. Fans call their Home Park ground the 'Theatre of Greens'.

PLYMOUTH'S TEAM OF THE CENTURY

GK   Jim Furnell
DEF Gordon Nisbet
DEF Graham Coughlan
DEF Jack C`hisholm
DEF Colin Sullivan
MID Kevin Hodges
MID Ernie Machin
MID Johnny Williams
MID Sammy Black/Garry Nelson)*
ATT Paul Mariner
ATT Tommy Tynan

* The vote between Black and Nelson was tied.

HODGES A HERO

Kevin Hodges earned a place in the Plymouth history books as a player and then went on to manage the club after hanging up his boots. Hodges holds the record for the most league appearances for the Pilgrims – 530 in total. He spent 14 years with Argyle, helping them to reach the semi-finals of the FA Cup in 1984. He took on the manager's role from 1998–2000 and in 2004 was voted part of Argyle's Team of the Century to mark their 100th anniversary as a professional club.

← Kevin Hodges' loyalty to Plymouth was rewarded with two testimonial matches, one in 1988 and another in 1992.

SHILTON'S LANDMARK IN SAFE HANDS

England goalkeeping great Peter Shilton is Plymouth's oldest-ever debutant, having made his bow for the club aged 42 years and 199 days. His last appearance at 44 years and 21 days also makes him the oldest player ever to have played for Argyle.

← Peter Shilton joined Plymouth as player-manager only 19 months after captaining England in the World Cup semi-final.

EIGHT IS GREAT FOR GREENS

The club's record victory is 8–1. They have achieved that feat twice, beating Millwall at home in January 1932 – Jack Vidler scoring a hat-trick – and more recently Hartlepool at Victoria Park in May 1994. Richard Landon scored three times in that game, while winger Paul Dalton netted a brace against his former club.

PILGRIMS' RECORD RUN

Argyle set a club record when they went 19 consecutive league games in one season without losing on their way to winning the fourth-tier title in 2001/02. Their memorable run started with a 3–2 victory at Rushden & Diamonds on August 27 2001, with their 19th game unbeaten coming when they defeated Darlington 1–0 on December 15. The honour of ending their record-breaking sequence went to Scunthorpe, who finally found a way to halt the Pilgrims' progress when they secured a 2–1 victory at Glanford Park a week later courtesy of two goals from midfielder Lee Hodges.

Preston North End

Preston have not played in the top flight since 1961, but they have an illustrious history that has seen some of the greatest players of all time grace Deepdale. They were the first English champions, the first double winners, and went a whole season without losing a game in 1888/89, although success has been harder to come by of late.

AFFINITY WITH FINNEY

The name of Sir Tom Finney is synonymous with Preston. The legendary forward was a one-club man, spending 14 years at Deepdale between 1946 and 1960, during which time he emerged as one of the finest players of his generation. He is North End's all-time leading goalscorer, having netted 210 goals for the club in 473 games. Finney also won 76 caps for England during that time, scoring 30 goals for his country. He is ranked fifth in the list of England's top goalscorers, level with Nat Lofthouse and Alan Shearer. Finney received a knighthood in 1998, while there is also a stand named after him at Deepdale and a sculpture in his honour outside the ground.

There is no argument about who is the greatest player in Preston North End history – Sir Tom Finney stands head and shoulders above all others.

PRESTON MANAGERS SINCE DAVID MOYES

Craig Brown	2002–2004
Billy Davies	2004–2006
Paul Simpson	2006–2007
Alan Irvine	2007–2009
Darren Ferguson	2010–Present

Preston fans hope that manager Darren Ferguson can be as successful as his famous father, Sir Alex.

MAGIC MOYES

Everton boss David Moyes started his managerial career at Preston, enjoying a successful spell at Deepdale between 1998 and 2002. He led North End to the play-offs in 1998/99 and the third-tier title in 1999/00, with the club racking up their best-ever points total in the process – 95. The play-offs were achieved again in 2000/01 before Moyes left for Goodison Park in March 2002.

PRESTON FIRST PAST THE POST

Preston hold the distinction of being English football's first champions. North End were founder members of The Football League in 1888, and they beat 11 other teams to win the title in its inaugural season. Preston also became the first team to achieve a league and FA Cup double in the 1888/89 campaign. They won the championship again the following year and finished as runners-up in 1890/91, 1891/92 and 1892/93.

NUGENT NETS A BUNDLE

David Nugent's departure to Portsmouth for a fee reported to be £6million in the summer of 2007 makes him the record sale by Preston. Striker Nugent was a goalscoring sensation at Deepdale, netting 37 times in 107 matches over three seasons before earning his move to Fratton Park. He spent 2009/10 on loan at Burnley playing in the Barclays Premier League.

David Nugent's goalscoring exploits – here celebrating a goal against Manchester City – made him a hot commodity in 2006/07.

Queens Park Rangers

QPR can count themselves among the wealthiest clubs in English football thanks to multi-millionaire owners, but they are still striving to get back to the top flight following their relegation in 1996. The west London club initially moved to their Loftus Road ground in 1917 but did not settle there permanently until 1963.

RAY OF LIGHT

Ray Wilkins is the oldest player to have featured in the Premier League for QPR aged 39 years and 352 days. Wilkins, who is currently assistant manager of Chelsea, made his last appearance for the Hoops on September 1 1996 – a 2–1 defeat at home to Bolton.

⟶ *Ray Wilkins made 208 appearances for the Loftus Road club towards the latter end of his distinguished 24-year playing career.*

BRILLIANT BAILEY DESTROYS UNITED

Dennis Bailey wrote himself into QPR folklore when he scored a hat-trick against Manchester United at Old Trafford on New Year's Day 1992 – the last player to achieve that feat domestically against the Red Devils on their own ground. United topped the table at the time, but they were stunned 4–1 by a rampant Rangers side. Andy Sinton had opened the scoring before Bailey took over, with Brian McClair pulling a goal back for the home side. Since Bailey, only one other player has scored a hat-trick against United at Old Trafford – Ronaldo, who bagged a treble for Real Madrid in the Champions League in 2003.

HOOPS HIT GOAL TON

QPR scored an amazing 111 league goals during the 1961/62 season – but only finished fourth in the third tier. That total was 24 more than champions Portsmouth, but Alec Stock's men finished six points behind the south-coast club. The Hoops ended the season having scored 129 goals in 52 matches in all competitions, with Brian Bedford netting 39 times, including six hat-tricks and four in a 5–3 win against Southend.

↓ *Neil Warnock was the third Queens Park Rangers manager of 2009/10 and he eventually steered them to Championship safety.*

HOT ROD

Rodney Marsh scored 44 goals in all competitions as QPR claimed the title in the third tier and won the League Cup in 1966/67. Striker Marsh fired 30 goals in the league – seven shy of George Goddard's club record – three in the FA Cup and 11 on the way to the League Cup triumph. Marsh, who went on to become a TV pundit after he finished playing, scored Rangers' equaliser in the cup final against West Brom as they came from two goals down to win 3–2.

⟶ *Les Ferdinand spent eight seasons at Loftus Road before Newcastle paid QPR a club-record £6million for his services in 1995.*

ARISE SIR LES

Les Ferdinand went for QPR's biggest-ever transfer fee when he joined Newcastle for £6million in 1995. Former England striker Ferdinand scored a total of 91 goals in 183 games for the Hoops – an average strike rate of almost a goal every other game. 'Sir Les', as he was known by fans throughout his career, was awarded an MBE by the Queen in 2005. His big-money switch to St James' Park proved a huge success as he scored 50 times in 83 games for the Magpies.

Queens Park Rangers and Reading

Reading

Reading are one of the oldest clubs in England, although they didn't join The Football League until 1920. They created their own piece of history in 2005/06 when they were promoted to the top flight for the first time, and although they were relegated at the end of their second term, the Royals remain a club with big ambitions.

RECORD-BREAKING READING

Reading enjoyed their best-ever season in 2005/06 when they won the Championship title with a massive haul of 106 points – a Football League record. The Royals also broke a host of other records during that 46-game campaign as they lost just two league matches – one of those away from home – conceded the fewest goals (32) and secured the most wins (31). With Steve Coppell in charge, Reading also became the team to have clinched promotion the earliest, beating Plymouth by one day and Notts County by three.

← *Reading's domination of the Championship in 2005/06 broke many long-standing Football League records, and their Barclays Premier League debut season was pretty good too.*

ROYALS KEEP IT CLEAN

The Royals created more Football League history when they went 1103 minutes without conceding a goal in 1979. The run began on March 24 when they kept a clean sheet for 84 minutes of their clash with Rochdale. They didn't concede for 11 more games that season before goalkeeper Steve Death was finally beaten 29 minutes into the start of the 1979/80 campaign against Brentford. Edwin van der Sar has since broken that record for Manchester United, although that is classed as a Premier League statistic.

A RECORD RUN

Reading started the 1985/86 season with 13 consecutive league wins – a Football League record. Here's how they did it:

v Blackpool	1–0
v Plymouth	1–0
v Bristol Rovers	3–2
v Cardiff	3–1
v Walsall	2–1
v Rotherham	2–1
v Brentford	2–1
v Swansea	2–0
v Doncaster	1–0
v Chesterfield	4–2
v Bolton	1–0
v Newport	2–0
v Lincoln	1–0

KITSON MAKES HIS MARK

Striker Dave Kitson scored Reading's first Barclays Premier League goal in a 3–2 win against Middlesbrough on the opening day of the 2006/07 season. The Royals were 2–0 down when Kitson struck, and that sparked an impressive comeback as goals from Steve Sidwell and Leroy Lita earned the newcomers victory.

DOYLE DEPARTS

Reading received their club-record transfer fee in the summer of 2009 when striker Kevin Doyle moved to Wolves in what was reported to be a £6.5million deal. That was £1million more than Stoke had paid for fellow forward Dave Kitson a year earlier.

⋯→ *Kevin Doyle scored more than 50 league goals for Reading in four seasons before joining Wolves.*

Scunthorpe United

Scunthorpe United enjoyed their highest finish since 1961/62 as they secured the right to play another campaign in the Championship in 2009/10, ultimately ending the season in a creditable 20th place. The club was known as Scunthorpe & Lindsey until 1958 and they moved to Glanford Park from the Old Showground 30 years later.

RAZOR-SHARP BILLY

The Iron received a club-record £2million fee when hot-shot striker Billy Sharp left for Sheffield United in July 2007. Sharp had joined from the Blades for just £100,000 in August 2005 and quickly established himself as a first-team regular for the club. However, after scoring 53 goals in just 82 league games over two seasons at Glanford Park, he returned to his roots and headed back to Bramall Lane in a deal that also saw winger Jonathan Forte move in the opposite direction.

IRON ON SMOKING RUN

Scunthorpe's promotion from The Football League's bottom division in 2004/05 sparked a real purple patch for the club that saw them playing in the second tier just two years later. They followed up their initial success with yet more glory the following season and went a club-record 19 games unbeaten on their way to winning the League 1 title in 2006/07 to complete their remarkable ascent.

↑ Scunthorpe's players celebrate with the 2006/07 League 1 championship trophy. It was the first time the Iron had finished top of the table for 49 years, when they won the final Division 3 North crown.

DUO SHINE IN GREAT EIGHT

Barrie Thomas and Andy McFarlane both put in outstanding individual displays on the two occasions that Scunthorpe recorded 8–1 wins – their biggest-ever victories. Luton were the opponents on April 24 1965 as Thomas, who is second on the list of the Iron's top scorers (his 93 goals in 143 matches in two spells is bettered only by Steve Cammack) netted five times – a club record for the most goals in a single game. McFarlane grabbed four goals as Torquay were beaten by the same scoreline at Plainmoor 30 years later.

↑ When Scunthorpe sold Barrie Thomas to Newcastle in 1962, the club was top of the second tier, but they fell away and missed promotion.

TAKING THE CARMICHAEL

Matt Carmichael set a club record for the most goals in consecutive league matches between December 1993 and February 1994. Carmichael got his name on the scoresheet in eight straight games, starting in a 2–2 draw at home to Chesterfield and ending after he was on target twice in a 3–2 defeat against Mansfield at Glanford Park.

SCUNTHORPE'S RECORD TRANSFER SALES

Billy Sharp	Sheffield United	£2million
Martin Paterson	Burnley	£1.6million
Andy Keogh	Wolves	£750,000
Neil Cox	Aston Villa	£350,000
Chris Hope	Gillingham	£250,000
Richard Hall	Southampton	£250,000

Sheffield United

The Blades, who earned their nickname due to Sheffield's long and proud history of steel production, were formed in 1889, but their real golden era came shortly afterwards between 1896 and 1925 when they won the top-flight title, finished runners-up twice and were FA Cup winners four times.

SHEFFIELD UNITED'S LAST FIVE MANAGERS

Steve Bruce	1998–1999
Adrian Heath	1999
Neil Warnock	1999–2007
Bryan Robson	2007–2008
Kevin Blackwell	2008–Present

† Kevin Blackwell took Sheffield United to the Championship Play-Off Final at Wembley in 2009.

INTERNATIONAL BLADES

United broke new ground in January 2006 when they bought a controlling stake in Chinese club Chengdu Five Bull, becoming the first foreign owners of a Chinese team in the process. The link-up saw the Asian outfit renamed Chengdu Blades in honour of their new owners, while United have since helped to establish training facilities and a new academy in the Far East. Chengdu are not the only foreign team with links to the Yorkshire outfit, however, with former Hungarian champions Ferencvaros and Australian A-League side Central Coast Mariners also enjoying a close relationship with the Blades.

BLADES CHOPPED DOWN

United have won the FA Cup four times – in 1899, 1902, 1915 and 1925 – but their best-ever run in the League Cup came more recently in 2003. The Blades reached the semi-finals, where they were beaten over two legs by Liverpool. Two goals from Michael Tonge had given them a slender 2–1 lead at Bramall Lane going into the return, but the Reds claimed a 2–0 victory to progress 3–2 on aggregate. Neil Warnock also led the club to the last four of the FA Cup that year.

FESTIVE FRUSTRATION

It was an unhappy Christmas for Sheffield United fans in 1993 when their team failed to score for a club-record six consecutive games. The run started on December 4 with a goalless draw at Swindon and continued until New Year's Day when the Blades secured a 2–1 win against Oldham. The club were playing Premier League football at the time, with games against Manchester United, Everton, Liverpool and Arsenal all included in that tough run of festive fixtures.

← Michael Tonge fires home the winner in the Carling Cup semi-final first leg against Liverpool at Bramall Lane.

⟶ What might have been.... Diego Maradona found fame and glory in the stripes of Argentina and Barcelona, but not the stripes of Sheffield United.

NO GO FOR 'HAND OF GOD'

Legend has it that Diego Maradona was close to signing for Sheffield United in the late 1970s. Maradona was 17 when then Blades boss Harry Haslam spotted him playing for Argentinos Juniors. There are conflicting reports as to why a deal fell through, but ultimately Maradona never pulled on a red-and-white-striped shirt. Fellow Argentinian playmaker Alex Sabella arrived at the club instead for a then record fee of £160,000, but he managed just eight league goals in 76 appearances.

Sheffield Wednesday

Sheffield Wednesday, nicknamed the Owls because their Hillsborough stadium is located in the Owlerton area of the city, have bounced between the divisions in recent times, going down again in 2010, but the club is still one of the most famous and best-supported in The Football League, boasting average attendances of well over 20,000.

↑ Hillsborough has been Sheffield Wednesday's home for more than 110 years. It is one of the most famous stadiums in England.

DEJA VU FOR OWLS

The Owls completed a remarkable achievement in 1993 when they reached both the FA Cup and League Cup finals in the same season, although their joy was shortlived, as they suffered defeat to Arsenal on both occasions. It is the only time in the history of the professional game that both of England's major domestic cup finals have been contested by the same two teams in the same season. Wednesday lost out in both matches to the same scoreline, 2–1.

SHEFFIELD WEDNESDAY'S GROUNDS

1867	Highfield
1869	Myrtle Road
1877	Sheaf House
1887	Olive Grove
1899	Owlerton (renamed Hillsborough in 1912)

WHY WEDNESDAY?

Wednesday rank as one of the more unusually named teams in The Football League. They actually started life as a cricket club, initially being formed as The Wednesday Cricket Club after the day of the week on which they held their matches. The local craftsmen who founded the club used to take half a day off on the same afternoon each week to play. It wasn't until June 1929 that the club's name was officially changed to Sheffield Wednesday.

MAGNIFICENT MARTIN

Goalkeeping legend Martin Hodge holds the club record for the most consecutive league and cup appearances. Hodge, who spent five years at Hillsborough between 1983 and 1988, played in 214 unbroken games. He made more than 240 appearances in total for Wednesday before moving to Leicester for £250,000 in August 1988.

SHERI THE TOAST OF SHEFFIELD

Sheffield Wednesday were in the second tier when they beat Manchester United to win the League Cup for the first and only time in their history in 1991. They knocked top-flight trio Derby, Coventry and Chelsea out of the competition on their way to reaching the Wembley showpiece. The Owls were promoted in the same season, while United finished sixth in Division One. A single goal from midfielder John Sheridan won the cup for the South Yorkshire side.

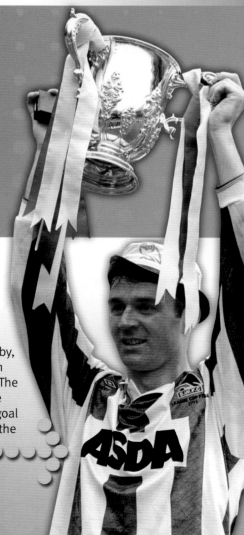

⤳ John Sheridan scored the only goal for Sheffield Wednesday when they won the 1991 League Cup. It was the Owls' first cup final victory since they beat West Brom to win the FA Cup in 1935.

Swansea City

As one of Wales' representatives in The Football League, Swansea have a proud history that has taken in plenty of highs as well as some painful lows. They have endured mixed fortunes since their best-ever finish to a season in 1981/82, when they were sixth in the top flight, but they have made steady progress in the second tier in recent times.

SWANS' ANFIELD MISERY

Liverpool inflicted Swansea's heaviest cup defeat in January 1990. The 8–0 reverse came in a replay in the third round of the FA Cup after the Swans had held their top-flight opponents to a goalless draw at the Vetch Field. Welsh goalscoring legend Ian Rush netted a hat-trick and John Barnes grabbed two as the Reds went goal crazy. Swansea suffered the same fate against Monaco in the European Cup Winners' Cup in October of the following year. Arsenal manager Arsene Wenger was in charge of the French side at the time.

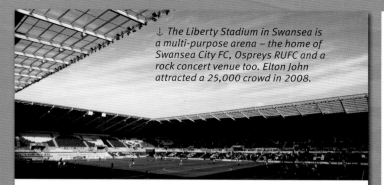

↓ *The Liberty Stadium in Swansea is a multi-purpose arena – the home of Swansea City FC, Ospreys RUFC and a rock concert venue too. Elton John attracted a 25,000 crowd in 2008.*

HOME COMFORTS

The club moved into the Liberty Stadium in time for the 2005/06 season. They had played their home matches at the Vetch Field since 1912, but the all-seater stadium, which can normally hold just over 20,500 spectators, became their new home in July 2005. The first match to take place there was a pre-season clash against Fulham which ended 1–1. The first league game was a 1–0 success against Tranmere, with Adebayo Akinfenwa scoring the only goal.

STATUE OF LIBERTY

Ivor Allchurch is Swansea's record goalscorer, having netted 164 times in almost 450 appearances for his home-town club in two separate spells between 1949 and 1968. He jointly held the record as Wales' all-time leading scorer with Trevor Ford until 1986, when the duo were overtaken by Ian Rush. A statue of Allchurch stands outside the Liberty Stadium to commemorate his achievements.

↓ *Jason Scotland's 45 league goals from 2007 to 2009 earned him a transfer to top-flight Wigan, the £2million fee being a Swansea club record.*

DE VRIES KEEPS IT OUT

Swansea, aided by goalkeeper Dorus De Vries, broke a 10-year-old club record during the 2009/10 campaign as they surpassed a clean-sheet mark set by Roger Freestone and the title-winning side of 1999/2000. The new milestone was set on April 5 when Dutchman De Vries made it 23 games without conceding in the 3–0 victory at home to Scunthorpe. 'To keep a clean sheet and break the record of a Swansea legend is absolutely amazing,' De Vries said.

↑ *Dorus De Vries proved to be a hard man to beat as the Dutch goalkeeper set a Swansea club record for clean sheets in a season with 25 in 2009/10.*

SCOTLAND THE BRAVE

Jason Scotland finished as League 1's top goalscorer in 2007/08 as Swansea claimed the title with a club-record points total. Scotland's 24 goals helped the Swans to a 92-point haul, 10 more than runners-up Nottingham Forest. Scotland scored 21 goals in the Championship the following term before moving to Wigan for £2million in July 2009 – a record fee received by the Welsh outfit.

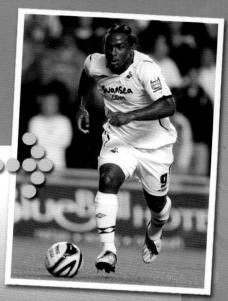

Watford

Watford were a top-flight club just three years ago, beating Leeds in the Play-Off Final to secure their promotion. However, 2009/10 was one of struggle in the second tier for the Vicarage Road side. It was in stark contrast to the glory years of the early 1980s when Elton John was chairman and Watford were competing for the top-flight title.

YOUNG IS OLD FAVOURITE

Ashley Young's move to Aston Villa in January 2007 is the record transfer fee the club have received. England international winger Young left for Villa Park for £9.65million, having scored 22 goals for the Hornets in all competitions. Young scored on his debut for Villa in a 3–1 defeat at Newcastle and went on to make his international bow in November 2007 in a friendly against Austria.

† It took almost £10million for Aston Villa to sign Ashley Young from Watford, the biggest transfer fee the Hornets have received.

HORNETS STUNG IN FINAL

Watford reached the FA Cup final for the only time in their history in 1984. Unfortunately for the Hornets, though, they were beaten 2–0 by Everton. Goals from Andy Gray and Graeme Sharp earned the Toffees their victory.

--> Under Graham Taylor, Watford went from the fourth tier of English football in 1977/78 to top-division runners-up in 1982/83.

ELTON CALLS THE TUNE

Superstar singer-songwriter Elton John has been chairman of Watford on two separate occasions. Taking over in 1976, the multi-million selling artist was then bought out by Jack Petchey in 1987. Sir Elton resumed the role in the late 1990s but stepped down again in 2002, although he is still an avid follower of the Hornets. He has also held the position of club president.

LEGEND LUTHER

Luther Blissett holds the Watford club records for both the most Football League appearances and the most Football League goals. Blissett appeared in 415 league games for the Hornets across three separate spells, scoring 148 goals in that time. He finished as the top scorer in the top flight in 1982/83 and as a result secured a £1million move to Italian giants AC Milan. He failed to make an impact at the San Siro, though, and promptly returned to Vicarage Road.

<-- Luther Blissett's first spell at Vicarage Road coincided with the Hornets' meteoric rise up the English football ladder.

TAYLOR-MADE FOR TOP FLIGHT

Watford finished as runners-up in their first-ever season in the top flight in 1982/83. Graham Taylor was in charge as the Hornets finished the campaign a point ahead of Manchester United but 11 behind champions Liverpool. It completed a meteoric rise by the club under Taylor's management as Watford had been playing in the fourth tier just five years previously. Taylor enjoyed a second spell as manager of the club between 1996 and 2001, leading them to the Premier League.

West Bromwich Albion

Formed in 1878, West Brom were top-flight title winners in 1919/20 and have also lifted the FA Cup on five occasions. More recently, they have yo-yoed between the second and top tiers, which has made for some exciting – if at times nervous – watching for the club's loyal supporters. The Baggies are back in the Barclays Premier League again in 2010/11.

ASTLE THE CUP KING

West Brom have won the FA Cup five times. The Baggies were victorious in 1888 – the year The Football League was formed – and followed that up with further success in 1892, 1931, 1954 and 1968. Alan Ashman led the club to glory against Everton in the 1968 final, with Jeff Astle scoring the only goal of the game in extra time. Striker Astle scored in every round of the competition that year.

⤏ *As well as his cup exploits for West Brom, Jeff Astle was a prolific marksman in The Football League, scoring 137 goals in 292 games for the Baggies from 1964 to 1974.*

BOMBER BROWN WINGS IN

Tony Brown holds plenty of records for West Brom. The forward is the club's all-time leading goalscorer, having scored 279 from an 18-year spell between 1963 and 1981, with 218 of those coming in the league – also a Baggies record. 'Bomber', as he was known by fans, was involved in 720 games for West Brom in total – an overall club appearance landmark – and featured 574 times in league matches.

ALBION STROLL ON

West Bromwich Albion is one of the most famous names in English football, but the club has not always been called as such. They were originally known as West Bromwich Strollers after their founders had to walk to Wednesbury to buy a match ball! They took on the name Albion in 1880.

WEST BROM'S 10-YEAR LEAGUE RECORD

2000/01 **(Second tier)**	6th
2001/02 **(Second tier)**	2nd
2002/03 **(Premier League)**	19th
2003/04 **(Second tier)**	2nd
2004/05 **(Premier League)**	17th
2005/06 **(Premier League)**	19th
2006/07 **(Second tier)**	4th
2007/08 **(Second tier)**	1st
2008/09 **(Premier League)**	20th
2009/10 **(Second tier)**	2nd

BOING, BOING BAGGIES

West Brom have developed an amazing ability to bounce back following relegation from the Premier League. The Baggies were promoted to the top flight in season 2001/02, and since then they have experienced the joy of promotion or the agony of relegation in seven of the last nine seasons, latterly as runners-up in the Championship in 2009/10. It's never dull at The Hawthorns!

CAPTAIN MARVEL

Bryan Robson's switch from West Brom to Manchester United in October 1981 was a British transfer record at the time. Robson followed manager Ron Atkinson and team-mate Remi Moses to Old Trafford in a £1.5million deal. That figure for a transfer between two British clubs was not beaten until Liverpool paid Newcastle £1.9million to sign striker Peter Beardsley in the summer of 1987. Robson returned to West Brom as manager from 2004–2006, keeping the club in the top flight in his first season in charge.

⤏ *Midfielder Bryan Robson had made almost 200 league appearances for West Brom, and made his full England debut, when Manchester United broke the British transfer record to sign him in 1981.*

npower League 1
Club Records

Several former Premier League clubs have found themselves in League 1 in recent times, with the likes of Southampton, Norwich, Charlton and Leeds having all played in the third tier. The Yorkshire derby between Leeds and Huddersfield at Elland Road was one of the highlights of 2009/10 and attracted a huge crowd of 36,723, while Southampton regularly played in front of over 30,000 spectators and Norwich 25,000, proving just how well-supported some of the teams in the lower divisions of English football are.

Jermaine Beckford's goals helped to propel Leeds United back to England's second tier in 2009/10, but his strike to knock Manchester United out of the FA Cup made bigger headlines. He later moved to Everton.

Akpo Sodje (centre) scores for Charlton in their 2–1 home defeat against Brighton in February 2010.

Brentford

ALL RHODES LEAD TO GOALS

Jordan Rhodes joined an elite group of players to have scored a 'perfect' hat-trick when he netted a treble for Brentford at Shrewsbury in January 2009. The young striker, who is now banging in the goals for Huddersfield, scored three in a row – the first with his right foot, the second with his left foot and the final one a header – as the Bees claimed a 3–1 victory.

⟵ Jordan Rhodes was on loan from Ipswich when he netted a 'perfect' hat-trick for Brentford at Shrewsbury in a League 1 match in January 2009. Rhodes become the Bees' youngest-ever hat-trick scorer.

HOME COMFORTS FOR BEES

Griffin Park was a fortress during the 1929/30 season as the Bees won all 21 of their home matches. That was still not enough for them to win the title, though, as they finished runners-up to Plymouth, who they had beaten 3–0 at home earlier in the campaign.

THE ICE MAN

Brentford paid a club-record £750,000 to sign defender Hermann Hreidarsson from Crystal Palace in September 1998, but he only stayed for 13 months before creating more Bees history. The Iceland international's performances in helping the club to the fourth-tier title in 1998/99 saw him make a £2.5million move to the Premier League with Wimbledon – the biggest fee received by Brentford.

Brighton & Hove Albion

SEAGULLS SOARING HIGH

Brighton claimed back-to-back promotions as champions in 2000/01 and 2001/02. Micky Adams was in charge as the Seagulls soared to the fourth-tier title. They finished the campaign with 92 points – their best total since three points for a win was introduced. Adams left for Leicester in October the following year but Peter Taylor successfully completed the job.

⟵ Danny Cullip celebrates after scoring for Brighton against Cheltenham during the Seagulls' run to the fourth-tier championship in 2000/01.

BOBBY DAZZLER

Fulham striker Bobby Zamora shot to prominence while playing for Brighton. He moved to the club from Bristol Rovers in August 2000 following a successful loan spell and left for Tottenham in a club-record £1.5million switch three years later having netted 77 goals in 130 league and cup appearances.

WARDY WONDERLAND

Peter Ward holds the record for the most goals scored in a single season by a Brighton player. Seagulls legend Ward netted 32 times in the league during the 1976/77 campaign as Albion finished runners-up to Mansfield in the third tier.

⬆ Bobby Zamora was an instant hit for Brighton after leaving Bristol Rovers in 2000 and he earned the Seagulls a club-record £1.5million transfer fee when Spurs signed him in 2003.

Bristol Rovers

BRADFORD BONANZA

Geoff Bradford holds a number of goalscoring records for Bristol Rovers. He is the club's all-time top scorer, having netted 242 times in the league during a 15-year stay between 1949 and 1964. Bradford also scored the most league goals in a single season for Rovers in 1952/53, grabbing 33 as the club claimed the third-tier title. He scored four goals in one game against Rotherham in March 1959 – a feat he shares with 10 other players.

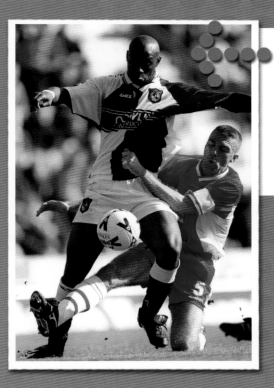

→ Jason Roberts of Rovers tries to evade the challenge of City's Shaun Taylor during a 1999 Bristol derby. The match ended in a goalless draw.

CITY RIVALRY

Bristol Rovers last faced bitter rivals Bristol City when they fought for a place in the final of the Johnstone's Paint Trophy in 2007. The Pirates claimed a 1–0 win over two legs but went on to lose to Doncaster at the Millennium Stadium. There have been 103 games between the two sides in all competitions, with Rovers winning 28 and City 42 while 33 have ended all-square.

PIRATES STEAL VICTORY

Bristol Rovers equalled their best run in the FA Cup in 2008 when they reached the quarter-finals. The highlight was a penalty shootout victory in the third round against top-flight Fulham after the Pirates had forced a replay. Rovers slipped to a 5–1 home defeat against West Brom in the last eight – the first time they had reached that stage since 1958.

Carlisle United

→ On-loan goalkeeper Jimmy Glass (red shirt) runs away in celebration after his last-minute goal against Plymouth at Brunton Park preserved Carlisle's Football League status in 1999.

THE TOP AND BOTTOM OF IT

Carlisle were in dreamland at the start of the 1974/75 season as they led the top flight after the opening three games. They claimed 2–0 victories at Chelsea and Middlesbrough in their first two matches and followed that with a 1–0 success at home to Tottenham. Unfortunately for the Cumbrians, they ended their one and only top-flight campaign at the bottom of the table.

CARLISLE MANAGERS SINCE 2000

Ian Atkins	2000–2001
Roddy Collins	2001–2002, 2002–2003
Paul Simpson	2003–2006
Neil McDonald	2006–2007
John Ward	2007–2008
Greg Abbott	2008–Present

TOUCH OF GLASS

Goalkeeper Jimmy Glass earned a place in Carlisle folklore when he scored an injury-time winner against Plymouth on the last day of the 1998/99 season to secure the club's Football League status in dramatic fashion. There were just 10 seconds of the Brunton Park clash remaining when shot-stopper Glass, who had come up for a corner, volleyed home after Scott Dobie's header had been parried. That was enough to earn the Cumbrians the win they needed to avoid the drop as Scarborough were relegated to the Conference instead.

Charlton Athletic

CHARLTON'S CENTENARY AWARDS

Greatest Manager	Alan Curbishley
Greatest Goalkeeper	Sam Bartram
Greatest Defender	Richard Rufus
Greatest Midfielder	Mark Kinsella
Greatest Striker	Derek Hales
Greatest Overseas Player	Eddie Firmani

MENDONCA'S THE MAN

Charlton were involved in one of the most memorable Play-Off Finals ever in May 1998. The Addicks beat Sunderland 7–6 on penalties after a ding-dong battle had finished 4–4 at the end of extra time. Clive Mendonca scored a hat-trick for the Londoners – his third coming in the 103rd minute to send the game to penalties. Michael Gray missed the crucial kick for Sunderland to send Charlton into the Premier League.

BARTRAM STANDS TALL

There is a nine-foot statue of Charlton goalkeeping legend Sam Bartram outside The Valley. Bartram is the club's record appearance holder, having featured 623 times in all competitions from 1934–1956. He was immortalised as part of the Addicks' centenary celebrations in 2005, when he was also voted as Charlton's greatest goalkeeper.

← Clive Mendonca slides in to score his third and Charlton's fourth goal in their memorable 1998 Play-Off Final against Sunderland at Wembley.

Colchester United

LEEDS LEFT REELING

Colchester reached the quarter-finals of the FA Cup in 1970/71 – their best-ever run in the competition. In the fourth tier at the time, they were drawn against Leeds in the fifth round, who were flying high in the top flight under manager Don Revie. Colchester pulled off one of the greatest shocks in the competition's history with a 3–2 victory. Everton proved too strong for them in the last eight, however, running out 5–0 winners.

COMMUNITY SPIRIT

The Us left their home of 71 years to move into a new £14million all-seater stadium in July 2008. Richard Cresswell was the last player to score at Layer Road as they were beaten 1–0 by Stoke. Athletic Bilbao striker Aritz Aduriz netted the first goal at the new Colchester Community Stadium in a pre-season friendly in August 2008.

Us RIDING HIGH

Colchester enjoyed their highest league finish in 2006/07 when they ended the season in 10th place in the Championship. The Us had been tipped to make an instant return to the third tier having gained automatic promotion in 2005/06. But they defied the pundits, with Jamie Cureton ending the campaign as the league's top scorer with 23 goals.

← Jamie Cureton acknowledges the Colchester fans. His 23 goals helped the Us to a best-ever league finish in 2006/07.

Exeter City

GRECIANS HOLD FIRM

Exeter recorded one of the most famous results in their history in 2004/05 when they held mighty Manchester United to a goalless draw in the FA Cup third round at Old Trafford. The Grecians were in the Conference at the time, but they held their own against a United side featuring the likes of Cristiano Ronaldo, Paul Scholes and Ryan Giggs before losing out in a replay.

 Kwame Ampadu (left) and Gary Sawyer (3) combine to frustrate Manchester United's Ryan Giggs during Exeter's 0–0 FA Cup draw at Old Trafford in 2005.

MOVING ON UP

The Grecians returned to The Football League after a five-year absence in 2008, and they made it back-to-back promotions the following term. A stunning comeback in the semi-final of the Conference play-offs against Torquay – they scored four second-half goals to win 5–3 on aggregate – set up a Wembley date with Cambridge. A single goal from Rob Edwards was enough to secure victory, and in 2008/09 they finished second in the fourth tier to move up again.

THE BOY DONE GOOD

Goalscoring great Cliff Bastin was handed his Football League debut by Exeter at the age of 16 years and 31 days – making him the youngest player to feature for the club. Winger Bastin was sold to Arsenal for £2,000 when he was 17 and went on to become the Gunners' all-time leading goalscorer in the league until he was surpassed by Thierry Henry in 2006.

Rob Edwards' goal in the Conference Play-Off Final against Cambridge restored Exeter's Football League status in May 2008.

Gillingham

STRIKER SUCCESS

Goalscoring duo Robert Taylor and Carl Asaba hold Gillingham's transfer records. Taylor scored 39 goals in 70 matches for the club between August 1998 and November 1999 before Manchester City splashed out £1.5million to sign him – a record transfer fee received by the Gills. The club's biggest outlay was £600,000 to sign Asaba from Reading in August 1998.

Gillingham's most expensive signing was Carl Asaba, for £600,000, from Reading. He scored 40 goals for the Gills.

CASCARINO SUITS GILLS

In 1982, Tony Cascarino moved to Gillingham from non-league side Crockenhill in exchange for a set of tracksuits! Republic of Ireland striker Cascarino went on to become a Gills great, scoring 110 times for the club before moving to Millwall for £225,000 in 1987.

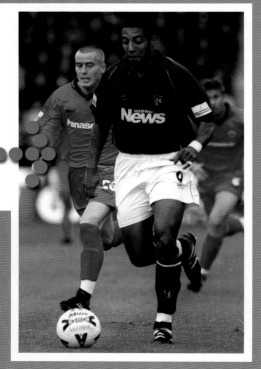

WEMBLEY AGONY TO ECSTASY

Gillingham endured the agony of losing a Play-Off Final in heartbreaking fashion in 1999 but emerged victorious on their return to Wembley a year later. The Gills were leading 2–0 against Manchester City going into the last minute of normal time in the first final, but amazingly City scored twice to send the game into extra time and then snatched victory on penalties. However, Gillingham bounced back in 2000 – coming from behind to beat Wigan 3–2.

Hartlepool United

FINAL WOE FOR POOLS

Hartlepool's highest Football League finish is sixth in the third tier. They achieved that in both 2003/04 and again the following campaign. The 2004/05 season was the most successful in the club's history so far as they reached the Play-Off Final, where they were beaten 4–2 by Sheffield Wednesday after extra time at the Millennium Stadium in Cardiff. Pools were relegated from the third tier the following year.

↪ *No one could question former England Under-21 international Ritchie Humphreys' loyalty to the Hartlepool cause.*

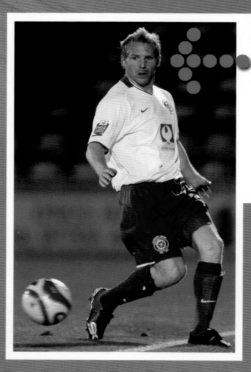

RITCHIE'S RECORD RUN

Ritchie Humphreys holds the record for the most consecutive league appearances in a Hartlepool shirt – a feat that earned him recognition from Buckingham Palace! He didn't miss a game in his first five years at the club and was honoured by the Queen for a remarkable run of 234 unbroken matches. Humphreys, who has played at left-back, in midfield and attack for Pools, was also named Hartlepool's Player of the Century in May 2008.

THAT WINNING FEELING

Season 2006/07 was one of the most memorable in Hartlepool's history. It started poorly, with the club taking six games to secure their first league win, but just when it looked like their promotion dream was struggling, a 2–1 victory at Accrington on November 18 2006 sparked a club-record run of nine consecutive league wins, the following eight without conceding, which carried Pools to a second-place finish.

Huddersfield Town

STRIKER MAKES HIS MARC

Marcus Stewart became Huddersfield's record signing when he arrived at the club from Bristol Rovers in July 1996. The striker made over 130 appearances and scored 68 goals for the Terriers before he claimed the record for Huddersfield's biggest transfer fee received in February 2000 when he moved to Ipswich for £2.75million. He helped his new club secure promotion to the Premier League at the end of that season.

← *Marcus Stewart was Huddersfield's record signing when he joined them in 1996. Four years and 68 goals later, the Terriers were paid a club-record £2.75million by Ipswich for his services.*

TRIPLE WHAMMY FOR TOWN

In 1926, Huddersfield became the first team in history to win three successive top-flight titles, a feat that only three other clubs – Arsenal, Liverpool and Manchester United – have been able to match.

UNLUCKY SEVEN FOR TERRIERS

Huddersfield were the losing side in one of the most amazing comebacks in Football League history in December 1957. The Terriers were leading 5–1 at Charlton with half an hour to go against 10 men, but they ended up losing 7–6! Bill Shankly was manager of Huddersfield as they allowed Johnny Summers to score five goals – including a quick-fire hat-trick – and set up two more to snatch Charlton a stunning victory.

← *Bill Shankly would not have been a happy man when his Huddersfield team lost 7–6 at Charlton in 1957.*

Leeds United

FOND MEMORIES FOR LEEDS

Leeds may have been playing in the third tier recently, but it was not so long ago that they were competing in a Champions League semi-final. In season 1999/00, the Yorkshire club finished third in the Premier League to qualify for Europe's top competition. They went on to reach the last four in May 2001, where they were beaten 3–0 over two legs by Spanish club Valencia.

--→ *John Charles is a Leeds legend. The 'Gentle Giant' made a brief return to the club in 1962, between spells at Juventus and Roma.*

LEEDS' LONGEST-SERVING MANAGERS

Don Revie	1961–1974
Billy Hampson	1935–1947
Howard Wilkinson	1988–1996
Dick Ray	1927–1935
Arthur Fairclough	1920–1927

GOALSCORING GIANT

John Charles is second in the list of Leeds' all-time Football League goalscorers, but he does hold the club record for the most goals in a single season. The 'Gentle Giant', as he was affectionately known, netted 42 times in the league in Leeds' 1953/54 campaign. He left Elland Road for Italian giants Juventus in 1957 for a then British-record transfer fee of £65,000.

Leyton Orient

LAST FOUR FOR ORIENT

Leyton Orient reached the semi-finals of the FA Cup while playing in the second tier in 1977/78. They finished 14th in the league that season, but an impressive cup run saw them beat then top-flight teams in Norwich, Chelsea and Middlesbrough along the way before they lost 3–0 to Arsenal at Stamford Bridge in the last four.

←--- *Defender Gabriel Zakuani was 20 years old when Fulham paid Leyton Orient £1million for him, but he didn't start a league match for the Cottagers.*

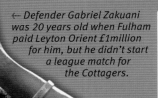

Os ON THE RUN

Between October 1993 and September 1995, Leyton Orient failed to win a single game away from home in The Football League. Following Colin West's goal at Hull in a 1–0 triumph on October 30 1993, Orient embarked on a 42-game winless run on the road which resulted in them being relegated from the third tier. They failed to win any of their first three games of the 1995/96 season in the fourth tier, before goals from Ian Hendon and Alex Inglethorpe finally secured a 2–1 victory at Northampton.

GIFT OF THE GAB

The biggest transfer fee ever received by Leyton Orient is £1million from Fulham for Gabriel Zakuani in July 2006. Defender Zakuani made more than 90 appearances for the club between 2002 and 2006, scoring three goals.

Millwall

LIONS HUNGARY FOR EUROPE

Millwall made it all the way to the FA Cup final in 2004 and as a result qualified for the UEFA Cup the following year. The Lions avoided Premier League opposition until the FA Cup final, where they lost 3–0 to Manchester United. Their European adventure ended at the first hurdle, as they were beaten 4–2 over two legs by Hungarian champions Ferencvaros.

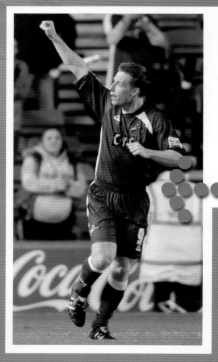

┄┄► *Neil Harris overcame illness and injury to become Millwall's all-time leading scorer. This goal celebration was in the FA Cup against AFC Wimbledon in 2009.*

HARRIS ROARS INTO HISTORY BOOKS

Neil Harris is Millwall's all-time leading goalscorer. Harris, who turned 33 in 2010, overtook Teddy Sheringham's record with his 112th goal for the Lions in an FA Cup tie against Crewe in January 2009. He improved the mark to 117 by the end of that campaign and has since continued to extended his run. He scored two hat-tricks alone during the first two months of the 2009/10 season.

GRAHAM HAS MILLWALL MOVING UP

George Graham began his managerial career at Millwall. The Lions were bottom of the third tier when he took over during 1982/83 and, after saving the club from relegation, he guided them to promotion two years later. Graham left the club for Arsenal in 1986, where he went on to spend nine successful years.

MK Dons

McLEOD HAS SILVER LINING

Izale McLeod is MK Dons' all-time leading scorer, having netted 60 goals in a three-year spell at the club between 2004 and 2007. McLeod scored on his Dons debut against Barnsley and went on to score 17 more times in his first season. A haul of 24 goals in 2006/07 helped the Dons to a play-off place, but they were beaten at the semi-final stage by Shrewsbury.

┄┄► *No one has scored more goals for the MK Dons since the club was formed than Izale McLeod. His form earned him an England Under-21 cap in 2006.*

FIVE-STAR DONS

The Dons equalled their record margin of victory when they beat Hartlepool 5–0 at Victoria Park in 2009/10. Jermaine Easter opened the scoring against one of his former clubs, with a Gary Liddle own goal and further strikes from Peter Leven, Sam Baldock and Jason Puncheon securing a memorable win. They had won by the same scoreline in December 2007 when Accrington were the opponents.

ROVERS AND OUT

Keith Andrews created a new transfer record for the MK Dons when he left for Blackburn in 2008. Paul Ince, then in charge at Rovers having previously been with the Dons, took his former captain to Ewood Park with him in a £1.2million deal.

Norwich City

LAMBERT WALKS TO CITY

The Canaries suffered the heaviest home defeat in their history on the opening day of the 2009/10 campaign when they were beaten 7–1 by Colchester. Club legend Bryan Gunn, in charge of Norwich at the time, parted company with the club soon after and was replaced by Paul Lambert – the man who had been in the Colchester dug-out for that game!

CANARIES FLYING HIGH

Norwich secured their highest-ever league finish under manager Mike Walker in 1992/93. They ended what was the first Premier League campaign in third place, two points behind Aston Villa and 12 behind champions Manchester United.

←⋯ Mike Walker guided Norwich to their best-ever league finish in 1993. The Canaries then enjoyed a UEFA Cup run that included a victory over Bayern Munich.

ASHTON UNDER THE HAMMER

Norwich made a tidy profit from the sale of Dean Ashton to West Ham in January 2006. The £3million paid by the Canaries to Crewe for the striker in January 2005 is a club record, but when he left for Upton Park in a £7.25million switch a year later he broke the record for the biggest transfer fee received by the Carrow Road club. An ankle injury forced Ashton to retire in December 2009, aged just 26.

⋯→ Dean Ashton seemed destined for great things when Norwich paid Crewe £3million for his signature in 2005 and collected a club-record fee of £7.25million from West Ham a year later, but injuries ensured it wasn't to be.

Oldham Athletic

OLDHAM MANAGERS SINCE 1982

Joe Royle	1982–1994
Graeme Sharp	1994–1997
Neil Warnock	1997–1998
Andy Ritchie	1998–2001
Mick Wadsworth	2001–2002
Iain Dowie	2002–2003
Brian Talbot	2004–2005
Ronnie Moore	2005–2006
John Sheridan	2006–2009
Joe Royle	2009
Dave Penney	2009–2010

PLASTIC LATICS

Oldham were one of four English clubs to install a plastic pitch during the 1980s. Artificial surfaces were also introduced at QPR, Luton and Preston in an effort to reduce maintenance costs and limit the number of postponements. However, they had their critics and Oldham got rid of their plastic pitch in 1991.

BY ROYLE APPOINTMENT

Joe Royle established his managerial reputation with Oldham, leading the club to the top flight in 1991 and also taking them to the final of the League Cup, where they lost to Nottingham Forest. Oldham also reached the last four of the FA Cup on two occasions during Royle's 12-year spell in charge, losing both times to Manchester United.

←⋯ Joe Royle ended Oldham's 68-year absence from England's top division when he took the Latics up in 1991, and his cup record was also quite impressive. He returned to Boundary Park briefly in 2009.

Southampton

DELL BOYS

The Saints moved from The Dell to their current St Mary's Stadium in 2001. Matt Le Tissier scored the last goal at their old ground as they beat Arsenal 3–2. Marian Pahars was the first home player to score a league goal at St Mary's, but Southampton lost 3–1 to Aston Villa.

LE TISS IS SPOT ON

Matt Le Tissier is a Southampton legend. The attacking midfielder joined the club as a youngster in 1986 and played for the Saints until his retirement in 2002. Le Tissier is second only to Mick Channon in the list of all-time Southampton goalscorers, while he was also incredibly reliable from the penalty spot. He took nearly 50 spot-kicks for the club and missed just once!

⟵ When they moved into St Mary's, Southampton may have had a beautiful new ground, but the tight confines of The Dell, their old home, had been a big advantage.

SAINTS MARCH TO GLORY

Southampton won the FA Cup for the only time in their history in 1976, stunning Manchester United 1–0 at Wembley. United had finished third in the top flight that year but a late Bobby Stokes goal snatched victory for the unfancied Saints.

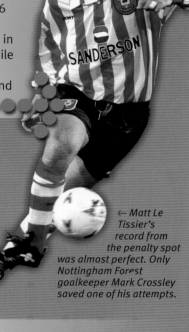

⟵ Matt Le Tissier's record from the penalty spot was almost perfect. Only Nottingham Forest goalkeeper Mark Crossley saved one of his attempts.

Southend United

SHRIMPERS MAKE PROGRESS

Steve Tilson led the Shrimpers to back-to-back promotions in 2005 and 2006 as they climbed from the fourth tier to the second tier in impressive fashion. They beat Lincoln 2–0 after extra time in the 2005 Play-Off Final as goals from Freddy Eastwood and Duncan Jupp gave them the edge. The following season they won the League 1 title, pipping rivals Colchester by three points.

⟶ Freddy Eastwood's Football League debut for Southend against Swansea at Roots Hall in October 2004 was spectacular. He scored after seven seconds and finished with a hat-trick.

EASTWOOD GUNS FOR UNITED

Southend stunned holders Manchester United in the fourth round of the Carling Cup in 2006/07 on their way to reaching the quarter-finals – the club's best-ever run in the major cup competitions. A Freddy Eastwood free-kick was enough to see off the Red Devils.

MILLENNIUM MISERY

Southend reached the final of the Football League Trophy two years in a row but lost out on both occasions in 2004 and 2005. They were beaten 2–0 by Blackpool the first time around before their return visit to Cardiff's Millennium Stadium the following season ended with a 2–0 defeat against Wrexham after extra time.

Stockport County

GIANTS CUT DOWN TO SIZE

Stockport reached the semi-finals of the League Cup in 1997, despite being in the third tier at the time. County, who gained promotion that season, had already knocked out top-flight opposition in Blackburn, West Ham and Southampton when they came up against Middlesbrough in the last four. After losing the first leg 2–0 at home, they claimed an impressive 1–0 win on Teesside in the return, but it wasn't enough to progress.

BITTER PILL FOR PALMER

The Hatters suffered a club-record number of consecutive defeats in season 2001/02 when they were relegated to the third tier. They finished the campaign having taken just 26 points, with second-bottom Barnsley on 48. County, under the management of Carlton Palmer at the time, lost 10 consecutive games between November 24 2001 and January 13 2002 and conceded 102 goals that season.

HATS OFF TO DUO

Stockport broke both of their transfer records in 1998, with strikers heading into and out of Edgeley Park. Middlesbrough paid County £1.6million for prolific forward Alun Armstrong in February – the largest fee received by the club. The Hatters then splashed half of that cash on Ian Thomas-Moore from Nottingham Forest that summer, setting a new record for a transfer fee paid.

↓ West Ham's Croatian defender Slaven Bilic struggles to deal with Stockport striker Alun Armstrong in 1996. Two years later, Middlesbrough paid County a record £1.6 million to sign him.

Swindon Town

YOUNG ROBIN RIDEOUT

Paul Rideout became the youngest player to turn out for Swindon when he made his debut aged 16 years and 107 days against Hull on November 29 1980. He scored four goals that season and netted 38 in 95 appearances overall. Rideout went on to score the winning goal for Everton in the 1995 FA Cup final.

SWINDON'S LEADING GOALSCORERS

Harry Morris	229
Harold Fleming	203
Don Rogers	178
Maurice Owen	165
Archie Bown	139

ROBINS ROCKED

Swindon made it to the Premier League in 1993, but their top-flight adventure lasted just one season. Glenn Hoddle led the Robins to promotion via the play-offs as they beat Leicester 4–3 at Wembley. However, under Hoddle's replacement, John Gorman, Swindon managed just five wins and conceded 100 goals – a Premier League record – as they were relegated with 30 points.

← Glenn Hoddle was player-manager at Swindon when he guided the Robins through the play-offs and into the Premier League in 1993. By the time the following season had kicked off, Hoddle was Chelsea's manager.

Tranmere Rovers

ALDRIDGE ON FORM

John Aldridge holds the post-war record for scoring the most goals in a season for Tranmere. The former Republic of Ireland striker, who also holds the club record for the most international caps, with 30, netted 40 times during the 1991/92 campaign.

⤑ *John Aldridge scored 138 goals in 221 league games for Tranmere and later managed the club.*

ROVERS OUT-FOXED

Tranmere recorded one of the most memorable achievements in their history when they reached the final of the League Cup in 2000. Having edged past Blackpool in the first round, Rovers beat Premier League Coventry 6–4 on aggregate. Wins against Oxford and Barnsley followed before a quarter-final against Middlesbrough and a semi-final with Bolton, which they won 4–0 over two legs. However, their dream run ended when they were beaten by Leicester at Wembley.

IN SAFE HANDS

Goalkeeper Eric Nixon kept a club-record 25 clean sheets as Rovers finished runners-up in the fourth tier and gained promotion in 1989. Nixon spent nine years at Prenton Park between 1988 and 1997 and, when he returned to the club for a second spell in 1999, he became the oldest player to appear for the club aged 39 years and 352 days.

⟵ *Eric Nixon played his final competitive match for Tranmere in September 2002, just two weeks before his 40th birthday.*

Walsall

DANN'S THE MAN

The biggest transfer fee received by Walsall is the £750,000 Coventry paid to sign Scott Dann in January 2008. Having come through the ranks, Dann established himself in the Saddlers' defence before being snapped up by the Sky Blues. He moved on again to Birmingham in the summer of 2009 for a fee thought to be around £3.5million.

HARRISON HITS 500

Colin Harrison is Walsall's record all-time appearance holder in The Football League, having turned out for the club 467 times between 1964 and 1981. He is one of three players to have made over 500 appearances for the Saddlers in all competitions, with Nick Atthey and Colin Taylor also achieving the feat.

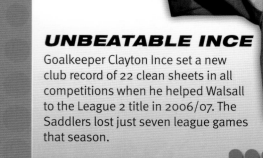

UNBEATABLE INCE

Goalkeeper Clayton Ince set a new club record of 22 clean sheets in all competitions when he helped Walsall to the League 2 title in 2006/07. The Saddlers lost just seven league games that season.

⤑ *Walsall's Trinidad & Tobago international goalkeeper Clayton Ince kept 22 clean sheets during the Saddlers' League 2 championship campaign of 2006/07.*

Wycombe Wanderers

WYCOMBE'S FOOTBALL LEAGUE MANAGERS

Martin O'Neill	1993–1995
Alan Smith	1995–1996
John Gregory	1996–1998
Neil Smillie	1998–1999
Lawrie Sanchez	1999–2003
Tony Adams	2003–2004
John Gorman	2004–2006
Paul Lambert	2006–2008
Peter Taylor	2008–2009
Gary Waddock	2009–Present

⟶ *Martin O'Neill took his first real steps in football management at Wycombe in 1990. It took him just three seasons to guide the Chairboys into The Football League and win two FA Trophies.*

O'NEILL EARNS HERO STATUS

Martin O'Neill was responsible for taking Wycombe into The Football League in 1993, and he cemented his hero status by guiding the club to a second successive promotion via the play-offs the following season. The Chairboys finished sixth in the third tier the season after that before O'Neill left to take charge at Norwich.

EXTRAORDINARY ESSANDOH

Wycombe famously reached the semi-finals of the FA Cup in 2001, thanks in no small part to a striker signed via a television text service! Lawrie Sanchez, who was Wanderers' manager at the time, placed an advert appealing for a new forward and Roy Essandoh's agent got in touch. Essandoh came off the bench to score a 90th-minute winner against Leicester and set up a semi-final clash with Liverpool at Villa Park, although the dream ended there as they were beaten 2–1.

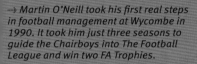

Yeovil Town

PHIL YOUR BOOTS

Phil Jevons holds the distinction of scoring the most league goals in a single season for Yeovil. The former Everton trainee netted 27 times in 2004/05 to help the Glovers claim the League 2 title. Jevons, who left the club to link up with his former Yeovil boss Gary Johnson at Bristol City in the summer of 2006, also boasts the club record for the most Football League goals in total with 42.

PLAY-OFF WOE FOR GLOVERS

Yeovil's highest-ever league finish came in 2006/07 when they reached the play-offs after ending the season in fifth place in League 1. The Glovers made it to the final by overcoming Nottingham Forest 5–4 over two legs, but they were beaten 2–0 by Blackpool at Wembley.

SKIVERTON BOSSES RECORDS

Yeovil manager Terry Skiverton holds the club record for the most Football League appearances. A talismanic captain during his playing days at Huish Park, Skiverton made 195 appearances before he stopped playing to focus on his managerial duties. He replaced Russell Slade in the Yeovil dugout in February 2009.

⟶ *Terry Skiverton, here playing in an FA Cup tie against Liverpool in 2004, is a Yeovil legend. As a player, he is the club's record Football League appearance holder and in 2009, he took over as boss at Huish Park.*

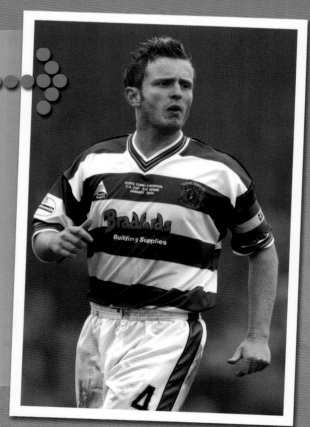

npower League 2 Club Records

There is always a lot to play for in League 2, with automatic promotion extending to the top three places in the table while relegation sends the bottom two teams out of The Football League. New faces such as Burton Albion, Dagenham & Redbridge and Morecambe have arrived in the fourth tier over recent seasons, while Bradford City were playing in the Premier League a decade ago.

Kasper Schmeichel, playing for Notts County, guesses correctly and saves Steven Schumacher's penalty during the Magpies' 2–0 defeat of Crewe at Meadow Lane in October 2009. Schmeichel later moved to Leeds.

Marvin Bartley (left) of Bournemouth tries to tackle Rochdale's Chris Dagnall during the goalless draw between two of the teams who were ultimately promoted from League 2 in 2009/10.

Accrington Stanley

ACCRINGTON STANLEY, WHO ARE THEY?

Accrington resigned from The Football League in 1962 after suffering financial difficulties, but they returned after a 44-year gap in 2006. Their first game back in the fourth tier was away at Chester, where they lost 2–0. They finished their comeback season in 20th place.

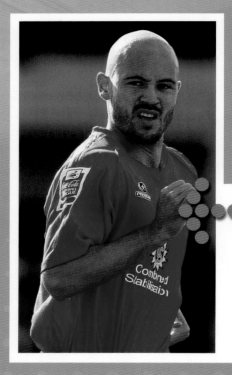

⟶ Paul Mullin's goals helped the reformed Accrington Stanley return to The Football League in 2006.

STANLEY GO OUT FIGHTING

Stanley enjoyed their best FA Cup run since their reformation in season 2003/04. Having knocked Huddersfield out of the competition, they then got the better of Bournemouth in the second round. Paul Mullin was on the scoresheet in a 1–1 draw at Dean Court and following a goalless draw in the replay, Accrington went through on penalties. They were beaten 2–1 by Colchester in the next round.

MULLIN'S THE MAN

Paul Mullin was the first player since Accrington's reformation to top 400 appearances for the club. The veteran striker is a Stanley hero, having scored almost 200 goals in an eight-year spell. After a loan spell at Bradford, Mullin finally left Accrington to join Morecambe in August 2009.

Aldershot Town

DONNELLY EARNS DISTINCTION

Scott Donnelly scored Aldershot Town's first-ever Football League goal at Accrington on August 9 2008. The Shots won the game 1–0 and followed that with a 1–1 draw against Bournemouth – Louie Soares scoring the club's first home Football League goal.

⟵ Goalkeeper Nikki Bull was first choice for Aldershot in the Ryman League, Blue Square Premier and League 2, and he played in 173 consecutive games between 2005 and 2009.

TOWN'S LEADING GOALSCORERS

Mark Butler	155
Gary Abbott	120
Steve Stairs	75
Roy Young	75
John Grant	57

BULL GRABS THE RECORD

Nikki Bull holds the record for the most consecutive appearances in an Aldershot shirt since the club's formation in 1992. Goalkeeper Bull played 173 matches in a row for the Shots from August 13 2005 to April 15 2009. Bull, who moved to Brentford on a free transfer in August 2009, is second on Aldershot's list of all-time appearance holders with 313 – 176 less than Jason Chewins, who played 489 games for the club.

Barnet

BEES BUZZING

Barnet's first campaign in The Football League in 1991 got off to an amazing start when they were beaten 7–4 at home by Crewe. Barry Fry's side then drew 5–5 at home to Brentford in the first leg of their debut League Cup game!

FREEDMAN ON FIRE

Dougie Freedman holds Barnet's record for scoring the most league goals in a season. The 1994/95 campaign saw the prolific striker score 24 times in the fourth tier as the Bees finished 11th. Freedman also shares the club record for the most goals in a single game, scoring four in a 6–2 victory over Rochdale in September 1994. Lee Hodges also netted four against Dale two years later. Freedman moved to Crystal Palace for a club-record fee of £800,000 in September 1995.

⟵ Barry Fry's first match as a Football League boss, with Barnet in 1991, saw 11 goals; his first game in the League Cup brought another 10.

GRAZIOLI SHOOTS DOWN BEES

Barnet suffered their record defeat in September 1998 when they lost 9–1 to Peterborough at Underhill. Giuliano Grazioli, who went on to play over 130 games for the Bees, scored five goals that day in a stunning all-round display. All was forgiven in season 2004/05 when the hot-shot striker helped the club gain promotion back to The Football League.

⟶ Giuliano Grazioli scored five goals for Peterborough in Barnet's record Football League defeat, but he later joined the Bees and helped them to reach League 2.

Bournemouth

CHERRIES PICK OFF BIG GUNS

Bournemouth enjoyed their greatest FA Cup run in 1956/57, reaching the sixth round, where they were narrowly beaten by Manchester United. Having knocked out Burton, Swindon and Accrington, the Cherries landed a trip to Wolves, who were third in the top flight at the time. They went on to claim a stunning 1–0 win at Molineux and earn a home game against Tottenham. Another superb performance brought a 3–1 victory and a meeting with United. However, the dream ended there, although Bournemouth did gain revenge in 1984 when, under manager Harry Redknapp, they stunned the reigning FA Cup holders 2–0 to record one of their most famous results.

† Darren Anderton's Bournemouth career began with a 40-yard goal on his debut in 2006 and ended with a match-winning volley in 2008, after which he retired.

ANDERTON GOES OUT ON A HIGH

Former England international midfielder Darren Anderton enjoyed a fairytale end to his career at Bournemouth in December 2008. Having come on as a substitute just before the hour mark, Anderton scored the only goal of the game against Chester with two minutes remaining – a stunning volley. Anderton made almost 500 league appearances for five different clubs.

MIDFIELD MAESTROS

Bournemouth have received club-record £800,000 transfer fees for both Joe Parkinson and Matt Holland. Parkinson moved to Everton, where he formed part of the team that won the FA Cup in 1995. Sadly, he was forced to retire through injury in November 1999 aged just 28. Former Cherries captain Holland, also a midfielder, left Dean Court for Ipswich in the summer of 1997, helping his new club to the Premier League.

Bradford City

← The first English club for Aussie goalkeeper Mark Schwarzer was Bradford City, and he helped them to avoid relegation to the third tier in 1996/97.

SOUTHALL TURNS BACK THE CLOCK

Neville Southall is the oldest player to have turned out for Bradford. The former Everton goalkeeper was 41 years and 178 days old when he made his only appearance for the Bantams in a 2–1 defeat to Leeds at Valley Parade on March 12 2000. That one-off display made Southall the fourth oldest player ever to appear in the Premier League.

SELECTION POSER

The Bantams used a total of 42 players in the 1996/97 campaign – a club record that still stands. Their squad that year was made up of players from 11 different nations, including two Australians (Mark Schwarzer and George Kulcsar) a Finn, two Swedes, a Norwegian, a Brazilian (Edinho) and players from Portugal and Holland, as well as the home nations.

BANTAMS ON THE RUN

Bradford's record number of consecutive victories is 10, achieved during the 1983/84 season. Their impressive run started on November 26 1983 against Brentford, with the last win coming on February 3 the following year. They finished that season in seventh place in the third tier.

Burton Albion

BREWERS MAKE THE BIG TIME

Burton Albion were promoted to The Football League for the first time in their history in 2008/09. Nigel Clough was in charge at the start of the campaign, helping them to open up a 13-point lead at the top of the Conference. When he left to take over at Derby, Roy McFarland was placed in charge until the end of the season, and he extended their advantage to 19 points. However, Burton's season stuttered and they eventually won the title by just two points from Cambridge following a tense finish.

← Nigel Clough spent 10 years as Burton Albion manager, but left them a few months before they won promotion to League 2.

UNITED HELD

Albion held Manchester United to a goalless draw in the third round of the FA Cup in 2005/06 – one of their most famous results. They were up against a team containing the likes of Ole Gunnar Solskjaer, Louis Saha and Giuseppe Rossi, while Cristiano Ronaldo and Wayne Rooney came on for United with an hour gone. Battling Burton held their own to secure a memorable draw and a replay at Old Trafford, where they were eventually beaten 5–0.

ROBINS LEAVE ALBION RED-FACED

Burton were involved in one of the most bizarre games in Football League history in 2009/10 when they were beaten 6–5 at home by Cheltenham. The hosts were leading 5–3 with just five minutes remaining but incredibly lost the game when Justin Richards completed an astonishing comeback in injury time. Substitute Michael Pook was the Cheltenham hero, scoring a hat-trick in six minutes.

Bury

JOHNSON HITS THE TOWN

David Johnson's £1.1million move to Ipswich in November 1997 is the record transfer fee received by Bury. Johnson scored 18 league goals in 97 appearances in a highly-successful two-year spell with the Shakers.

⇢ *Released by Manchester United in 1995, David Johnson spent two excellent seasons at Bury before the future Jamaica international joined Ipswich.*

CRAIG'S GOAL MAD

Craig Madden netted the most league goals for Bury in a single season on his way to becoming the Shakers' all-time leading scorer. Madden scored 35 times in the 1981/82 season as the club finished ninth in the fourth tier. In eight years at the club, Madden netted 129 league goals.

LANDMARK SEASON FOR SHAKERS

Bury celebrated their 125th anniversary in 2010. The club was formed in 1885, with the first match at Gigg Lane taking place in September of that year – a 4–3 friendly win against Wigan. To mark the anniversary, the Shakers wore a brown and sky blue shirt with white shorts for the 2009/10 campaign – the same colours they wore in their very first season.

⇢ *Scorer Daniel Nardiello (right) and Danny Racchi celebrate in Bury's 125th anniversary shirts against Notts County at Gigg Lane in November 2009.*

Cheltenham Town

CHELTENHAM TOWN FC

HAPPY RETURNS

Julian Alsop's return to Cheltenham paved the way for him to become the club's record goalscorer in The Football League. Following a successful three-year spell with the Robins between 2000 and 2003, during which he scored 35 goals in 117 games, the big striker was brought back to the club by Martin Allen at the age of 36 in July 2009. He went on to beat Martin Devaney's 38-goal record in the 2009/10 campaign.

VICTORY FOR JAMIE

Jamie Victory has made the most Football League appearances for Cheltenham, playing 258 games in 11 years. Club legend Victory, who made the left-back spot his own between 1996 and 2007, retired from football in 2008 due to injury. Roger Thorndale is the Robins' all-time record appearance holder with 702 to his name.

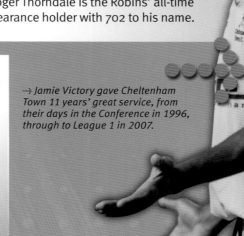

⇢ *Jamie Victory gave Cheltenham Town 11 years' great service, from their days in the Conference in 1996, through to League 1 in 2007.*

MIDDLE MAN ARRIVES IN STYLE

Cheltenham paid a club-record fee of £50,000 to sign midfielder Grant McCann from West Ham in January 2003. He played almost 200 games for the Robins, scoring more than 30 goals between 2003 and 2007. McCann is also Cheltenham's most capped player, having made seven starts and 22 substitute appearances for Northern Ireland while at the club. Cheltenham equalled their transfer record by paying Stoke £50,000 for Brian Wilson in March 2004.

Chesterfield

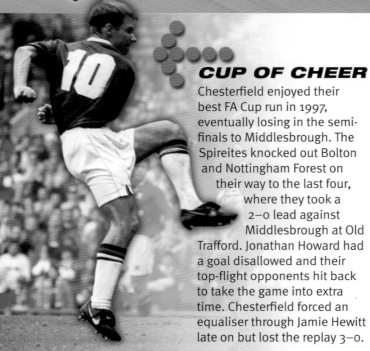

CUP OF CHEER

Chesterfield enjoyed their best FA Cup run in 1997, eventually losing in the semi-finals to Middlesbrough. The Spireites knocked out Bolton and Nottingham Forest on their way to the last four, where they took a 2–0 lead against Middlesbrough at Old Trafford. Jonathan Howard had a goal disallowed and their top-flight opponents hit back to take the game into extra time. Chesterfield forced an equaliser through Jamie Hewitt late on but lost the replay 3–0.

DAVIES STARTS AS A SPIREITE

Barclays Premier League striker Kevin Davies began his career at Chesterfield and ranks as one of their most famous former players. Davies scored 22 goals in 129 league games for the Spireites before making a club-record £750,000 move to Southampton in May 1997. Blackburn then paid £7.5million to take him to Ewood Park just over a year later. He is now captain of Bolton.

← *A disallowed goal from Jonathan Howard denied Chesterfield the chance to lead Middlesbrough 3–0 in their 1997 FA Cup semi-final. Boro hit back and eventually won the tie after a replay.*

GILLS GO GOAL CRAZY

Gillingham inflicted Chesterfield's record league defeat when they scored 10 past them without reply in 1987/88. There were six different Gills scorers that day, with George Shipley, Howard Pritchard, Dave Shearer and Karl Elsey all netting twice. The Spireites' post-war record victory in the league stands at 8–0, against Crewe in 1955/56.

Crewe Alexandra

CREWE'S CONVEYOR BELT

Crewe have earned a reputation for producing top-quality young players through their youth system or signing them from other clubs at a very young age and turning them into stars. David Platt, Robbie Savage and Neil Lennon all made their names with the Alex, while Danny Murphy, Seth Johnson and most recently Dean Ashton all came through the ranks at Gresty Road before moving to top-flight clubs.

↑ *Dario Gradi became Crewe manager before any member of the Alexandra squad at the end of the 2009/10 season was born.*

GRADI'S LONG LEGACY

Long-serving boss Dario Gradi and Crewe have become almost inseparable. Gradi took charge of the club in June 1983 and celebrated his 1,000th game in charge against Norwich in November 2001. He continued as manager until 2007, when he was appointed technical director. Gradi resumed his role as manager for a short spell before the arrival of Gudjon Thordarson and took charge again when the Icelander was sacked. The veteran tactician was still going strong with Alex at the end of the 2009/10 season after almost three decades with the club!

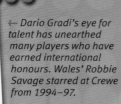

← *Dario Gradi's eye for talent has unearthed many players who have earned international honours. Wales' Robbie Savage starred at Crewe from 1994–97.*

TONY NAILS RECORD

Tony Naylor holds the record for the most goals in a single game for Crewe. Striker Naylor scored five times as Colchester were beaten 7–1 at Gresty Road in April 1993, just a few years after he had joined the professional ranks from non-league Droylsden.

Dagenham & Redbridge

DUO'S DOUBLE DEAL

The biggest transfer fee ever received by Dagenham came from a double deal involving Craig Mackail-Smith and Shane Blackett. Peterborough paid £250,000 to sign the pair in January 2007. Mackail-Smith had scored 38 goals in the Conference for Daggers prior to his departure.

DAGGERS PUT CHESTER TO THE SWORD

Dagenham clearly enjoyed playing Chester City, who went out of business in 2009/2010, with their two biggest Football League victories having come against the Blues. A 6–0 opening-day win on August 9 2008 was secured thanks to goals from Sam Saunders (two), Paul Benson, Dominic Green, Mark Nwokeji and Ben Strevens. Chester were also on the receiving end of the Daggers' second biggest win, 6–2 in February 2008.

ROBERTS REWRITING HISTORY

Tony Roberts is creating history with every game he plays for Dagenham. Goalkeeper Roberts, who made his debut in August 2000, is already the club's record appearance holder, turning out for the 450th time on March 16 2010 at Lincoln. He saved a penalty on his 400th Daggers appearance to earn his side a hard-fought point against Accrington.

⟵ Tony Roberts won Welsh international caps and spent 11 years at QPR before being forced to retire because of injury in 1998. But he came back to the game with Dagenham & Redbridge in 2000 and, now aged 40, is still the club's No. 1.

Darlington

DARLO DROP OUT

Relegation from the fourth tier in 2009/10 ended Darlington's proud record as the second longest-serving club in the division. The Quakers dropped back into the bottom tier of The Football League in 1992 having been promoted the season before, and they stayed there until the end of the recent campaign, as Simon Davey was unable to prevent them from slipping into the Conference.

⟵ Simon Davey arrived in April 2010, by which time the Quakers' fate had been all but sealed, and they suffered a second relegation from The Football League.

DARLINGTON APPEARANCES

Ron Greener	490
John Peverell	465
Brian Henderson	463
Kevan Smith	440
Hughie Dickson	433

QUAKERS ARE LUCKY LOSERS

Darlington hold the dubious honour of having been knocked out of the FA Cup twice in the same season in different rounds of the competition. Manchester United pulled out of the tournament in 1999 due to their FIFA World Club Championship commitments, meaning a Lucky Loser draw took place. The Quakers, who had been beaten by Gillingham in the second round, were subsequently reinstated, but they lost 2–1 to Aston Villa in the third round.

Grimsby Town

MARINERS ARE SUNK

The Mariners created an unfortunate club record on their way to relegation from The Football League in 2009/10. They went 25 league games without a win from September 26 to February 27 before that sequence was finally broken with a 3–0 win over Shrewsbury at Blundell Park.

WEMBLEY DOUBLE

Grimsby were Wembley winners twice in 1998 as they won the Football League Trophy and then secured promotion via the play-offs. They beat Bournemouth 2–1 with a golden goal from Wayne Burnett in April and returned to the national stadium a month later to snatch a 1–0 win against Northampton courtesy of Kevin Donovan's goal.

↑ *Jubilant Grimsby players show off The Football League trophy after the first of their two victories at Wembley in 1998.*

McDERMOTT IS THE MAN

John McDermott spent his entire career with Grimsby, making a club-record 753 appearances in a 20-year spell from 1987 to 2007. Defender McDermott experienced promotion or relegation nine times with the Mariners, and he captained the club for several seasons towards the end of his career. He made his last appearance at Shrewsbury on May 5 2007 and has since gone on to coach at the Grimsby Institute. He was presented with a Merit Award by the PFA in 2009 for his achievements in the game.

⋯→ *John McDermott's amazing Grimsby career had its ups and downs, enjoying or enduring multiple promotions or relegations with the Mariners.*

Hereford United

GRAHAM TURNED HIS HAND TO ANYTHING

Graham Turner ended a 15-year association with Hereford in June 2010 when he left the club to take charge at Shrewsbury. Turner had held numerous positions at Edgar Street, including chairman and director of football as well as resuming his role as manager following the departure of John Trewick during the 2009/10 campaign. He was first appointed as Hereford boss in 1995 and bought the club in 1998. Arguably his biggest achievement came in 2008 when he was named League 2 Manager of the Year.

←⋯ *Graham Turner has spent 46 seasons in football. He made his Wrexham debut in 1964, became Shrewsbury player-manager in 1978 and Hereford boss in 1995.*

FAB FOUR FOR STRIKER

Hereford suffered their record defeat in a League Cup clash at Middlesbrough in September 1996. Boro's Italian striker Fabrizio Ravanelli netted four times, while Brazilian duo Emerson and Branco and defender Curtis Fleming were also on the scoresheet in a 7–0 victory. The Teesside club went on to reach the final of the competition that season, losing 1–0 to Leicester in a replay.

CUP MAGIC

Hereford shocked the world of football in 1972 when they belied their non-league status to knock top-flight Newcastle out of the FA Cup. Ronnie Radford's strike from distance is one of the most famous goals in the competition's history, with Ricky George also on the scoresheet for the Bulls in a memorable 2–1 success. Hereford were subsequently drawn against West Ham in the fourth round, where they were beaten in a replay.

Lincoln City

ALEXANDER THE GREAT

Keith Alexander is fondly remembered as one of Lincoln's best-loved bosses after he led them to the fourth-tier play-offs in four consecutive seasons between 2003 and 2006. Unfortunately for the Imps, they failed each time to win promotion. They were beaten 5–2 by Bournemouth in the final in 2002/03 and lost to Huddersfield at the semi-final stage the following year. They made it an unwanted treble when they suffered a 2–0 defeat after extra time against Southend at the Millennium Stadium in 2004/05 and they missed out to Grimsby 12 months later. Alexander left the club in 2006 and was manager of Macclesfield Town when he sadly died in March 2010 aged 53.

Lincoln centre-back Gareth McAuley (17) averaged a goal every nine games for the Imps, including one in a play-off semi-final against Macclesfield in 2005.

CAP FITS FOR McAULEY

Gareth McAuley earned five caps for Northern Ireland during his time at Lincoln from 2004–2006, making him the most capped Imps player. The defender, who joined the club from Coleraine, made 72 league appearances for Lincoln before moving on to Leicester and more recently Ipswich.

LINCOLN LEAGUE APPEARANCES

Grant Brown	407
Tony Emery	402
Dave Smith	371
Alan Marriott	351
Phil Neale	335

Macclesfield Town

SILKMEN BOX CLEVER

Macclesfield's record league victory came against Stockport on Boxing Day 2005 when they ran out 6–0 winners at Moss Rose. Strike duo Clyde Wijnhard and Jon Parkin both scored twice, with Martin Bullock and substitute John Miles completing the scoring.

ROOM FOR PARKIN

Jon Parkin has scored the most league goals in a single season for Macclesfield. The big striker netted 22 times in 2004/05. He scored a total of 30 goals in 67 league appearances for the club before joining Hull City in January 2006.

Jon Parkin's 22 goals for Macclesfield in 2004/05 was the best return by a Town player since they joined The Football League in 1997.

LAMBERT WALKS THE WALK

Rickie Lambert's career has gone from strength to strength since he first made his name at Macclesfield. Lambert was the subject of the biggest transfer fee received by the club when he left for Stockport in a £300,000 deal in April 2002. More recently, he has been banging in the goals for Southampton, and in 2010 he was voted the 30th best player outside of the Premier League.

Morecambe

CHAMPIONSHIP DUO STUNNED

Morecambe's maiden Carling Cup campaign made the headlines when they stunned Preston and Wolves. The Shrimps travelled to Deepdale in the first round and claimed a 2–1 victory, with Jim Bentley and David Artell sending North End out of the competition. A trip to Molineux followed, where Morecambe claimed a 3–1 win after extra time. Carl Baker, Jon Newby and Garry Thompson were on the scoresheet. Their run ended in the third round when they were beaten 5–0 by Sheffield United.

⟵ Goalscorers Danny Carlton (left) and Garry Thompson flank manager Sammy McIlroy after Morecambe had beaten Exeter 2–1 in the Conference Play-Off Final in 2007 to win promotion to The Football League.

WEMBLEY GLORY

The biggest day in Morecambe's history came on May 20 2007 when they were promoted to The Football League for the first time. The Shrimps made it to the Conference play-offs, where they beat York over two legs to set up a Wembley date with Exeter. Having fallen behind early on, Morecambe rallied to claim a 2–1 win thanks to goals from Garry Thompson and Danny Carlton. The club played their first Football League match on August 11 2007 – a goalless draw against Barnet.

SHRIMPS CATCH CARL

Carl Baker is the club's record signing, having cost £40,000 from Southport in June 2007. Baker scored 11 goals in his first season with the Shrimps and went on to secure a move to Stockport for an undisclosed fee, which is thought to have matched the club-record £175,000 received when Justin Jackson moved to Rushden & Diamonds in June 2000.

Northampton Town

GRAYSON IS QUICK OFF THE MARK

Neil Grayson holds the record for the fastest hat-trick in a Northampton shirt. Striker Grayson scored three goals in five minutes against Hartlepool at Sixfields on January 25 1997. The Cobblers went on to secure promotion to the third tier that season, beating Swansea in the Play-Off Final at Wembley with an injury-time goal from John Frain.

COBBLERS KEEP IT TIGHT

Northampton suffered just three away league defeats in their promotion-winning season of 2005/06 – a club record. Town finished runners-up to Carlisle in the fourth tier thanks in no small part to their record on the road.

⟵ Neil Grayson scored one of the fastest hat-tricks in football history when he netted three times in five minutes for Northampton against Hartlepool in 1997.

A LUCKY ESCAPE

The Cobblers finished bottom of The Football League for the only time in their history in season 1993/94, but they still managed to escape relegation. Conference champions Kidderminster were not allowed to take their place as their Aggborough ground did not meet the necessary requirements.

Notts County

WARNOCK WORKS HIS MAGIC

Neil Warnock led Notts County to back-to-back promotions in 1989/90 and 1990/91. They secured a play-off spot with a third-place finish in 1989/90, beating Tranmere 2–0 in the final with goals from Tommy Johnson and Craig Short. Seven consecutive wins towards the end of the following campaign earned County another play-off appearance, and Johnson was the goal hero again, scoring twice in a 3–1 win against Brighton to send them up. The Magpies were relegated in season 1991/92, however.

⤍ *Neil Warnock's first league job was as Scarborough manager, but he became well-known as Notts County boss.*

COUNTY'S RECORD GOALSCORERS

Les Bradd	137
Tony Hateley	114
Jackie Sewell	104
Tommy Lawton	103
Tom Keetley	98
Don Masson	97
Tom Johnston	92
Ian McParland	90
Harry Daft	81
Gary Lund, Trevor Christie, Mark Stallard	79

⬆ *Mark Stallard is equal 10th on the list of Notts County goalscorers. His 79 came between 1999 and 2005.*

OLD TIMERS

Notts County hold the honour of being the oldest league club in the world. They were first formed in 1862 – although their official formation came two years later – and they were one of the founding members of The Football League in 1888.

Port Vale

KEEPING IT IN THE FAMILY

Roy Sproson is Port Vale's record appearance holder with 836 in all competitions. Defender Sproson, who played for the club for 22 years between 1950 and 1972, is joint ninth in the list of all-time Football League appearances with 760 to his name. Roy's nephew, Phil, is Vale's second highest appearance maker with 500.

BIG FEAT BY LITTLEWOOD

Vale's record win came in September 1932 when they beat Chesterfield 9–1. Another club record was created that day as striker Stewart Littlewood scored six of those goals, the most any Vale player has netted in a single game.

A SOCA WARRIOR

Chris Birchall earned 22 caps for Trinidad & Tobago during his time at Port Vale, making him the most capped player in the club's history. Midfielder Birchall was the first white player to represent the Soca Warriors for over 60 years, and he lined up against England in the 2006 World Cup finals. He left Vale Park for Coventry in August of that year.

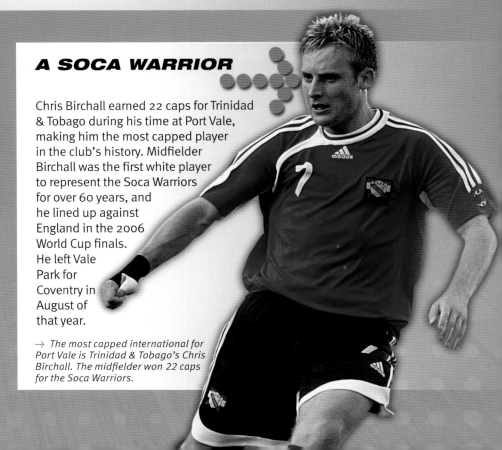

⤍ *The most capped international for Port Vale is Trinidad & Tobago's Chris Birchall. The midfielder won 22 caps for the Soca Warriors.*

Rochdale

JONES KEEPING UP APPEARANCES

Gary Jones became Rochdale's record appearance holder in 2007/08 and is increasing his tally with every game he plays for the club. Jones, who has already written himself into the history books at Spotland, surpassed Graham Smith's previous landmark of 345 appearances in all competitions in March 2008 and he was still going strong as a regular in the promotion-winning side of 2009/10.

←··· At the heart of Rochdale's first promotion for 41 years in 2010 was Gary Jones, who holds the club record for appearances. In all competitions, he has more than 400 to his name.

DALE MOVE ON UP

Rochdale fans will not forget 2009/10 in a hurry after the club were promoted for only the second time in their history. Dale spent a total of five seasons in the third tier on their first visit to that level before they were relegated at the end of the 1973/74 campaign. However, they finally had cause to celebrate for a second time on April 17 2010 as Chris O'Grady's close-range strike against Northampton secured their first promotion since 1969. They had been the longest-serving club in the bottom division of The Football League.

WHITEHURST GOAL BURST

Albert Whitehurst scored a club-record 44 league goals during the 1926/27 season. He netted 117 times in the league in total for Dale – two less than all-time top scorer Reg Jenkins – and also bagged 10 hat-tricks for the club.

Rotherham United

ROTHERHAM'S LEAGUE RECORD
(as Rotherham United)

Second tier: 1951–1968, 1981–1983, 2001–2005

Third tier: 1925–1951, 1968–1973, 1975–1981, 1983–1988, 1989–1991, 1992–1997, 2000–2001, 2005–2007

Fourth tier: 1973–1975, 1988–1989, 1991–1992, 1997–2000, 2007–Present

CHUCKLES A VISION AT MILLMOOR

The Chuckle Brothers are honorary presidents of Rotherham. The comedy duo are the club's most famous fans and regularly watch their home-town team. An episode of their TV series, *Chucklevision*, entitled 'Football Heroes' was filmed at Millmoor in 1995/96 in which the pair played for the club, with Barry Chuckle crossing for brother Paul to head home what they thought was the winning goal, only to find out that they had scored at the wrong end!

MOORE THE MERRIER

Ronnie Moore led Rotherham to successive promotions in 2000 and 2001. The Millers finished one point behind champions Swansea to move up to the third tier and then secured another second-place finish the following season. The latter promotion was secured with a 2–1 home win against Brentford, with Alan Lee snatching a last-gasp winner.

↑ Ronnie Moore is a Rotherham legend, having managed the Millers to successive promotions in 2000 and 2001. He then took the team to Wembley in the 2010 League 2 Play-Off Final.

Shrewsbury Town

↑ *Nigel Jemson was Shrewsbury's two-goal hero as Everton were shocked in a 2003 FA Cup third-round tie at Gay Meadow.*

TOFFEES TAMED BY SHREWS

Shrewsbury caused a huge FA Cup upset in 2003 when a double from Nigel Jemson earned them a 2–1 win against Premier League Everton – one of the most memorable results in the Shrews' history. A total of 80 places separated the two teams in the league ladder at kick-off, but the hosts claimed victory when captain Jemson opened the scoring with a superb free-kick and then headed a late winner after Niclas Alexandersson had levelled.

ROWLEY RANKS HIGHEST

Arthur Rowley holds the record for the most goals scored in The Football League. The prolific striker netted 152 times for Shrewsbury between 1958 and 1965 to take his career tally to 433 overall. That puts him 54 ahead of the legendary Dixie Dean in the all-time stakes. Rowley managed the Shrews as player-boss for seven years and then stayed on for three seasons after hanging up his boots.

CITY TAKE HART

England goalkeeper Joe Hart started his career at Shrewsbury and the £600,000 Manchester City paid to sign him in 2006 remains a Shrews record. Goalkeeper Hart played 54 games for his home-town club, having made his first-team debut just a day after his 17th birthday in April 2004.

⤍ *Shrewbury's record transfer fee was paid by Manchester City for 19-year-old goalkeeper Joe Hart in 2006.*

Torquay United

TORQUAY'S TOP SCORERS

Sammy Collins	219
Tommy Northcott	150
Robin Stubbs	133
Ron Shaw	106
Ernie Pym	94

IN AT THE SHARPE END

Former Manchester United and England winger Lee Sharpe started his career at Plainmoor. Sharpe was only 16 when he was handed his debut by then Torquay boss Cyril Knowles, but he only played a handful of games before moving to Old Trafford in a £180,000 switch.

⤍ *Lee Sharpe's Torquay career comprised only 11 starts, but he did enough as a 16-year-old for Manchester United boss Alex Ferguson to pay £180,000 to sign him.*

McNICHOL FEELING RUFF

A dog helped to save Torquay from relegation in 1987! During the last game of the campaign against Crewe – a match Torquay could not afford to lose – Jim McNichol, who had earlier made it 2–1, was bitten by a police dog who thought that the right-back was running towards his handler as he tried to prevent the ball from going out of play. The treatment to McNichol meant a lengthy period of injury time, during which Paul Dobson equalised to keep the Gulls in The Football League!

Cup Competitions

There is something special about a cup final, whether you are watching two of Europe's finest teams going head to head in the Champions League or League 1 rivals battling it out for the Johnstone's Paint Trophy.

Fans up and down the country dream of a grand day out at a sun-drenched Wembley – the pre-match anticipation, the electric atmosphere inside the stadium and the memories that such occasions inevitably bring.

English football boasts the oldest knockout extravaganza in the world in the shape of the FA Cup, and every year that competition provides some memorable shocks and incredible matches which make it a truly worldwide spectacle.

There are very few other tournaments where a non-league side – with a team possibly made up of tradesmen – can get the chance to pit their wits against an established team from the Barclays Premier League, and every so often pull off a famous victory.

The 92 Football League and Barclays Premier League clubs are also involved each year in the League Cup (currently known as the Carling Cup) – Manchester United retained the trophy last season by beating Aston Villa – while teams from League 1 and 2 compete annually for the Football League Trophy (currently known as the Johnstone's Paint Trophy). Southampton won that particular prize in 2009/10, securing their first piece of silverware since 1976 with a 4–1 victory over Carlisle to give their loyal fans something to celebrate.

Further afield, appearing in the Champions League final counts as the pinnacle of most footballers' careers, and in recent times we have been lucky enough to see a number of English clubs grace that stage.

The so-called 'Big Four' of Manchester United, Chelsea, Arsenal and Liverpool have all featured in the showpiece over the last five years, with varying degrees of success, but there have also been some remarkable games along the way.

Over the decades, English clubs – and not just the perceived 'big' names – have also excelled in other European competitions, such as the Cup Winners' Cup, the UEFA Cup (now known as the Europa League) and the Intertoto Cup.

Norwich, Ipswich and most recently Fulham have stunned some of the biggest names in the business. The Cottagers, for example, enjoyed one of the most amazing nights in their history in the Europa League in 2010. Roy Hodgson's men overturned a 3–1 first-leg deficit to knock out Italian giants Juventus 5–4 on aggregate following a stunning comeback at Craven Cottage in the return encounter.

Cup competitions, both domestically and in Europe, offer something different from the regular routine of league combat for players and supporters alike – and with plenty of knockout action both at home and abroad, we have never had it so good!

↑ England's main football trophies, from left to right: Barclays Premier League trophy, FA Cup, Carling Cup, Football League Trophy.

↓ Wembley Stadium hosts all of England's major cup finals, from the FA Vase to the FA Cup and npower Football League Play-Off Finals. FA Cup semi-finals are also played at the famous venue, and in 2009 Everton and Manchester United fans packed it out.

FA Cup

The FA Cup is one of the oldest and most famous competitions in football. Over the years it has seen many great teams, historic moments and memorable upsets. From the first winners, Wanderers, to the current holders, Chelsea, every single season the 'Magic of the Cup' guarantees drama, passion and plenty of excitement.

MOST FA CUP WINS

Manchester United	11
Arsenal	10
Tottenham Hotspur	8
Aston Villa	7
Liverpool	7
Blackburn Rovers	6
Chelsea	6
Newcastle United	6
Everton	5
The Wanderers	5
West Bromwich Albion	5

GOLDEN OLDIE

The FA Cup is the oldest domestic cup competition in the world, having been an integral part of English football for more than 100 years. The first competition was played in 1871/72 and had just 15 entrants (compared to more than 700 who took part in the 2009/10 season). Wanderers, a team formed by ex-public school and university pupils, won the first final 1–0 against Royal Engineers at Kennington Oval, although the game was almost unrecognisable from today as back then matches were played without crossbars or nets and the pitch markings did not include a centre circle or a half-way line.

↑ The FA Cup adorned with the ribbons of the sponsor, e.on. A popular quiz question asks: 'What is taken to every FA Cup final but is never used?' The answer? The losers' ribbons.

↓ Steve Bruce shows off the FA Cup after Manchester United had beaten Chelsea 4–0 in the 1994 final. Excluding replays, It was the most one-sided final since Bury beat Derby County 6–0 in 1903.

FAMILIAR FOES

The most common FA Cup final pairing has been Arsenal v Liverpool, Arsenal v Newcastle and Aston Villa v West Brom, with each having met three times in the showpiece.

WESTON THE LION CUB

Millwall midfielder Curtis Weston is the youngest player to have appeared in an FA Cup final. The Lions ace, now with Gillingham, broke one of the longest-standing records in football when he appeared as a second-half substitute in the 2004 final against Manchester United. He was 17 years and 119 days old at the time, beating the record of James Prinsep, who was 17 years and 245 days old when he played for Clapham Rovers in the 1879 final against Old Etonians.

QUICK AS A FLASH

Jimmy Kebe scored after just nine seconds in Reading's fifth-round clash with West Brom in 2010 to make his mark on the competition. Although records are incomplete, the winger's strike is believed to be the fastest goal in the FA Cup proper, although his time has been bettered in the qualifying rounds by window fitter Gareth Morris, who scored after just four seconds for Ashton United in the preliminary stages in 2001.

⤳ Jimmy Kebe's goal after nine seconds is believed to be the fastest in the FA Cup proper. Reading drew 2–2 with West Brom, but they won the replay 3–2 after extra time.

⤙ Hereford United players celebrate with a beer after their 2–1 defeat of Newcastle United in 1972. The winner came from Ricky George (middle row, far left).

BEASANT LEADS THE CRAZY GANG

Dave Beasant shot into footballing folklore in 1988 when he became the first goalkeeper to save a penalty in a Wembley final. The shot-stopper dived full length to turn away John Aldridge's spot-kick as 'The Crazy Gang' beat reigning league champions Liverpool in one of the greatest final upsets of all time.

⤳ Dave Beasant shows off the FA Cup after Wimbledon's shock victory over Liverpool in 1988. Behind him are Dennis Wise and Andy Thorn.

WHAT A SHOCKER

Everybody loves surprises, and the FA Cup is normally full of them as small teams look to get the better of big-name opponents. These shocks, known as 'giantkillings', are what football fans look forward to every year... unless they support the team that has just been knocked out, of course! Arsenal were beaten 2–1 by Wrexham, who were bottom of the fourth tier at the time, in January 1992 in what was one the biggest FA Cup shocks of all time. Liverpool, Everton and Newcastle are three more teams who have been dumped out of the competition by clubs from lower divisions, while more recently, Manchester United were stunned by League 1 side Leeds at Old Trafford in January 2010, with hot-shot striker Jermaine Beckford scoring the only goal.

A CRICKET SCORE

Preston hold the record for the biggest win in the FA Cup, having scored 26 goals without reply against Hyde in 1887. Striker Jimmy Ross was their hero that day, netting eight times. He scored six more against Bolton in the fourth round and went on to finish the season with 19 in the competition overall – also a record.

THE GIANTKILLERS

Hereford	2–1	Newcastle	(1972)
Wrexham	2–1	Arsenal	(1992)
Yeovil	2–1	Sunderland	(1949)
Sutton	2–1	Coventry	(1989)
Barnsley	1–0	Chelsea	(2008)
Liverpool	1–2	Barnsley	(2008)
Bournemouth	2–0	Manchester United	(1984)
Sunderland	1–0	Leeds	(1973)
Burnley	0–1	Wimbledon	(1975)

DOUBLE DELIGHT

Seven clubs have won the FA Cup as part of a league and cup double: Preston (1889), Aston Villa (1897), Tottenham (1961), Arsenal (1971, 1998, 2002), Liverpool (1986), Manchester United (1994, 1996, 1999) and Chelsea (2010).

THE WORLD'S GAME

The FA Cup final is one of the most watched sporting events in the world with around 484 million people tuning in from all four corners of the globe to watch the 2005 clash at the Millennium Stadium, Cardiff as Arsenal beat Manchester United on penalties.

FA CUP FINAL VENUES

1872	Kennington Oval
1873	Lillie Bridge, London
1874–1892	Kennington Oval
1893	Fallowfield, Manchester
1894	Goodison Park
1895–1914	Crystal Palace
1915	Old Trafford
1920–22	Stamford Bridge
1923–2000	Wembley Stadium
2001–2006	Millennium Stadium, Cardiff
2007–Present	New Wembley Stadium

⟵ *The arch over the New Wembley Stadium has rapidly become a famous landmark, even if some traditionalists mourn the passing of the old venue's Twin Towers.*

KING LOUIS THE 25TH

Louis Saha scored the fastest goal in FA Cup final history when he put Everton ahead against Chelsea after just 25 seconds in May 2009. The Frenchman got on the end of Marouane Fellaini's headed knockdown and beat Petr Cech with a well-struck shot into the bottom corner. Unfortunately for the Toffees, Chelsea hit back to claim a 2–1 victory. Everton's defeat meant that they finished as FA Cup runners-up for the eighth time, more than any other club.

I CAN'T BELIEVE IT'S NOT BUTTERFIELD

Defender-turned-striker Danny Butterfield scored a hat-trick in seven minutes for Crystal Palace against Wolves in the fourth round of the 2009/10 FA Cup. However, there have been quicker hat-tricks in the competition, with the fastest recorded at two minutes and 20 seconds when Andy Locke scored three times for Nantwich against Droylsden in a qualifier in 1995.

↓ *Everton played in five FA Cup finals in 11 years, 1984–1995, winning two. When Louis Saha gave them the lead after 25 seconds of their first final for 14 years in 2009, it led to a record eighth defeat as Chelsea hit back to win.*

FIVE-STAR COLE

Ashley Cole became the first player since the 19th Century to win the FA Cup on five separate occasions when he was part of the Chelsea team that beat Everton 2–1 in May 2009. Cole had already lifted the trophy once with the Blues in 2007 when Didier Drogba's extra-time goal secured a 1–0 victory over Manchester United. The England left-back also won the competition three times with Arsenal in 2002, 2003 and 2005. The Gunners were 2–0 winners against Chelsea in Cardiff in 2002, beat Southampton 1–0 a year later and claimed a penalty shootout victory against Manchester United in 2005, with Cole scoring from the spot. He has since won a sixth medal following Chelsea's victory over Portsmouth in 2010.

PLAY IT AGAIN, FULHAM

Fulham hold the record for the most games played in one FA Cup campaign to reach the final. Ties used to be played over and over again until one team won rather than a replay followed by extra time and penalties if the game remained all-square. The Cottagers, playing in the second tier at the time, played 12 games over six rounds of the competition on their way to being losing finalists against West Ham back in 1975.

← Eric Cantona of Manchester United was the first player to convert two penalties in an FA Cup final, doing so in 1994. In 2010, Portsmouth and Chelsea both failed with a spot-kick – another FA Cup final first.

HAMMERS ARE ALL-ENGLAND CLUB

West Ham's FA Cup-winning side of 1975 was the last all-English line-up to lift the trophy. Alan Taylor scored both goals as the Hammers claimed a 2–0 win against Fulham at Wembley. Their team that day also featured the likes of Billy Bonds, Frank Lampard Snr and Trevor Brooking.

SPOT-ON ERIC AT THE DOUBLE

Eric Cantona made history in 1994 when he became the first player to score two penalties in an FA Cup final. 'King Eric', who was also voted PFA Player of the Year that season, was spot on for Manchester United as they claimed a 4–0 win against Chelsea at Wembley. Cantona's two penalties and a Mark Hughes strike in nine second-half minutes put the Red Devils in control before Brian McClair added a fourth goal late on. Frenchman Cantona also scored the winning goal in the 1996 final as Manchester United beat Liverpool 1–0.

MOST APPEARANCES IN FA CUP FINALS

Manchester United	18
Arsenal	17
Everton	13
Liverpool	13
Newcastle	13
Aston Villa	10
West Brom	10
Chelsea	10
Tottenham	9

↑ Alan Taylor of West Ham was the two-goal hero of the 1975 FA Cup final, the last time the FA Cup winners contained only England-eligible players.

A CLASSIC ENCOUNTER

Liverpool's victory over West Ham in 2006 was arguably the most exciting FA Cup final of modern times – with Steven Gerrard proving to be the Reds' hero that day. The Merseysiders were twice forced to come from behind to take the game into extra time, with Gerrard completing the comeback in injury time with a stunning 30-yard volley to haul his side back to 3–3. Both sides went close again in a thrilling extra period before Liverpool goalkeeper Pepe Reina saved from Bobby Zamora, Paul Konchesky and Anton Ferdinand in the penalty shootout.

WELSH WONDERS

The FA Cup has only been won by a non-English team once. Cardiff claimed that honour in 1927 when they beat Arsenal 1–0 at Wembley. They came close to repeating the feat when they made it to the final again in 2008, but they were ultimately beaten by Portsmouth.

← Steven Gerrard's performance for Liverpool in the 2006 FA Cup final cemented his legendary status at Anfield. The 3–3 draw against West Ham was one of the greatest finals ever.

Carling Cup

The League Cup, currently known as the Carling Cup, still holds a special place in the domestic football calendar. Traditionally the first major piece of silverware of the domestic season, the competition is still going strong beyond its 50th year.

NEW FORMAT FOR FINAL

The 1967 League Cup final between Queens Park Rangers and West Brom was the first to be staged at Wembley. Six two-legged finals had been contested before the decision was made to switch the tie to a one-off showpiece at the home of football. QPR claimed a 3–2 victory in the first game under the famous Twin Towers – the only time that the London club have won the competition.

VILLANS TO HEROES

Aston Villa beat Rotherham to win the first League Cup in 1961. The final was played over two legs, with the first at Millmoor ending 2–0 to Rotherham, who were in the second tier at the time. Villa mounted a superb comeback in the second game, winning 3–0 at Villa Park after extra time to lift the trophy.

⋯→ *Keith Cooper has just brandished the first red card in a League Cup final, Andrei Kanchelskis of Manchester United being the unfortunate recipient in the defeat against Aston Villa in 1994.*

↓ *Jon Arne Riise scored for Liverpool in the first minute of the 2005 Carling Cup final at the Millennium Stadium in Cardiff, but Chelsea hit back to win 3–2.*

KAN YOU HANDLE IT?

Andrei Kanchelskis became the first player to be sent off in a League Cup final in March 1994. Manchester United were losing 2–1 to Aston Villa when Russian winger Kanchelskis used his hand to clear the ball off the goalline from Dalian Atkinson's shot. United went on to lose the game 3–1 as Villa's Wales international striker Dean Saunders scored from the resulting penalty.

RIISE LEAVES BLUES RED-FACED

Jon Arne Riise holds the record for the quickest goal in the final. It took the Norway international defender just 45 seconds to open the scoring for Liverpool against Chelsea in 2005. It was the Blues who were celebrating at the end of the game, though, as Mateja Kezman's strike in extra time secured a 3–2 victory.

REDS RULE

Liverpool are the most successful side in League Cup history and have won the competition a total of seven times. The Reds won the trophy four years in a row between 1981 and 1984 to cement their status. Aston Villa are their nearest challengers, having won the title five times in all. Nottingham Forest and Manchester United, who have both won the competition four times, are the only other teams to have won consecutive finals. United achieved that feat in 2010 when they claimed victory over Villa at Wembley to follow up their 2009 success.

RECENT ALAN HARDAKER TROPHY WINNERS

2010	Antonio Valencia	(Manchester United)
2009	Ben Foster	(Manchester United)
2008	Jonathan Woodgate	(Tottenham)
2007	Didier Drogba	(Chelsea)
2006	Wayne Rooney	(Manchester United)
2005	John Terry	(Chelsea)
2004	Boudewijn Zenden	(Middlesbrough)
2003	Jerzy Dudek	(Liverpool)
2002	Brad Friedel	(Blackburn)
2001	Robbie Fowler	(Liverpool)

↑ *Manchester United's Ben Foster won the 2009 Alan Hardaker Trophy, as much for his penalty shootout heroics against Tottenham as for any saves in the 120 minutes.*

HESKEY MAKES HIS MARK

England striker Emile Heskey shares the record for the most appearances in finals. Heskey has played for Leicester three times (1997, 1999 and 2000), Liverpool twice (2001 and 2003) and Aston Villa (2010). The big forward has been a winner on four of those occasions – twice with Leicester and twice with the Reds. Ian Rush also appeared in six finals, claiming five winners' medals with Liverpool.

↓ *Carlos Tevez celebrates his sixth and final goal of the 2009/10 Carling Cup, Manchester City's only strike in a semi-final second-leg loss to rivals United.*

HARD ACT TO FOLLOW

In 1990 The Football League introduced The Alan Hardaker Trophy, presented to the man of the match in the final. Hardaker was the former secretary of the League who conceived the idea for the cup competition back in 1960. Nottingham Forest defender Des Walker was the first man to receive the prize, while Manchester United winger Antonio Valencia claimed the trophy in 2010 following a superb display as United defended their title.

BUNN HITS BORO FOR SIX

Frankie Bunn holds the record for the most goals in a single League Cup tie. Striker Bunn scored six goals for Oldham in a 7–0 win against Scarborough in the third round in October 1989. The Latics went on to reach the final, where they were beaten 1–0 by Nottingham Forest. Bunn was forced to retire in 1990 through injury.

···▸ *Frankie Bunn was fantastic on plastic and his six goals for Oldham in the 7–0 rout of Scarborough on the artificial turf at Boundary Park in 1989 remains the competition's individual scoring record.*

TEVEZ TOPS THE CHARTS

Carlos Tevez was the top goalscorer in the competition for the second successive season in 2009/10 as he finished the campaign with six goals. The Argentinian striker netted twice in the first leg of Manchester City's semi-final clash against his former club Manchester United and scored again in the return encounter as City lost out on aggregate. He had previously netted against Crystal Palace, Scunthorpe and Arsenal in the earlier rounds.

MOST FINAL APPEARANCES

Liverpool	10
Aston Villa	8
Manchester United	8
Tottenham	7
Arsenal	6
Nottingham Forest	6
Chelsea	6

GLOBAL APPEAL

Now into its 51st season, the competition continues to capture the imagination of football fans right across the globe. The 2010 final between Manchester United and Aston Villa was screened around the world on television to a total of 137 different countries, meaning it was watched by supporters across several different time zones.

⇢ *Silverware is not the only reward for the winners: victory also guarantees a place in the Europa League.*

HURST HOLDS GOAL RECORD

England's 1966 World Cup hero Geoff Hurst shares the landmark for scoring the most League Cup goals in a career. Hurst, who famously netted a hat-trick for England against West Germany, scored 49 goals overall in the competition playing for West Ham and Stoke. He holds the record jointly with Ian Rush, who managed the same feat with Chester, Liverpool and Newcastle.

⇠ *Geoff Hurst was a real cup star. His 49 goals is a League Cup record, but he also won the FA Cup and European Cup Winners' Cup with West Ham, to say nothing of his 1966 World Cup final hat-trick for England.*

CAPTAIN VENISON

Barry Venison is the youngest player to have captained a side in a League Cup final. The midfielder was 20 years, seven months and eight days old when he led Sunderland out at Wembley in 1985. Unfortunately for Venison, he ended up on the losing side as Norwich claimed a narrow 1–0 victory thanks to an own goal from Gordon Chisholm.

SCORING MADE EASY

Yeovil's Carling Cup tie against Plymouth in 2004 witnessed a memorable act of good sportsmanship. As he attempted to return the ball to Plymouth goalkeeper Luke McCormick following a break in play for an injury, Yeovil striker Lee Johnson managed to inadvertently lob his pass into the net. To compensate for the error, Yeovil's manager at the time, Gary Johnson (who also happens to be Lee's father), ordered his players to allow Argyle striker Stevie Crawford to run through unopposed from the kick-off and score the equaliser.

CLIVE IS GOAL MACHINE

Tottenham legend Clive Allen has scored the most goals in one League Cup campaign. He netted 12 in the 1986/87 season as Spurs reached the semi-finals. They were eventually beaten by arch-rivals Arsenal over three games – two legs and a replay – with Allen scoring three times in the process. The prolific striker scored 49 goals in total that season, with 33 coming in the league, as he was named the PFA Player of the Year.

⇢ *Clive Allen (arm raised) celebrates scoring the first goal of the 1987 League Cup semi-final second leg against Arsenal with Spurs team-mates Gary Mabbutt (left) and Paul Allen.*

MINSTERMEN MAKE LIGHT OF UNITED

The League Cup has thrown up its fair share of shocks over the years, although perhaps the most memorable came in 1995 when York City, playing in the third tier at the time, claimed a sensational 3–0 win against Premier League giants Manchester United at Old Trafford. David Beckham and Ryan Giggs were playing for the home side, but that didn't faze the Minstermen, who secured a remarkable upset thanks to two goals from striker Paul Barnes and a third from Tony Barras.

DENNIS THE MENACE

Dennis Tueart's acrobatic winner for Manchester City against Newcastle in the 1976 final was recently voted the greatest moment in League Cup history. The Football League asked fans to vote for their 50 golden memories to mark the competition's 50th anniversary in 2010. Goalkeeper Paul Robinson's heroic performance for Leeds against Swindon in 2003 came second. Having scored the equalising goal with 15 seconds of the game remaining to force extra time, the shot-stopper then saved two spot-kicks in the penalty shootout to send his side through!

DOUBLE DELIGHT FOR WHITESIDE

Norman Whiteside holds the record as the youngest goalscorer in a League Cup final at 17 years and 324 days old. The former Northern Ireland international opened the scoring for Manchester United against Liverpool at Wembley in 1983, but the Merseysiders hit back to claim the trophy in extra time as Ronnie Whelan made it 2–1. Whiteside is also the youngest FA Cup final goalscorer following his strike in a 4–0 replay win against Brighton that same season aged 18 years and 18 days.

DUO HIT DOUBLE FIGURES

Liverpool and West Ham share the record for the biggest wins in League Cup history. The Reds romped to a 10–0 victory against Fulham, then a third-tier team, on their way to the final in 1986/87. Steve McMahon scored four goals in that game and also missed a penalty. West Ham beat Bury by the same scoreline in October 1983, with Tony Cottee netting four times.

⇡ *Norman Whiteside (right) takes on Mark Lawrenson at Wembley in 1983 when he became the League Cup final's youngest goalscorer.*

⇢ *Dennis Tueart fills the League Cup with champagne after the Manchester City player's spectacular goal beat Newcastle in the 1976 final. Having swapped shirts, the ex-Sunderland legend looks odd in Newcastle stripes.*

English Clubs in Europe

Domestic action may still be the benchmark by which most clubs judge their season, but increasingly, European football plays an important role in the modern game. English clubs have enjoyed plenty of success on the continental stage over the years, although there have been some low points too.

CHAMPIONS LEAGUE IS BORN

The European Cup became known as the Champions League at the start of the 1992/93 season. The format of the competition changed to include a group stage, and a number of different variations have since followed. A second group stage was introduced in 1999, with eight third-place teams from the first round of action dropping down into the UEFA Cup (now called the Europa League). The current format of the competition was introduced in 2003/04, with one group stage leading straight to the last 16.

⬅ The UEFA Champions League trophy is the most prized piece of silverware in European club football.

ENGLISH CLUBS TO REACH THE CHAMPIONS LEAGUE GROUP STAGES

Manchester United
Liverpool
Arsenal
Chelsea
Leeds
Newcastle
Blackburn

⟶ Steven Gerrard lifts the UEFA Champions League trophy after the 'Miracle of Istanbul' saw Liverpool pull off the most unlikely of comebacks against AC Milan.

SILVA LINING

Gilberto Silva scored for Arsenal after 20.07 seconds of their Champions League clash with PSV Eindhoven in September 2002. However, the Brazilian's time has been bettered. Roy Makaay holds the record for the quickest goal in the competition, having netted after just 10.3 seconds for Bayern Munich against Real Madrid in March 2007. Manchester United were on the receiving end of the third fastest goal in Champions League history when Alessandro Del Piero scored after 20.12 seconds for Juventus at Old Trafford in 1997.

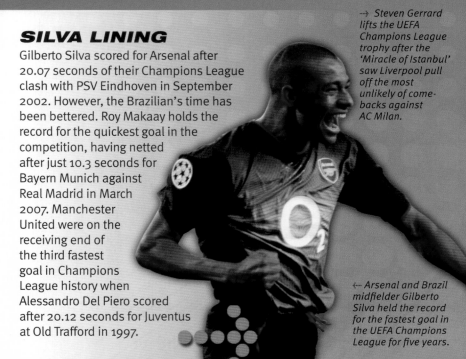

⬅ Arsenal and Brazil midfielder Gilberto Silva held the record for the fastest goal in the UEFA Champions League for five years.

FIVE-STAR REDS

Liverpool are among an elite group of clubs who have the won the European Cup five times. That meant they kept the trophy following their amazing comeback victory against AC Milan in 2005 and a new one was commissioned. The same thing also happens if a team wins the competition three times in a row. Real Madrid, Ajax, Bayern Munich and AC Milan also have trophies sitting in their cabinets.

VAN'S THE MAN

Former Manchester United striker Ruud van Nistelrooy holds the record as the top scorer in a single Champions League season. The Dutchman netted 12 times as the Red Devils reached the quarter-finals in 2002/03, where they were eventually beaten by Real Madrid. Van Nistelrooy also scored four times in one game for United in their Champions League clash against Sparta Prague in November 2004. That is also a record for the most goals by one player in a Champions League game, although he shares it with Marco van Basten, Simone Inzaghi, Dado Prso, Andriy Shevchenko and Lionel Messi.

GOODNIGHT VIENNA

Everton won the European Cup Winners' Cup in 1985 with a 3–1 victory against Rapid Vienna. A strong line-up, which included club greats such as Neville Southall and Peter Reid, secured victory thanks to goals from Andy Gray, Trevor Steven and Kevin Sheedy. Unfortunately, Everton were denied the chance to play in the European Cup the following season due to a ban imposed on all English clubs following the Heysel stadium tragedy.

NEWELL ON CLOUD NINE

Mike Newell scored the fastest hat-trick in Champions League history during Blackburn's only campaign in Europe's top competition in 1995/96. It took the Rovers striker just nine minutes to score his treble against Norwegian side Rosenborg. Blackburn won the game 4–1, although that is their only victory in the competition.

⤏ *Blackburn striker Mike Newell heads home the second goal of his nine-minute UEFA Champions League hat-trick against Rosenborg in 1995.*

CANARIES STUN GERMAN GIANTS

Norwich stunned the footballing world when they knocked mighty Bayern Munich out of the UEFA Cup in 1993 in one of the biggest upsets in European football history. The Canaries had qualified for Europe for the first time by finishing third in the Premier League the previous season. Jeremy Goss struck a stunning volley to open the scoring in the Olympic Stadium before Mark Bowen headed in a second. The first leg finished 2–1 to City and another strike from Goss in the return leg at Carrow Road sent them through 3–2 on aggregate. They were beaten by eventual winners Inter Milan in the next round.

FOREST SOW THE SEED

Nottingham Forest were the second English club to win back-to-back European Cups when they triumphed in 1979 and 1980. Forest enjoyed outstanding success under then manager Brian Clough, beating Swedish side Malmo 1–0 in Munich's Olympic Stadium in 1979 before retaining the trophy a year later with a 1–0 victory against Hamburg in Madrid. Current Aston Villa manager Martin O'Neill was in the Forest side that day, while Kevin Keegan was playing for the Germans. Liverpool were the first English back-to-back winners, having achieved the feat in 1977 and 1978.

⬇ *Trevor Francis scores Nottingham Forest's match-winner in the 1979 European Cup final against Malmo. Amazingly, Forest have won the European Cup twice and the top-flight title only once.*

ENGLISH EUROPEAN CUP WINNERS

Liverpool	5
Manchester United	3
Nottingham Forest	2
Aston Villa	1

TOFFEES CAUSE STICKY SITUATION

A record five English teams were involved in the 2005/06 Champions League. Liverpool, as reigning champions, were given special permission to feature in the competition despite having finished outside of the qualification places in the league. Merseyside rivals Everton had beaten them to fourth place to take the last automatic spot, although the Toffees failed to make it to the group stages after they were beaten 4–2 on aggregate by Spanish side Villarreal.

TEEN ROONEY RUNS RIOT

Wayne Rooney became the youngest player to score a hat-trick in the Champions League when Manchester United beat Fenerbahce at Old Trafford on September 28 2004. England striker Rooney, just 18 at the time, was making his debut for the club following his transfer from Everton. He marked his arrival with a superb treble to help his side to an emphatic 6–2 victory.

⋯⃗ Wayne Rooney marked his Manchester United debut in spectacular style with a UEFA Champions League hat-trick against Fenerbahce. At 18 years and 339 days he was the youngest player ever to achieve the feat.

IPSWICH ENJOY EURO GLORY

Legendary manager Sir Bobby Robson led Ipswich to UEFA Cup glory in 1981. In what was a golden era for the Suffolk club, Town beat Dutch side AZ Alkmaar 5–4 on aggregate over two legs to clinch the trophy. Frans Thijssen and John Wark scored in both games. Town qualified for the same competition again in 2001/02 and secured a famous 1–0 win against Italian giants Inter Milan in the first leg of their third-round tie before going on to lose 4–1 in the return.

↑ Ipswich may have been a relatively small club, but they had a giant reputation around Europe in the 1970s and 1980s, especially under coach Bobby Robson, who guided them to UEFA Cup glory in 1981.

REDS GO GOAL CRAZY

Liverpool's record European victory was an 11–0 triumph in the European Cup Winners' Cup against Norwegian side Stromsgodset in September 1974. What made the match even more memorable was the fact that nine of the 10 outfield players who started the game for the Reds managed to get on the scoresheet, with Brian Hall the only player to miss out!

BORO ARE COMEBACK KINGS

Middlesbrough reached the final of the UEFA Cup in 2006 following an amazing run in the knockout stages. Having beaten Stuttgart and Roma over two legs, The Teessiders managed to overturn 3–0 deficits against both Swiss side FC Basel in the quarter-final and then Romanians Steaua Bucharest at the semi-final stage. Italian striker Massimo Maccarone was the hero in both ties, scoring late goals to send them through 4–3 on aggregate. Boro's luck finally ran out in the final as they were beaten 4–0 by Spanish club Sevilla.

⚫⚫ Massimo Maccarone runs away in triumph after scoring Middlesbrough's match-winner against Steaua Bucharest in the 2006 UEFA Cup semi-final.

TURKISH DELIGHT

English clubs hold the record for both the biggest win in the group stages of the Champions League and also the largest margin of victory in the knockout stages. Liverpool beat Turkish side Besiktas 8–0 at Anfield in November 2007, with midfielder Yossi Benayoun scoring a superb hat-trick. The previous season, Manchester United had dismantled Italian side Roma 7–1 in the second leg of their quarter-final clash at Old Trafford, with Michael Carrick and Cristiano Ronaldo both scoring twice. United share that landmark with Bayern Munich, who beat Sporting Lisbon by the same scoreline in March 2009.

THE MIRACLE OF ISTANBUL

Liverpool were involved in one of the greatest European finals in history in 2005 when they came from behind to beat AC Milan on penalties after extra time. The Italian giants were leading 3–0 at half-time in Istanbul, only for Liverpool to score three goals in six minutes through Steven Gerrard, Vladimir Smicer and Xabi Alonso to haul themselves level. With no further goals, the game went to penalties and goalkeeper Jerzy Dudek saved from Andriy Shevchenko to seal an amazing victory for the Reds.

⚫⚫ Jerzy Dudek's outstretched legs block Andriy Shevchenko's penalty to give Liverpool their unlikely 2005 UEFA Champions League triumph over AC Milan in Istanbul.

GUNNERS ARE RUNNERS-UP

Arsenal became the first London club to feature in a European Cup final when they lost to Barcelona in Paris in May 2006. Chelsea missed the chance to become the first London club to win the trophy when they were beaten in the final by Barclays Premier League rivals Manchester United in 2008, losing out on penalties following a 1–1 draw.

EUROPEAN CUP RUNNERS-UP

Liverpool	2
Arsenal	1
Chelsea	1
Leeds	1
Manchester United	1

LEHMANN SEES RED

Former Arsenal goalkeeper Jens Lehmann became the first player to be sent off in a European Cup final when he was shown a straight red card for bringing down Samuel Eto'o in the 18th minute of the Gunners' 2–1 defeat to Barcelona in May 2006. However, that did not stop the German from being named the Champions League Goalkeeper of the Year after he played a key role in the run to the final.

⚫⚫ Jens Lehmann fouls Samuel Eto'o in the 2006 UEFA Champions League final. Although Barcelona put the ball in the Arsenal net before the whistle was blown, the goal was disallowed and Norwegian referee Terje Hauge dismissed Lehmann.

Johnstone's Paint Trophy

For those clubs further down the league pyramid, the Football League Trophy, currently the Johnstone's Paint Trophy, offers the chance of silverware, and a memorable day out at Wembley. The competition, which began in 1983, is popular with both players and supporters in the lower reaches of the English game.

FIFTH TIME UNLUCKY FOR CUMBRIANS

Carlisle hold the record for the most appearances in the final, with their 2010 clash with Southampton the fifth time they have been involved. Unfortunately for the Cumbrians, they have only won the trophy on one occasion, in 1997 when they beat Colchester on penalties following a goalless draw. Bristol City have featured in four finals, winning twice in 1986 and 2003.

SAINTS DRAW A CROWD

The highest attendance for a Trophy game other than the final came in the 2009/10 competition when Southampton hosted MK Dons at St Mary's Stadium in front of 29,901 spectators. The previous best was 24,002 at Birmingham City's St Andrew's in 1994/95.

LAST FIVE FINALS

2005/06	Swansea	2–1	Carlisle
2006/07	Doncaster	3–2	Bristol Rovers
2007/08	MK Dons	2–0	Grimsby
2008/09	Luton (extra-time)	3–2	Scunthorpe
2009/10	Southampton	4–1	Carlisle

MOST TROPHY WINS

Bristol City	2
Port Vale	2
Birmingham	2
Blackpool	2
Stoke	2
Swansea	2
Wigan	2

↓ *Dean Hammond lifts the Johnstone's Paint Trophy after Southampton's victory over Carlisle in the 2010 final.*

TO HULL AND BACK

The Football League Trophy was introduced in 1983/84. The first final was scheduled to be played at Wembley but damage to the pitch caused by the Horse of the Year show saw the game switched to Hull. Hull actually made it to the final that year, but they were beaten 2–1 by Bournemouth.

↑ *The Football League trophy in its current guise, the Johnstone's Paint Trophy. It was won in 2010 by Southampton, 4–1 against Carlisle at Wembley.*

PENALTY HEROES

Three finals have been settled by penalty shootouts. Mansfield beat Bristol City 4–3 after the game had finished 1–1 in 1987, while Swansea were 3–1 winners following a 1–1 draw with Huddersfield in 1994, with goalkeeper Roger Freestone the Welsh club's hero that day as he saved the decisive spot-kick. Carlisle won the trophy via a penalty shootout in 1997. They beat Colchester 4–3 after a goalless draw in normal time, with Peter Cawley and Karl Duguid missing from 12 yards for the losing side.

THREE-SY DOES IT

No team has won the Trophy by more than three clear goals. Bristol City beat Bolton 3–0 in the 1986 final, while Bolton claimed the title with a 4–1 victory against Torquay three years later and Blackpool inflicted the same scoreline on Cambridge in 2002. The 2009/10 competition also ended 4–1, with Southampton claiming their first silverware since 1976 with victory against Carlisle.

↑ *Swansea goalkeeper Roger Freestone helped his club win the trophy in 1994 with a crucial save in the penalty shootout.*

TROPHY MADNESS FOR HATTERS

Luton won the 2009 competition but were unable to defend their title after they were relegated from The Football League in the same season. The Hatters finished bottom of League 2 that year but at least had something to celebrate when they beat Scunthorpe 3–2 at Wembley. Claude Gnakpa was the Hatters' hero, scoring the winner in extra time.

FAMOUS NAMES

Some famous names have won the Trophy over the years, making it a prestigious piece of silverware for those in the lower reaches of English football. No fewer than four sides who competed in the top flight in 2009/10 have lifted the prize, with Wigan, Birmingham, Stoke and Bolton among the former winners.

INCE IS THE DON

MK Dons' success in 2008 was a landmark moment in the history of the club. Their 2–0 victory over Grimsby in the final secured the Dons their first piece of silverware. Paul Ince, in his first season as manager, saw his side cap a superb season by going on to win the League 2 title. However, the Dons could not repeat their heroics the following year and defend the Trophy. After receiving a bye into the second round, they were knocked out of the competition by Bournemouth.

⇢ *One of the highlights of Paul Ince's first spell in charge of MK Dons was victory in the 2008 Johnstone's Paint Trophy final, the first silverware collected by the club in its current guise.*

THE BOY DUNN GOOD

Iain Dunn was the first player in British football to score a golden goal in the Trophy of 1994. The golden goal method, which failed to catch on, meant that the game ended immediately after a goal was scored by either side in extra time. Striker Dunn earned Huddersfield a 3–2 victory against Lincoln, although the Terriers went on to lose to Swansea on penalties in the final.

⇠ *Golden goals (and silver ones, too) were a short-lived football innovation. Introduced in England for the 1994/95 Football League Trophy, Iain Dunn of Huddersfield was the first man to end extra time early when he scored against Lincoln.*

Index

Acknowledgements

This book would not have been possible without the help and co-operation of Football DataCo Limited, the Premier League, The Football League and the clubs themselves, as well as the talented and dedicated team of journalists and researchers at Press Association Sport.
On Behalf of Press Association Sport:
Author: Andrew Carless
Head of Content: Peter Marshall
Copy Editor: Andrew McDermott
Head of Research: Alaric Beaumont-Baker
Contributors: Duncan Bech, Mark Bowering, Roddy Brooks, Andrew Curry, John Curtis, Steve Davis, Wayne Gardiner, Ross Heppenstall, Simon Lovell, Simon Peach, Tom Rostance, Matthew Sherry, Andrew Sims, Damian Spellman, Sean Taylor, Jonathan Veal, Mark Walker, Stuart Walker, Drew Williams

Picture Credits